DISTINGUISHED WOMEN ECONOMISTS

DISTINGUISHED WOMEN ECONOMISTS

James Cicarelli and Julianne Cicarelli

GREENWOOD PRESS
Westport, Connecticut • London

Library of Congress Cataloging-in-Publication Data

Cicarelli, James.
    Distinguished women economists / James Cicarelli and Julianne Cicarelli.
      p. cm.
    Covers biographies from the 18th century to the present.
    Includes bibliographical references and indexes.
    ISBN 0–313–30331–2 (alk. paper)
    1. Women economists—Biography. 2. Women economists—United States—Biography. I.
Cicarelli, Julianne. II. Title.
    HB76.C53 2003
    330′.092′2—dc21   2003049136

British Library Cataloguing in Publication Data is available.

Library of Congress Catalog Card Number: 2003049136
ISBN: 0–313–30331–2

First published in 2003

Praeger Publishers, 88 Post Road West, Westport, CT 06881
An imprint of Greenwood Publishing Group, Inc.
www.praeger.com

Printed in the United States of America

The paper used in this book complies with the
Permanent Paper Standard issued by the National
Information Standards Organization (Z39.48–1984).

10 9 8 7 6 5 4 3 2 1

In memory of
Gelsomina Cicarelli and Dossie Todaro
women of distinction in their own right

CONTENTS

PREFACE AND ACKNOWLEDGMENTS

Women have played a vital role in the development of modern economics almost from its inception, which is generally agreed to have begun in 1776 with the publication of Adam Smith's *The Wealth of Nations*. For much of the last 227 years, women's contributions to the field were all but unrecognized, and even today their input is undervalued despite the fact that a full one-third of those who identify themselves as economists are female. This book has several purposes, but above all, it is an appreciation of the many and varied contributions women have made to the creation, practice, and applications of Western economic thought.

There are fifty-one biographees in this book; there could have easily been ten times that many and still some women who have made or are making significant contributions to the discipline would have been left out. This book is not comprehensive; rather, it highlights women whose range of historical and contemporary accomplishments have helped make economics what it is today. The economists in this volume represent a cross-section of the many high-performing women who have advanced economics in meaningful ways. Some have made important theoretical breakthroughs in the field, others have distinguished themselves through the dissemination of economic knowledge, and still others have been trailblazers in the applications of economic reasoning. They are *not* all equally important to the development of economics, but each has made a difference in the scope, depth, or use of economics, and in this sense every one is representative of how women in general have moved economics forward.

Each entry in the book includes a brief introduction, a biographical sketch, a summary of contributions, and a selected bibliography. The introduction is a short biographical tag that distinguishes the subject from the other fifty women featured here. The biographical section includes the exact date and location of birth (if available); information about the subject's family, education, career, achievements, and honors; and the exact date of death, if applicable. In the summary of contributions, the economist's life work is reviewed, characterized, and interpreted. Whenever possible, the individual's own words—from publications or speeches—are quoted to reveal what and how she thought or thinks. Quotations are from a representative sample of a subject's works over the span of her career. This selective summary of contributions is meant to give a flavor of the person's impact on the field and is neither exhaustive nor definitive.

The bibliographic section of each entry consists of two parts: works by the subject and works about the subject. The list of works by the subject is a selected sample of the individual's most prominent and/or most typical publications, presentations, or speeches, arranged in chronological order. The women in this book are by and large prolific authors, and a complete listing of the published works of each would be impractical. The list of works about each subject directs the reader to other sources of biographical and bibliographical information, some of which may include more extensive listings of her publications, presentations, and speeches. The list of works about the subject is arranged alphabetically by author, or by title when there is no author. There are few published sources on some of the younger economists included in the book, and as a result some entries do not include this section.

A few housekeeping details remain. An author's last name, a short title, or a page number in parentheses refers to an item cited in the bibliography at the end of the entry. A year in parentheses—for example, "(2001)"—is usually the date of a significant event or the year of publication of a work mentioned in the text but not cited in the bibliography, although in some cases these works are included in the bibliography too. A boldface name in an entry indicates a cross-reference to one of the women featured here. The entries in this volume are arranged in alphabetical order. The appendix lists the fifty-one economists in chronological order, beginning with the earliest birth year.

No matter how inclusive, acknowledgments never do justice to the many people and resources that make a book possible. All books are the product of a collaborative effort for which the authors of record take a disproportionate share of the credit. Our work is no exception. We want to thank those biographees who provided resumes, reprints of publications, and other vital pieces of information so necessary for the preparation of each entry. We also acknowledge the input of the relatives, friends, and acquaintances of biographees who supplied anecdotes and other insights into the lives and works of the women we selected to feature in this work.

In a book of this nature, librarians play a big role in locating source materials. We appreciate the efforts of the librarians at Roosevelt University's Robin Campus in Schaumburg—Mona Attia, Jo Ellen Brnusak, Marilyn Clark, Joe Davis, Linda Irmen, Karlotta Methews, Carolyn Nelson, Carol Rogowski, and Barbara Schoenfield—for their tireless efforts in finding even the most obscure writings by and about our biographees. A special thanks is in order for Rebecca Sharkey of the University of Chicago's Regenstein Library for tracking down material about the women in this book who were associated, in one way or another, with that university.

A legion of readers reviewed various portions of the text, and we acknowledge the input of each: Christie Ahrens, Marian Azzaro, Diane Baker, Susan Burroughs, Natalie Davila, Susan Dudish-Poulsen, Clara Gong, Linda Jones, Kristen Leckrone, Chunhui Ma, Mariano Magalhaes, Vicky McKinley, Josetta McLaughlin, Margaret Rung, Leon Stein, Marge Tauber, Kelly Tzoumis, Lynn Weiner, and Carl Witte. Their collective comments and criticisms improved the readability of the book immeasurably.

A special thanks to Cynthia Harris, our editor at Greenwood Publishing Group. She was the one who initially suggested this project. We want to acknowledge the efforts of the editors at Westchester Book Services: Agnes Priscsak and Halley Gatenby. The excellent computer work of Clara Gong and Marilyn Nance helped bring order to what for the longest time was a work in chaos. Finally, we thank Rose Carmellino for compiling the index.

This book is the joint effort of two individuals, each of whom brought different strengths and talents to the work. Working together, we have written a book that neither of us could have created on our own. Hopefully, the final product is better for this combined endeavor.

INTRODUCTION

In 1985, the University of Chicago Press published a desktop engagement calendar celebrating fifty-four late, great economists who had "achieved a measure of fame, and in at least one case, immortality" (Stigler and Friedland, preface). Of the fifty-four economists selected for recognition, only one was a woman: the indomitable Joan Robinson, one of the most famous economists of the twentieth century. Arranged in chronological order by year of birth, the economists showcased included those whose reputations transcend the discipline—Adam Smith and John Maynard Keynes—and others whose contribution to the field and personal celebrity—Sir James Steuart-Denham and Luigi Einaudi—are familiar only to scholars who possess a consummate knowledge of the history of economic thought.

The compilers of the calendar, George J. Stigler (who won the Nobel Memorial Prize in Economics* in 1982) and Claire Friedland, intentionally chose only deceased economists. "We have been warned not to make a calendar of living economists because at the margin of inclusion there would be several excluded economists whose rights to inclusion were at least as good as those of the chosen" (preface). Acknowledging that a similar problem exists even for departed economists, Stigler and Friedland concluded the calendar with an alphabetical list of birth and death dates and an editorial comment or quote from a published work of more than 250 economists, including the 54 singled out for special consideration with a photograph or a portrait. This extended list of great economists included the names of five women—less than 2 percent of the total. The dearth of women among the list of more than 250 deceased prominent economists would suggest that women did not play a significant role in the historical development of economics. Surely a listing of important living economists would show a greater representation of women among the notables in the field. The evidence does not support this supposition.

In the second edition of *Who's Who in Economics* (Blaug), published in 1986, only 31 of 1,400 entries were women (Ferber and Nelson, 2). By the third edition, published in 1999, things had changed marginally at best. With some 1,200 pages of text covering approximately 1,800 entries—more than a thousand of whom were still living at the time—the book featured 36 women. In absolute terms, the presence of women had increased, but in relative terms, it had declined. During the thirteen years between editions, the percentage of women appearing in one of the most comprehensive directories of economists actively engaged in scholarship had declined to 2 percent from just over 2.2 percent.

These data would seem to explain why no woman has ever received one of the major awards in economics. A woman has never won the Nobel Memorial Prize in Economics, an honor bestowed annually since 1969. The American Economic Association's (AEA) John Bates Clark Medal is given to accomplished American economists under age forty, and several past recipients have gone on to win the Nobel Memorial Prize in Economics. Since its inception in 1947, the Clark Medal has been awarded twenty-eight times, but never once to a woman. This despite the fact that about 30 percent of the AEA's members are female. Even the more modest recognition of delivering the AEA's distinguished Richard T. Ely Lecture, given at the association's annual meeting since 1962 and not restricted to an American, has only twice gone to a woman.

Despite outward appearances to the contrary, women constitute a vital component of the human resources within the economics profession. About 25 percent of the approximately 3,000 members of the National Association of Business Economists (NABE) are female, and women represent more than 30 percent of the 20,000 individual memberships of the American Economic Association. Survey data provided to the Committee on the Status of Women in the Economics Profession ("Report of the Committee") from 120 Ph.D.-granting economics programs in the United States and more than 100 liberal arts colleges show that women occupy about 30 percent of faculty positions in economics at the former and about 40 percent at the latter. Women are now approximately 30 percent of all new Ph.D. recipients in economics, and while precise figures are not available, it seems safe to assume that about one-third of policy economists in the United States are female. Wherever there is economics, there are women, and as the fifty-one stories in this book demonstrate, that has been the case for nearly the entire history of the discipline.

SELECTING BIOGRAPHEES

Economists, female and male, toil in one of three broad areas: cognitive economics, policy economics, and business economics. By far the largest category of economists—cognitive economists—are those engaged in creating and disseminating economic knowledge; that is, research and teaching. Cognitive economists are often associated with institutions of higher learning—community colleges, four-year colleges, and universities—or they work at think tanks such as the Brookings Institution or the Cato Institute. In addition to their institutional affiliations, these economists usually belong to academic associations such as the American Economic Association, more than half of whose individual members are affiliated with colleges or universities and most of whose institutional members are academic organizations. Jane Haldimand Marcet, Jean Trepp McKelvey, and Ann Dryden Witte exemplify the cognitive economists featured in this book.

In terms of sheer numbers, the next-largest concentration of economists would probably be those involved in policy economics. These economists advise public policy makers or are themselves decision makers of record. They often work for government—local, state, or federal—or for nongovernmental agencies that seek to influence public policy, such as the Institute for Women's Policy Research. Some policy economists are independent scholars whose influence on public officials is general in nature, as opposed to working to achieve a specific outcome or passage of a particular piece of legislation. The economists in this category are likely to be members of the same associations to which cognitive economists belong. Beatrice Potter Webb, Barbara M. Ward, and Nancy Hays Teeters are typical of the policy economists included in this volume.

Business economists are those who practice the craft on a day-to-day basis within the private sector. The smallest of the three categories, business economists are primarily found in relatively large corporations, in major banks, or in stand-alone consulting firms. Regardless of their place of work, these economists are usually involved in advising high-level executives about future economic conditions or the financial implications of key business decisions. Because their duties are sufficiently different from those of cognitive and policy economists, many business economists belong to associations that reflect their uniqueness, such as the Institute for Business Forecasting and NABE. M. Kathryn Eickhoff, Abby Joseph Cohen, and Diane C. Swonk are representative of the women who work as business economists.

Of the fifty-one women in this book, approximately 65 percent are cognitive economists, around 25 percent are policy economists, and about 10 percent are business economists. Naturally, any classification system, especially one applied to economists, has its shortcomings. Juanita M. Kreps was the first woman appointed U.S. secretary of commerce and the first professional economist to hold that particular cabinet post. Prior to her career in government, Kreps was a cognitive economist for more than thirty years, teaching at several colleges including Duke University and authoring a number of works in the field of labor economics. After her stint in government, Kreps returned to academic life. Clearly, her major contributions to the discipline came as a policy economist, yet her experience and accomplishments entitle her to be included among the ranks of cognitive economists as well.

Elizabeth Ellery Bailey can claim membership in all three categories. For more than a decade, she has been the John C. Hower Professor of Public Policy and Management in the Wharton School of Business at the University of Pennsylvania. She served on the Civil Aeronautics Board under Presidents Jimmy Carter and Ronald Reagan and worked for seventeen years at Bell Laboratories in a variety of positions, including as a founding member of the company's Economics Research Department. Conceptually, the categories in the tripartite classification system described above are mutually exclusive, and most women profiled in this book have achieved special distinction in just one of the three areas. As a practical matter, however, nearly every woman described in these pages has had a career that transcends a classification as simplistic as the one laid out here.

Selecting the individuals for inclusion in similar books has been done in a variety of ways. In *Adam Smith's Daughters*, Polkinghorn and Thomson wrote lengthy essays about the lives and contributions of eight women almost universally recognized as having played a prominent role in the development of economics from its early days. The editors of *The New Palgrave: A Dictionary of Economics* (Eatwell, Milgate, and Newman), a four-volume encyclopedia of the people, terminology, and theories that are or have been a significant part of economics since its inception, centered their brief biographical essays on persons who have advanced the field through the published word. In the second and third editions of *Who's Who in Economics,* M. Blaug applied a more quantitative approach, selecting subjects on the basis of an economist's having published a predetermined number of articles in prestigious economics journals or having produced a comparable volume of output in books and monographs. The editors of *A Biographical Dictionary of Women Economists* (Dimand, Dimand, and Forget) took a different tack in publishing a work that features the biographies of more than 100 women. They put out a call for contributors over the Internet, asking interested persons to write a short essay about the life and works and/or contributions of women they considered worthy of inclusion in the book. In *Engendering Economics,* P. I. Olson and Z. Emami created eleven oral histories of the lives of feminist economists who earned doctorates in economics at U.S. universities between 1950 and 1975.

Each approach for selecting biographees has its advantages and shortcomings. On the plus side, *Adam Smith's Daughters* and *The New Palgrave* include women whose names many cognitive economists would quickly recognize and thus deem deserving of inclusion. *Who's Who in Economics* has a quantitative criteria for selection, giving the appearance of objectivity, while *A Biographical Dictionary of Women Economists* has dimensions of democracy and inclusiveness not found in the other works. *Engendering Economics* presents the moving stories of women, all still alive, who through pluck and luck have created a prominent place for themselves in the discipline despite its persistent male chauvinism. On the negative side, all of these works focus on cognitive economists to the near exclusion of policy and business economists, two categories that have emerged in the post–World War II era and in which women have achieved relatively high levels of acceptance and recognition. Even the objectivity of *Who's Who in Economics* is suspect because its criteria for inclusion is based on publication in a select number of journals, many of which have had a historical bias against women economists as authors. The veneer of impartiality begs the question, and rationalizing the absence of women because of their lack of publication in top-ranked journals is tantamount to blaming the victims. Further, the very nature of the selection processes used in these works tend to favor women who are deceased, near the ends of their careers, relatively obscure and virtually unknown even among their peers, or who espouse a viewpoint that reflects a relatively narrow spectrum within the panorama of economic analysis. There is little indication in these books of the presence of relatively young women economists who have excellent credentials in the field but have yet to achieve the acclaim of those who have completed long and distinguished careers.

Our approach to selecting the women to be included in this book was not superior to the methods others have used, just different. We sought to have a balance of accomplished and emerging economists; deceased and living economists; cognitive, policy, and business economists—economists who cover virtually every philosophical perspective there is to economic reasoning. The underlying criterion is that the women we chose have performed or are performing at a high level, whether they made their mark teaching economics and publishing in professional journals, doing vital research for government agencies, or forecasting business and economic conditions for private-sector firms. Naturally, there is some duplication between the women described in this volume and those featured in similar works. Many of the lives we describe, however, are unique to this book. All the women included deserve to be considered, although we readily acknowledge that different authors would have selected a similar but not necessarily identical set of biographees for inclusion in a tome about *Distinguished Women Economists.*

DEMOGRAPHIC SKETCH OF BIOGRAPHEES

Of the fifty-one women profiled in this book, thirty-seven were born in the United States, nine in England, and one each in Romania, Czechoslovakia, Poland, Canada, and Germany. Twenty-eight of the biographees are living and twenty-three are deceased. Among the deceased, the earliest birth year is 1769 and the most recent is 1939, while the most recent death year is 2002 and the earliest is 1858. Their average age at death was sixty-eight, with a range from forty to ninety-five. Among the living biographees, the earliest birth year is 1915 and the most recent is 1966. Their average age is sixty, with a range from thirty-seven to eighty-eight as of 2003. With respect to race, at least two of the biographees are African American and the rest are probably Caucasian, although it is difficult to determine race with absolute precision.

The economic status of the families in which most of the biographees grew up was roughly homogeneous. Nearly all spent their childhood in middle- and upper-middle-income environments. Their fathers were farmers, coal miners, lawyers, merchants, professors, and executives, and their mothers were usually homemakers, although a few worked outside the home, often as teachers. Few biographees were reared in the lap of luxury or had to wrestle with the day-to-day financial problems that frequently beset the lives of the working class. There are exceptions. Jane Haldimand Marcet was born into privilege; Phyllis Ann Wallace's origins were so humble that we do not even know her exact date of birth.

Regardless of the financial status of their families, most of the biographees passed their early years in nurturing environments. At least one and usually both parents—defying prevailing conventions that limited the educational aspirations of women—encouraged their daughter to acquire as much formal schooling as possible, an enlightened attitude we take for granted in the twenty-first century but that has become common only since the late 1960s and the rise of the women's movement. Biographees born since the 1850s are almost all college graduates, and most went on to earn a doctorate or at least a master's degree. The thirty-seven American biographees attended a variety of undergraduate institutions, with multiple alumni from Radcliffe College, Cornell University, the University of Michigan, the University of Texas at Austin, Wellesley College, and Oberlin College. That the biographees are a bright group is evident in the fact that at least half of the Americans graduated Phi Beta Kappa. Graduate degrees, especially the Ph.D., were earned at a plethora of institutions, although collectively, Harvard University/Radcliffe College, the University of Chicago, and the Massachusetts Institute of Technology accounted for about one-third of the doctorates the biographees received.

The proclivity that the biographees had or have for family arrangements closely mirrors the pattern that could be expected of any group of fifty-one women chosen at random from the many cultures that the subjects represent. More than 80 percent have married at least once, a few have had life partners, and more than 60 percent have had one or more children. In that sense, the biographees are fairly typical. What is surprising is that, despite this collective commitment to family life, these fifty-one women economists still managed to have demanding and distinguished careers outside the home. While working women are commonplace today, most of the biographees were actively involved in the labor force long before it became a generally accepted norm.

As noted above, the career trajectories of the biographees place them into one of three basic classifications of professional economists: cognitive, policy, or business. Of the twenty-three deceased biographees, about two-thirds were cognitive and maybe one-third were policy economists. The qualifiers "about" and "maybe" are necessary because sharp delineation is impossible in many cases. Edith Abbott, for instance, began teaching at the University of Chicago in 1920 and remained there for more than thirty years before retiring in 1953. Prior to her long tenure as a cognitive economist, Abbott was a policy economist, having served one year as a research assistant for the Women's Trade Union League in Boston, Massachusetts, and was a teacher/scholar at the independent Chicago School of Civics and Philanthropy for nearly a dozen years. Similarly, Phyllis Ann Wallace was a cognitive economist from 1953 to 1957 while teaching at Atlanta University and again from 1972 to 1986 as a professor at MIT. In the intervening years, she worked at the Central Intelligence Agency, the Equal Employment Opportunity Commission, and the Metropolitan Applied Research Center, a think tank in New York City. Most of the cognitive economists among the deceased biographees, however, were like Katharine Coman and Ann Fetter Friedlaender, who, after completing their formal education, went directly into academe and a life of teaching and writing.

While several of the cognitive economists among the deceased biographees spent a portion of their professional lives as policy economists, the deceased policy economists as a group had careers with less variability. Beatrice Potter Webb was on a mission, and even though she and her husband, Sidney Webb, founded the London School of Economics, their purpose in life was to bring democratic socialism to England. Webb was a prolific author and probably did some teaching, but her life was dedicated to public service and consumed by the desire to create a modern welfare state. Selma J. Mushkin worked in the U.S. federal government from 1937 to 1960 and at the Urban Institute from 1968 to 1970, but she also spent seventeen years in academe at three different institutions: Johns Hopkins University (in the early 1960s), George Washington University (1963–68), and Georgetown University (1970–79). Selma F. Goldsmith spent virtually her entire work life, some twenty-five years, with the U.S. federal government, working for the Department of Agriculture, the National Resources Planning Board, and the Department of Commerce. About the only definitive statement one can make about the career choices of the deceased biographees is that none was a business economist.

The fusion of careers evident among some of the deceased biographees is even more pronounced in the cohort of living biographees. Indeed, the careers of some have placed them at one time or another in each of the three classifications of professional economists. Elizabeth Ellery Bailey's story has already been cited. Like Bailey, Marina von Neumann Whitman has been a cognitive economist, a policy economist, and a business economist at different times in her life. Since 1992 she has been a professor of business administration and public policy at the University of Michigan Business School. From 1979 to 1992 she was a senior executive with General Motors, and in 1972 she earned a unique distinction as the first woman appointed to serve on the president's Council of Economic Advisers. About one-third of the living biographees are like Caroline M. Hoxby, who has spent all of her professional life as a cognitive economist—in her case, just nine years. Virtually all the rest have careers that straddle two of the category designations for professional economists. Kathleen Bell Cooper was chief economist at Exxon Corporation and is now under secretary of commerce for economic affairs in the U.S. Department of Commerce. In 1993 Marianne A. Ferber retired after nearly forty years in higher education, teaching at the University of Chicago and the University of Illinois at Urbana-Champaign. Her first professional job in the 1940s was as an economist with Standard Oil of New Jersey. A long-time research associate with the Urban Institute, Isabel V. Sawhill taught for three years at Goucher College in Baltimore, Maryland.

Regardless of career choices, the fifty-one biographees are a group of prolific authors who have collectively received many awards and honorary recognitions. All together, the biographees have authored thousands of publications. Joan Robinson alone produced more than 300 books, articles, essays, monographs, pamphlets, op-ed pieces, book chapters, and book reviews. The sheer volume of her output made her one of the most preeminent economists of her time. Shirley Almon took a different path to acclaim, achieving a modicum of immortality within the discipline based on a career output that consisted of just two professional articles. Barbara M. Ward was a best-selling author, Nancy L. Schwartz and Anna J. Schwartz worked best as parts of teams, and Mabel F. Timlin and Marjorie S. Turner did not realize notoriety for their writings until late in their careers. Some biographees—e.g., Harriet Hardy Taylor Mill, Millicent Garrett Fawcett, and Mary Paley Marshall—were productive and original authors whose husbands, because of the social conventions of the time, were often credited for the works they penned.

As with publications, the awards and other recognition that the biographees accumulated over time are too numerous to quantify definitively. Acknowledged as one of the most important persons of letters in the nineteenth century, Harriet Martineau has been the subject of more biographical essays and books than just about any other woman associated with economics. Nancy Hays Teeters is representative of the women in the group who achieved a significant first—in her case, the first woman appointed to the U.S. Federal Reserve's Board of Governors. Many other biographees serve or have served on boards of directors of widely held public corporations or internationally recognized not-for-profit organizations. In toto, the biographees have received many honorary degrees from colleges and universities throughout the world, and at least a dozen of them hold or have held endowed, distinguished, or named professorships. Several biographees have been elected to the governing boards of prestigious professional associations such as NABE, the AEA, and the Eastern and Midwest Economic Associations. Many of the biographees have been designated fellows of illustrious learned societies, and a number have edited or been on the editorial boards of the field's top professional journals. Two biographees—Heidi I. Hartmann and Nancy Folbre—have received MacArthur Fellowships, often referred to as genius grants, and the combined dollar value of grants the biographees have received is in the millions.

Ironically, many of the awards the biographees have amassed have come from outside the discipline. All too often, our fifty-one biographees have had to wait inordinate lengths of time for their fellow economists to recognize their worth. Joan Robinson, for instance, did not occupy the one full professorship in the economics program at Cambridge University until her husband, Austin Robinson, whose credentials pale in comparison to hers, vacated the position upon his retirement. More typical is the experience of Ingrid H. Rima, who took fifteen years to make the transition to full professor from assistant professor; a man with a comparable publication record probably would have completed the journey in half the time.

CONTRIBUTIONS OF BIOGRAPHEES

If classifying the biographees according to the type of work that they do is difficult, summarizing their collective contributions is nearly impossible and is becoming more so with the proliferation of female economists and the growing diversity of their interests. When economics was new and female economists were few and far between, cataloging their contributions could be done with reasonably satisfactory results. From 1800 to 1850, two women—Jane Haldimand Marcet and Harriet Martineau—did more to create "political economy" as a stand-alone field of study separate and distinct from its roots as a branch of moral philosophy than just about any other writers of the period. Marcet published the first edition of *Conversations on Political Economy* in 1816. Sixteen years later, Martineau published the first installment of her subscription series *Illustrations of Political Economy*. Both works were educational, as each author sought to popularize economics rather than to add to the body of the existing canon, which they embraced. Their ultimate purpose was to transform political economy from a dull and difficult discipline into a practical, understandable subject accessible to the growing literate and educated middle class. Some of those producing economic doctrines at the time, such as J. R. McCulloch and Jean Baptiste Say, applauded the efforts of Marcet and Martineau, who were successful beyond their wildest expectations, becoming the best-selling economists of the first half of the nineteenth century.

The women in the field quickly moved from teaching economics to doing economics. Harriet Hardy Taylor Mill was the unacknowledged coauthor of one of the seminal works of the classical economic tradition, *Principles of Political Economy* (1848), a work whose authorship is attributed solely to her husband, John Stuart Mill. In all likelihood, she had a major hand in the writing of *On Liberty*, a book that lists J. S. Mill as the sole author, but the significance of her contribution to this work is disputed. Mary Paley Marshall was also an economist who, in keeping with the conventions of the times, chose to submerge her career in favor of that of her husband, Alfred Marshall. To a lesser extent, Millicent Garrett Fawcett followed a similar path, although her *Political Economy for Beginners* did have a publishing life quite independent of the publications of her husband, Henry Fawcett.

The era of women as stealth economists was short-lived, and by the last third of the nineteenth century, women began asserting themselves as economists actively involved in the transition of the discipline from a normative doctrine to a positive science. In the United States, Katharine Coman became an instructor of rhetoric at Wellesley College in 1880, and a decade later she organized the Department of Economics and Sociology at Wellesley, one of the watershed events in the opening of the economics profession to women. Besides teaching, Coman was an active scholar and one of the economists instrumental in the creation of the AEA. In the late nineteenth and early twentieth centuries, Rosa Luxemburg was pushing the envelope of women in economics in her quest to bring communism to eastern Europe. At the same time, Beatrice Potter Webb was drawing up blueprints for the welfare state in Great Britain.

This inclination to social action is a characteristic common to the lives of many women in economics. Mary Jean Bowman, Hazel Kyrk, and Margaret Gilpin Reid, contemporaries at the University of Chicago, combined long and productive careers as teachers and scholars with an unswerving commitment to issues affecting consumers in general and families in particular. Theresa Wolfson actively worked to promote the labor movement in the United States while publishing extensively on unionization in industries and occupations dominated by women. Barbara Mary Ward, Irma Glicman Adelman, and Frances Julia Stewart are representative of female economists who have centered their writings and professional activities on the problems and concerns of peoples living in the so-called third world. Carolyn Shaw Bell, Marianne A. Ferber, and Barbara Rose Bergmann advocated for women's interests, especially children, long before modern politicians discovered the focus group. Bell has been particularly instrumental in furthering the status of women in economics; she was the engine behind the creation of the AEA's Committee on the Status of Women in the Economics Profession. In honor of her efforts, in 1998 the AEA created the Carolyn Shaw Bell Award, given annually to an individual who has furthered the mission of the committee in measurable ways.

The advocacy of causes usually perceived as peripheral to the profession has often come with a price in that these causes, generally liberal in nature, become stigmatized as women's issues. Research on these topics is frequently dismissed as normative and not positive, as if women bring biases to scholarship that men do not. Despite the professional penalties, women economists, more than men, continued to be identified with causes, especially those concerning women, children, and persons of color. The irrefutable power and rigor of the research of Francine D. Blau, Nancy Folbre, Rebecca M. Blank, and economists of their ilk now commands peer respect and has legitimized the study of topics once deemed soft, inconsequential, or agenda-driven.

In the middle third of the twentieth century, as mathematics increasingly became the preferred language of economics, women readily shifted to a quantitative exposition from one based on a combination of narrative, graphs, and number crunching. Ann Horowitz, who majored in mathematics as an undergraduate, brings to her scholarship a level of quantitative sophistication that has become a de facto norm for those wishing to publish in the field's major journals. Ann Fetter Friedlaender used her mathematical skills to break new ground in the subfield of transportation economics, and Nancy L. Schwartz applied dynamic optimization to a potpourri of problems in managerial economics. Starting in the 1990s and continuing into the twenty-first century, Jennifer F. Reinganum has used mathematics to analyze the legal system in innovative and provocative ways.

The ascendancy of these mathematical economists came at the expense of those given to other forms of exposition. Anna J. Schwartz and Selma F. Goldsmith made a scientific art of sifting through mountains of data in search of recurring patterns of behavior. In *The Rhetoric of Economics*, Deirdre N. McCloskey relies almost exclusively on the written word to plumb the essence of economics and what it means to be an economist. Jean Trepp McKelvey used hard work and the power of her will to make labor and industrial relations an important subfield in the discipline.

At approximately the same time (roughly, the 1940s through the 1970s), women economists began to occupy policy positions of real substance and clout. In 1937, Selma J. Mushkin came to Washington, D.C., to begin an eleven-year term as chief of financial studies with the Social Security Administration. That job was a prelude to her appointment as an economist with the U.S. Public Health Service, a post she held until 1960. Nancy Hays Teeters began her long career in public service as a staff economist with the Federal Reserve in 1957. During the presidency of Lyndon B. Johnson, Alice M. Rivlin held a number of government positions, and she then worked for the Brookings Institution in the early 1970s before returning to the federal government in 1974 as director of the Congressional Budget Office. In 1968, Isabel V. Sawhill began her career in economics as a policy analyst in the U.S. Department of Health, Education, and Welfare. Four short years later, Marina von Neumann Whitman became the first woman to serve on the president's Council of Economic Advisers, paving the way for Laura D'Andrea Tyson, who became chair of the CEA in 1993 during Bill Clinton's presidency.

In the last twenty-five years, as the use of econometrics to test hypotheses and/or predict the likely probabilities of outcomes or events became widespread, economics made the transition to a stochastic science from a social science. Women did more than just follow the trend; they helped set the pace. Since the mid-1970s, Francine D. Blau has become a recognized expert on the causes and consequences of discriminatory pay differentials, especially those affecting women and African Americans. Rebecca M. Blank has earned a solid reputation for her technical, no-nonsense analysis of poverty and related topics—specifically, the economics of welfare. Equally impressive is the work of Caroline M. Hoxby, whose massive empirical studies on various aspects of education in the United States are forcing politicians and policy makers alike to rethink the whole process of public schooling in this country. These three women and others like them are cognitive economists operating on the cutting edge, and they have prized reputations among their peers. For the general public, however, the best-known practitioners of the craft are not those working in higher education or government, but economists toiling in the private sector.

The classification "business economists" is relatively new. Business economics emerged in the 1950s and 1960s as a viable career path for practitioners. Not surprisingly, the mean age of the business economists in this book is less than that of the cognitive and policy economists. M. Kathryn Eickhoff began her career as a business economist in the early 1960s working for the consulting firm of Townsend-Greenspan. (Alan Greenspan went on from that firm to become chair of the Board of Governors of the Federal Reserve.) Today, Eickhoff heads her owns nationally known consulting firm and serves on the board of directors of many well-known U.S. corporations. In 1971, Kathleen Bell Cooper began a thirty-year career as a corporate economist for a bank holding company. She moved to jobs of increasing responsibility and authority before becoming undersecretary of commerce for economic affairs in the presidential administration of George W. Bush.

Business economists are among the most recognized in the profession because of their frequent media exposure, especially on television. Appearing often on the Public Broadcasting System, CNN, CNBC, and MSNBC, Abby Joseph Cohen is a widely known and respected forecasting guru who did as much as any individual to fuel the stock boom of the 1990s. Named a "star forecaster" by the *Wall Street Journal* in 1999, Diane C. Swonk is frequently quoted in major U.S. business publications, and sound bites of her economic analyses are heard regularly on major broadcast and cable news networks in the United States. For most professional economists, the names and images that personify economics belong to the men (and all have been men) who have won the discipline's major prizes, but for the millions of people around the globe with equity positions in publicly held companies, the face of economics is a woman's.

*Initiated in 1901, Nobel Prize awards were originally limited to physics, chemistry, medicine or physiology, literature, and peace. In 1968, in conjunction with its tercentenary celebration, the Central Bank of Sweden instituted the Central Bank of Sweden Prize in Economic Science in the Memory of Alfred Nobel, first awarded in 1969. The Royal Swedish Academy of Science actually determines the recipients. Although technically not a Nobel Prize, the Economics Nobel is a difference without a distinction. Recently, however, some scientists have called for the discontinuation of the Nobel Memorial Prize in Economics, believing that the discipline lacks the scientific substance to warrant equal status with hard sciences such as physics and chemistry. The reality is that the Economics Nobel is here to stay, and for the foreseeable future, it will be awarded each October along with all the other Nobel Prizes (Nasar, 368).

BIBLIOGRAPHY

Blaug, M., editor. *Who's Who in Economics.* 2nd ed. Cambridge, MA: MIT Press, 1986.
———. *Who's Who in Economics.* 3rd ed. Northampton, MA: Edward Elgar, 1999.
Dimand, R. W., M. A. Dimand, and E. L. Forget, editors. *A Biographical Dictionary of Women Economists.* Northampton, MA: Edward Elgar, 2000.
Eatwell, J., M. Milgate, and P. Newman, editors. *The New Palgrave: A Dictionary of Economics.* New York: Macmillan, 1991.
Ferber, M[arianne]. A., and J. Nelson. A. *Beyond Economic Man: Feminist Theory and Economics.* Chicago: University of Chicago Press, 1993.
Nasar, S. *A Beautiful Mind.* New York: Simon & Schuster, 1998.
Olson, P. I., and Z. Emami, editors. *Engendering Economics: Conversations with Women Economists in the United States.* London: Routledge, 2002.
Polkinghorn, B., and D. L. Thomson. "Irma Adelman (1930–)." In *Adam Smith's Daughters,* 90–103. Northampton, MA: Edward Elgar, 1998.
"Report of the Committee on the Status of Women in the Economics Profession." *American Economic Review* 91(2), May 2001: 502–7.
Stigler, G. J., and C. Friedland, compilers. *Engagement Calendar, 1985: Great Economists.* Chicago: University of Chicago Press, 1984.

Edith Abbott
(1876–1957)

After becoming just the second woman to earn a Ph.D. in economics from the University of Chicago, Edith Abbott went on to have a long and distinguished career as a "social reformer, economic historian, and a pioneer in America of the study of the economic position of women" (Kerr). A social activist, she was deeply involved in efforts to protect and educate children and immigrants, improve housing, and ameliorate conditions in penal institutions. Her efforts in these areas mimic those of her sister, Grace, who "grew up to become a nationally recognized social reformer and Chief of the U.S. Children's Bureau" (Hammond, 1). Throughout their lives, the sisters were like bookends: "Edith Abbott was the scholar, Grace the sister who took the initiative in translating knowledge into action" (Costin, xi). Edith Abbott was an extraordinary teacher, spending more than thirty years at the University of Chicago, during which time she published widely in the areas of social and public policy and economic history. She was representative of a number of women economists who, in the first half of the twentieth century, combined social activism and life as a cognitive economist into a single career. With the increasing professionalization of economics, this merger of interests has lost legitimacy in the field.

BIOGRAPHY

Edith Abbott was born on September 26, 1876, in central Nebraska on the "grand island" between two channels of the Platte River (Costin, 3). Her father, Othman Abbott, was a veteran of the Civil War, a pioneer lawyer, and an author. Her mother, Elizabeth (Griffin) Abbott, was a teacher and a "respected high school principal in West Liberty, Iowa" before she married (4). Both parents believed in the value of education and tried to provide a college experience for Edith and Grace (who was two years younger than Edith), something that proved especially difficult during the depression of the 1890s. A natural scholar, Edith Abbott persisted in her undergraduate studies despite her family's financial problems. By combining high school teaching with summer and correspondence courses and full-time study, Abbott was able to earn a bachelor's degree from the University of Nebraska in Lincoln in 1901, graduating Phi Beta Kappa (17–18).

In 1902, Abbott enrolled in a summer session at the University of Chicago, an institution that had admitted women since its inception in 1891. There she attracted the attention of Professors J. Laurence Laughlin and Thorstein Veblen, who recommended her for a fellowship in political economy. Abbott became a full-time graduate student at the University of Chicago in 1903. She came under the influence of Laughlin, Veblen, and Veblen's prized student, Wesley Clair Mitchell, and she also took courses from Professor Sophonisba Breckinridge, "with whom she established a close, life-long professional association" (Hammond, 1). In 1905, Abbott earned her Ph.D. in economics, writing a dissertation on the wages of unskilled workers that became the basis of one of her earliest publications ("Wages of Unskilled Labor").

After graduating from the University of Chicago, "Abbott moved to Boston to work for the Women's Trade Union League and as a research assistant to the labour economist Carroll Wright" (Hammond, 3). In 1906, a Carnegie Institution fellowship with supplemental funding from the Association of Collegiate Alumnae financed a year of study at the London School of Economics and Political Science. While in England, Abbott investigated British employment and British experiments with poverty relief. She also interacted with some of England's most prominent social reformers, including Charles Booth and Sidney and **Beatrice Potter Webb**. Returning to the United States in 1907, Abbott took a teaching position at Wellesley College, where she stayed for one year.

In 1908, Abbott moved to Chicago to work for Breckinridge, then director of social research at the independent Chicago School of Civics and Philanthropy. Abbott was hired to teach statistics in its Department of Social Investigation. She joined her sister, Grace, and moved into Jane Addam's Hull House, which, "with its thriving reform-minded resident community, was a mecca for educated women" (Hammond, 3). While at the School of Civics and Philanthropy, Abbott published a steady stream of books and articles for scholarly and popular presses dealing with a variety of topics ranging from the housing problem in Chicago to juvenile delinquency.

The chronically underfunded School of Civics and Philanthropy was always on the verge of closing, and working there proved such a challenge for Abbott that she and Breckinridge convinced the University of Chicago to absorb the school. In 1920, renamed the Graduate School of Social Service Administration, it became the first graduate school of social work in the United States associated with a major research university. Abbott was hired as an associate professor of social economy in the University of Chicago's newest graduate school, and in 1924 she was named dean. Three years later, she and Breckinridge established *Social Service Review*, a distinguished and prominent academic journal published by the University of Chicago Press. Abbott and

Breckinridge were coeditors from 1924 to 1934, "when Grace Abbott was named editor upon her resignation as Chief of the Children's Bureau. Edith Abbott resumed as editor after her sister's death in 1939. She retained the position until 1952" (Hammond, 5). For more than thirty years, Abbott was a fixture at the University of Chicago, teaching and writing about myriad social issues until her retirement in 1953. On July 28, 1957, she died at her family home in Grand Island, Nebraska. Her passing marked the end of an era in more ways than one: "During the course of their childhood and early adult years, the Abbott sisters accepted for themselves special goals held for them by their parents, goals not common for girls or young women growing up in the late nineteenth century. As their careers advanced, Grace and Edith Abbott demonstrated qualities often found in creative individuals who became distinguished in their endeavors—an ability to grasp the global nature of problems, to see patterns and connect divergent ideas, a readiness to challenge existing assumptions and to take risks to advance the causes to which they were committed" (Costin, xiii).

CONTRIBUTIONS

Edith Abbott began her productive career as a research scholar in 1904 with the publication of her first major paper ("Wage Statistics"), which was essentially a review of D. R. Dewey's *Employees and Wages,* a special U.S. census report filled with an exhaustive set of wage data. In writing her review, Abbott sought to address three specific questions: "(1) How does the scope of the inquiry differ from that of previous census investigations into wages? (2) In what respect is the method of presentation and tabulation new, and what are the relative advantages or disadvantages of this method of treatment? (3) What conclusions are reached regarding the trend of wages during the decade?" (339). On the basis of her analysis, Abbott concluded, "There is, indeed, abundant evidence all through the volume to show that it is the result of much thought, painstaking care, and patience. Every possible effort was made to secure accuracy, and the four series of tables, covering more than 1,100 pages, are as nearly perfect in their way as the most critical statistician could desire." In her judgment, the book represented "the best collection of wage statistics ever published by the Federal Census" (361).

Her next major publication ("History of Industrial Employment") proved important in two ways. First, it examined statistically the prevailing "assumption that women in competing with men can 'work cheaper,' and that a sort of Gresham's law exists in the labor market, according to which women's labor which is cheap drives out men's labor which is dear, whenever they are brought into competition" (461). Second, the article became the basis for her seminal book *Women in Industry.* In it, Abbott analyzed wage data for women working in five industries: cotton, boots and shoes, cigar making, clothing, and printing. That work, while more extensive than the work done in the article, only reinforced the conclusions Abbott had arrived at four years earlier:

> Evidence has certainly been given to show that any theory that women are a new element in our industrial life or that they are doing "men's work" or that they have "driven out the men" is a theory unsupported by facts. Instead of coming in as usurpers, women have been from the beginning an important factor in American industry—in the early days of the factory system an indispensable factor—and fifty years ago there were more women relatively to the number of men employed than there are today. Additional evidence is offered . . . supporting a point . . . that the "women movement" of the nineteenth century belongs almost exclusively to middle-class women. The woman of the working classes was self-supporting and was expected to be self-supporting long before. . . . The efforts of the middle-class woman to realize a new ideal of pecuniary independence, which have taken her out of the home and into new and varied occupations, belong to recent if not contemporary history. But this history, for her, covers a social revolution and the world she faces is a new one. The woman of the working classes finds it, so far as her measure of opportunity goes, very much as her great grandmother left it. ("History of Industrial Employment," 501)

Of Abbott's more than fifty published articles, books, essays, and reviews, a plurality were about women, work, and wages. She was, nevertheless, concerned with other social issues. From 1910 to 1915, she penned a series of articles in the *American Journal of Sociology* on housing in Chicago. She also authored a number of pieces about crime, prisons, and punishment, including a historical essay about the post–Civil War crime wave ("Civil War"). That article was her contribution to the first volume of the *Social Service Review*. For more than fifty years, she actively fought for a number of causes. Like Jane Addams, Grace Abbott, Eleanor Roosevelt, and others, Edith Abbott devoted her life to reforming society and ameliorating the lot of the poor and dispossessed.

BIBLIOGRAPHY

Works by Edith Abbott

"Wage Statistics in the Twelfth Census." *Journal of Political Economy* 12(3), June 1904: 339–61.

"Wages of Unskilled Labor in the United States, 1850–1900." *Journal of Political Economy* 13(3), June 1905: 321–67.

"The History of Industrial Employment of Women in the United States: An Introductory Study." *Journal of Political Economy* 14(8), October 1906: 461–501.

Women in Industry: A Study in American Economic History. New York: D. Appleton and Co., 1910.

"The Civil War and the Crime Wave of 1865–70." *Social Service Review* 1, June 1927: 212–34.

Works about Edith Abbott

Costin, L. B. *Two Sisters for Social Justice: A Biography of Grace and Edith Abbott*. Urbana: University of Illinois Press, 1983.

Deegan, M. J., and Hill, M. R. "Edith Abbott." In *Women in Sociology: A Bio-*

Bibliographical Sourcebook, edited by M. J. Deegan, 29–36. Westport, CT: Greenwood Press, 1991.

Hammond, C. H. "Edith Abbott (1876–1957)." In *A Biographical Dictionary of Women Economists,* edited by R. W. Dimand, M. A. Dimand, and E. L. Forget, 1–8. Northampton, MA: Edward Elgar, 2000.

Kerr, P. "Abbott, Edith." In *The New Palgrave: A Dictionary of Economics,* edited by J. Eatwell, M. Milgate, and P. Newman, 1. New York: Macmillan, 1991.

Irma Glicman Adelman
(1930–   )

· ·

Irma Glicman Adelman is one of those rare economists whose work reflects a combination of compassion and technical expertise par excellence. Drawn to the study of economics by a desire to contribute to the solution of the problems of worldwide poverty, Adelman produced a body of scholarship that is as analytical as that of those economists who train their highly developed quantitative skills on topics that are arcane, irrelevant, or both. A master of mathematics, econometrics, and statistics and of the interplay of all three, Adelman nearly always applied her intellectual prowess to human problems whose solution would make a perceptible difference in the quality of the lives of average people.

BIOGRAPHY

Irma Glicman was born in Cernowitz, Romania, on March 14, 1930. The daughter of Jacob Max Glicman, a merchant, and Raissa (Ettinger) Glicman, she married physicist Frank L. Adelman in 1950. The couple had one child, a son, and divorced in 1979. The Glicmans immigrated to the United States in 1949, and six years later Irma Adelman became a naturalized U.S. citizen.

Adelman earned her bachelor of science in business administration from the University of California-Berkeley in 1950, graduating Phi Beta Kappa. She remained at UC-Berkeley, where she received her M.A. in economics in 1951 and her Ph.D. in 1955. Continuing at Berkeley, Adelman became a teaching associate in 1955–56, an instructor in 1956–57, and a lecturer with the rank of assistant professor in 1957–58. She then moved to Mills College in Oakland, California, serving as a visiting assistant professor in 1958–59.

In 1959, Adelman became an assistant professor at Stanford University, where she stayed until 1962, moving to Johns Hopkins University in Baltimore, Maryland, where she was an associate professor from 1962 to 1965. She then moved on to Northwestern University in Evanston, Illinois, as a professor of economics from 1966 to 1972. In 1972, she became a professor of economics and agricultural economics at the University of Maryland, staying there until 1977 and becoming the Cleveringa Chair at Leiden University and a fellow at the Netherlands Institute of Advanced Studies in 1977–78. Adelman returned to UC-Berkeley in 1979 as a professor of economics, remaining there as a full-time faculty member until 1994, when she retired as professor emeritus.

In addition to her academic career, Adelman held numerous positions in research-oriented nonprofit agencies and professional economic organizations. She was associated with the United Nations' Division of Industrial Development in 1962–63, the U.S. State Department's Agency of International Development from 1963–72, and the World Bank beginning in 1968. Adelman served on several editorial boards, including the *Journal of Economic Literature* (1969–75), the *American Economic Review* (1976–78), the *Journal of Policy Modeling* (since 1979), and the *Journal of Comparative Economics* (since 1980). She was a vice president of the American Economic Association in 1979–80 and was selected as a fellow of the American Academy of Arts and Sciences, the Econometric Society, and the Royal Society for the Encouragement of Arts, Manufacturing and Commerce. In 1994 Adelman was named to the University of California-Berkeley Women's Hall of Fame.

CONTRIBUTIONS

A major theme running through Adelman's scholarship is an interest in quantifying the qualitative phenomena associated with economic growth and development, particularly among less-developed and emerging economies. The quantitative force of her research was readily apparent in her first major publication, but the topic was as far afield from development economics and the problems of worldwide poverty as could be imagined. Her "Stochastic Analysis of the Size Distribution of Firms" is clearly a contribution to the subdiscipline of industrial organization and structure and not remotely related to the themes that would become the hallmark of Adelman's later publications. Using the probabilistic method called the Markov chain process, the paper sought to predict the long-term equilibrium size-distribution of firms within a given industry if certain existing trends were to continue into the foreseeable future. The resulting probability distribution allowed Adelman to forecast correctly a tendency toward deconcentration in the U.S. steel industry as well as a growth in the size of the median firm, but the issues that would be the center of her research for the next thirty years—economic development and social welfare—were not addressed in this paper, even obliquely.

That first major article showcased Adelman's technical prowess but not her compassion, and certainly not her passion. By contrast, her first major book—*Theories of Economic Growth and Development*—did it all, combining her humanity, zeal, and analytical skills. The basic purpose of the book was "to examine, in the context of modern economic theory and with the aid of modern economic tools, the evolution of economic thought in the field of economic

growth and development" (vii). Adelman began her effort with a definition
of economic development that is still operational: "...the process by which
an economy is transformed from one whose rate of growth of per capita income is small or negative to one in which a significant self-sustained rate of
increase of per capita income is a permanent long-run feature" (1). She then
developed a general framework for analyzing theories of growth and development in the form of a mathematical model that included a combination of
traditional variables—capital, labor, and natural resources—and nontradi-
tional variables—society's fund of applied knowledge and the sociocultural
milieu within which the economy operates.

Against the empirical backdrop of per capita income and other economic
and sociodemographic characteristics of fifty-two nations, Adelman applied
her growth model to the development theories embedded in the works of
Adam Smith, David Ricardo, Karl Marx, Joseph Schumpeter, and a composite
neo-Keynesian model of a growing economy. The analysis of these theories of
economic development led Adelman to conclude that "there is no single explanation for underdevelopment" (*Theories of Economic Growth*, 145). Despite
the popular inclination to ascribe underdevelopment to a deficiency of capital,
a lack of entrepreneurial talent, a hostile cultural-political environment, or
some other single factor, Adelman argued that no one-dimensional theory can
explain why some economies develop and others do not. Neither, she concluded, can a single factor—a high savings/income ratio or the rate of innovation—explain the phenomenon of continuous economic growth. Despite this
everything-depends-on-everything-else conclusion, Adelman did settle on one
axiom: A pattern of shocks to behavioral practices is more likely to trigger the
changes necessary to sustained economic growth than is a gradualist approach
(145).

Long convinced that economic development and sociopolitical change are
interdependent, in 1965 Adelman published a seminal article ("Factor Analysis") that demonstrated the empirical connectivity between growth and the
noneconomic aspects of the development process. To gain semiquantitative
insights into the interaction of various types of social and political change
with the level of economic development, Adelman and her coauthor used
factor analysis to examine the interrelatedness of per capita income and a large
number of indexes representing the social and political structure of seventy-
four less-developed countries for the period 1957–62: "The results...show
that a remarkably high percentage of intercountry variations in the levels of
economic development (66 percent) are associated with differences in non-
economic characteristics. Thus it would appear that it is just as reasonable to
look at underdevelopment as a social and political phenomenon as it is to
analyze it in terms of intercountry differences in economic structure" (556).
Adelman noted that it would be imprudent to conclude that economic forces
play no role in cross-country variations in the development process. Equally
inappropriate would be to conclude that the relationships discovered are
causal in nature: "The results of the factor analysis neither demonstrate that
economic growth is caused by socio-political transformations nor indicate that
variations in development levels determine patterns of social and political

change. Rather they suggest the existence of a systematic pattern of interaction among mutually interdependent economic, social and political forces, all of which combine to generate a unified complex of change in the style of life of a community" (557).

In *Economic Growth and Social Equity in Developing Countries*, a sequel to her earlier work on the interrelatedness of sociopolitical factors and development, Adelman and her coauthor applied regression analysis on cross-sectional data for forty-three underdeveloped countries for 1950–63 to test hypotheses concerning the impact of economic growth and institutional change on social equity in those countries. Conventional thinking held that economic growth is unambiguously beneficial to most nations, especially in equalizing the distribution of wealth and earnings opportunities while raising the average level of economic welfare. Adelman's conclusions about the distribution of income in noncommunist nations proved at odds with prevailing wisdom. Specifically, Adelman found that capitalist societies have increased the concentration of wealth and income, creating "the persistence of significant hard-core poverty for large minorities in the midst of growing affluence for the majority . . ." (141).

Two years later, Adelman revisited the whole question of the goals and values of economic development. In light of her book on growth and social equity (*Economic Growth*), she challenged the unswerving mainstream belief that economic development is a rising tide that lifts all boats. The very definition of economic development—creation of conditions for self-sustained growth of capita GNP—was found wanting: "To the extent that growth in GNP and concomitant changes, on the one hand, and improvements in the welfare of the poor, on the other, are monotonically and positively related . . . , this [conventional] definition of development could offer an acceptable working definition. If, however, as is suggested by the work described above, a U-shaped relation exists, then the accepted definition of development is . . . badly misleading as a focus for thought and practice in the field" ("Development Economics," 306).

Much of Adelman's research involved pioneering the use of multivariate techniques to quantify the interactions of economic planning and the long-term relationship among economic development, social equity, and the sociopolitical environment within emerging nations. Her scholarship interests eventually focused on the interplay of land reform, agricultural and industrial development, and the modeling of institutional change under conditions of uncertainty. An article in the *Journal of Policy Modeling* ("Some Thoughts") exemplified the convergence of these issues. In it, Adelman advanced a number of original policy recommendations, including the idea of a land-reform fund, a rural and industrial development package for developing nations, and the easing of trade restrictions on imports from countries that implement land reform. As always, her goal in advancing these and other proposals was to create an economic environment in which the likelihood of sustained growth would be maximized while the economic and social disruptions associated with development were minimized.

BIBLIOGRAPHY

Works by Irma Glicman Adelman

"A Stochastic Analysis of the Size Distribution of Firms." *Journal of the American Statistical Association* 53(284), December 1958: 893–904.

Theories of Economic Growth and Development. Stanford, CA: Stanford University Press, 1961.

"A Factor Analysis of the Interrelationship between Social and Political Variables and per Capita Gross National Product" (with C. T. Morris). *Quarterly Journal of Economics* 79(4), November 1965: 555–78.

Economic Growth and Social Equity in Developing Countries (with C. T. Morris). Stanford, CA: Stanford University Press, 1973.

"Development Economics: A Reassessment of Goals." *American Economic Review* 65(2), May 1975: 302–09.

"Some Thoughts on the Restructuring of North-South Interaction." *Journal of Policy Modeling* 2(2), 1980: 291–305.

Works about Irma Glicman Adelman

"Adelman, Irma." In *Who's Who in Economics,* edited by M. Blaug, 10–11. 3rd ed. Northampton, MA: Edward Elgar, 1999.

Polkinghorn, B., and Thomson, D. L. "Irma Adelman (1930–)." In *Adam Smith's Daughters,* 90–103. Rev. ed. Northampton, MA: Edward Elgar, 1998.

Rodgers, Y. V. D. M., and Colley, J. C. "Outstanding Female Economists in the Analysis and Practice of Development Economics." *World Development* 27(8), August 1999: 1397–1411.

Shirley Almon
(1935–1975)

Shirley Almon was to econometrics what the mythical Helen of Troy was to the Greek navy. Although she published only two professional papers, Almon launched a total reevaluation of lagged analysis, one of the mainstays used in testing quantitatively the validity and predictive value of theoretical models. She influenced a generation of econometricians, and the impact of her work still reverberates today.

BIOGRAPHY

Shirley Ann Almon was born to Harold and Dorothea (Pfleuger) Montag on February 6, 1935, in Saxonbury, Pennsylvania. Her father grew up on a farm and attended school through the eighth grade. Originally an automotive mechanic, he became an entrepreneur, owning a new-car dealership in Butler, Pennsylvania, and, later, a hardware store in New Castle, Pennsylvania. Sensing that western Pennsylvania was becoming a chronically depressed area, Montag moved his family to Cincinnati, Ohio, where he operated a convenience store and eventually became the production manager in a factory making outdoor advertising signs. Dorothea Montag was a homemaker and mother of seven, of whom Shirley was the oldest.

While Almon was growing up, her family lived in Jefferson Center, Pennsylvania, where she attended a one-room Lutheran school for eight years. About the time her family moved to Butler, Almon began attending Butler High School, from which she graduated in 1952. She went on to Goucher College in Baltimore, Maryland, graduating in 1956 with a B.A. in economics. As an undergraduate, Almon had two internships. In the summer of 1955, she worked in the Women's Bureau of the Department of Labor in Washington, D.C., writing a report on the demand for women mathematicians and statisticians. One year later, she served as a research assistant at the National Bureau of Economic Research in New York City.

In 1957, Almon became a research assistant at the Federal Reserve Bank in San Francisco, California. She married Clopper Almon Jr., who was serving in the army in the Washington, D.C., area, on June 14, 1958. She transferred to the Federal Reserve in Washington, where she helped create the index of industrial capacity and capacity utilization, now a regularly published Federal Reserve data set. In September 1959, Almon and her husband entered the Ph.D. program in economics at Harvard University. While working on her degree, Almon became an instructor at Wellesley College; she then became an assistant professor at Wellesley when she received her Ph.D. in economics in 1964. She also taught at Harvard University for the 1965–66 academic year. In 1966, Clopper Almon began teaching at the University of Maryland in College Park, and Shirley took an assignment with the Council of Economic Advisers in Washington, D.C.

Always deeply interested in economics, Almon preferred to study how businesses worked rather than theory per se. Her first major paper was published in 1965 when she was teaching at Wellesley, and her second paper was completed when she was in Washington, D.C. An accomplished pianist, a talented ballroom dancer, and a good tennis player, Almon read the *Wall Street Journal* religiously until the end of her life. In December 1967, after four years of various symptoms, doctors discovered that Almon had a brain tumor. An operation to remove the tumor was done on December 21, and the presiding surgeon thought she would live four to six months. In fact, she lived until September 29, 1975. Almon was in fairly good health during most of this time, and in those precious years, she and her husband traveled to France, Germany, Austria, Switzerland, Italy, and Russia

CONTRIBUTIONS

Shirley Almon published two papers in the 1960s representing the sum total of the professional output of her brief yet stellar career. The first paper ("Distributed Lag") involved the application of a new distributed lag model in "predicting quarterly capital expenditures in manufacturing industries from present and past appropriations" (178). Using National Industrial Conference Board survey data for the period 1953–61 for all manufacturing, for durables and nondurables separately, and for their fifteen constituent industries, Almon concluded that "the distributed lag on appropriations, plus estimated seasonal coefficients, gives a good explanation of the variance in expenditures, with the best lags centering around 8 and 9 quarters in length" (178). Based on her 1964 Ph.D. dissertation of the same title, the paper did not attract much attention among scholars studying future capital investments by firms because rival models, especially those employing variable lags as opposed to fixed coefficients, had equal or greater predictive value (Popkin).

In her second publication ("Lags"), Almon investigated the determinants of the decision to invest. Specifically, she developed a model that estimated the time lag relationships between investment appropriations as reflected in National Industrial Conference Board data for 1955 through 1966 and the basic stimulants to invest—expected output, available capacity, cash flow, and interest rates. Summarizing her results for all manufacturing, Almon concluded:

1) Output and interest rate variables, when given a four-quarter distributed lag, have very significant weights in the current quarter only, while negative weights toward the end of the lag on output do fit into the accelerator theory. Positive weights on lagged values of the interest rate are reasonable; they indicate that a given rate causes more investment if proceeded by a high, rather than a low Rate.

2) Cash flow—retained earnings plus depreciation—promotes decisions to spend over the whole year. The weight at the end is almost half as large as that in the current quarter. Money can be saved.

3) Several other financial variables tested—the debt-asset ratio, the ratio of debt minus cash flow to assets, and stock prices—were not very useful for explaining appropriations. (193)

As with her first publication, the results of Almon's second work did not generate much enthusiasm among economists studying the determinants of investment, primarily because her "distributed lag models did not compete well against other neoclassical explanations . . . of investment" (McDonough-Dumler, 12). By contrast, econometricians—economists and statisticians who study the ways in which statistics and modeling can be combined to quantify economic relationships—were instantly captivated by the power and elegance of her quantitative technique, which was immediately dubbed the "Almon distributed lag."

The beauty of the Almon distributed lag was twofold. "The technique was a success with the applied econometric community for its ease of estimation and parsimonious representation of data" (McDonough-Dumler, 13). Prior to Almon, most lag models of the 1950s and 1960s were natural extensions of adjustment models such as the accelerator theory of investment. These models, for example, the Koyck lag model, while effective, either violated some of the basic statistical requirements to estimate models efficiently or lacked predictive power because of data limitations. By developing a method wherein the weights of the lag function are assumed to lie on a Lagrangian interpolation polynomial, Almon created an estimating technique that conserved data requirements while avoiding the problem of collinearity, a statistical drawback of many pre-Almon distributed lag models.

Eventually, the Almon distributed lag model gave way to more powerful and statistically sophisticated approaches to the same problem, but not before her research altered fundamentally the way econometricians view lags. The impact of Almon's work was evident in the frequency with which others cited her papers. Through the early 1980s, Almon's 1965 paper had been cited nearly 200 times, and by the early 1990s, "more than 370 citations appeared in the economics, sociology, and political science literature—as well as in the sciences" (McDonough-Dumler, 12). Rarely in the history of economics has a single idea had such a pronounced effect on the methodology of research.

BIBLIOGRAPHY

Works by Shirley Almon

"The Distributed Lag between Capital Appropriations and Expenditures." *Econometrica* 33(1), January 1965: 178–96.
"Lags between Investment Decisions and Their Causes." *Review of Economics and Statistics* 50, May 1968: 193–206.

Works about Shirley Almon

McDonough-Dumler, C. "Shirley Ann Montag Almon." In *A Biographical Dictionary of Women Economists,* edited by R. W. Dimand, M. A. Dimand, and E. L. Forget, 11–15. Northampton, MA: Edward Elgar, 2000.
Popkin, J. "Comment on 'The Distributed Lag between Capital Appropriations and Expenditures.' " *Econometrica* 34(3), July 1966: 719–23.

Elizabeth Ellery Bailey
(1938–)

Elizabeth Ellery Bailey's contributions to economics have been so significant and varied that she may well become the first woman to receive the Nobel Memorial Prize in Economics. She began her career as a researcher at Bell Laboratories, studying the effects of regulation on the telecommunications industry and public utilities, among other things. Her efforts at Bell helped broaden the theoretical structure of industrial organization. A staunch supporter of airline deregulation, Bailey took her practical business experience to Washington, D.C., in 1977, when she was the first woman appointed to serve on the Civil Aeronautics Board (CAB). Her position on the CAB gave her a unique opportunity to put economic theory into practice. After her tour in Washington, Bailey entered academe, making her one of the few economists in the profession, man or woman, to have a career with service in all three branches of the discipline: business, policy, and cognitive economics.

BIOGRAPHY

Elizabeth Ellery Bailey was born in New York City on November 26, 1938, to Irving Woodward Raymond and Henrietta Dana (Skinner) Raymond. Her father was a professor of medieval history and Elizabeth grew up in a family with four sisters. She married James Bailey, a professor of computer science, and the couple had two sons, James Jr. and William. The couple was divorced in 1978. Bailey received her B.A. in economics, magna cum laude, from Radcliffe College in 1960 and her M.S. in computer science from Stevens Institute of Technology in 1966. In 1972, she became the first woman to receive a Ph.D. in economics from Princeton University. After graduation from Radcliffe, she began a seventeen-year career at Bell Laboratories in New Jersey, working and going to school at the same time.

Bailey has been a trailblazer in the advancement of women in academic and management positions. She began at Bell in the technical programming department, where she developed a hands-on knowledge of computers but had little chance to work through her ideas about their relationship to management. After she earned her Ph.D., Bailey transferred to Bell's economics department and became one of the founding members of the economics research section. In 1973, she became head of the department, the first woman at Bell to hold such a position. She angrily recalls going to a meeting at Bell in which a male colleague asked her if she was there to take notes, and to this day, she continues to have a strong antipathy to what she sees as sexism in the workplace. During her years at Bell, Bailey also served as an adjunct professor at New York University and began her publishing career.

In 1977, President Jimmy Carter appointed Bailey the first woman to hold a seat on the CAB, and in 1981, President Ronald Reagan appointed her the agency's first woman vice chair. Bailey had built her career around relevant research, starting with her doctoral dissertation, titled *Economic Theory of Regulatory Constraint*. When the chance came to serve at the CAB, she saw it as a unique opportunity to put economic theory into practice. She also viewed the position as one of public responsibility, noting that economists often take potshots at public programs without ever having worked in government and thus not really understanding how it functions and what competing pressures government is subject to.

Bailey served on the CAB until 1983, when another first opened up to her. After much persuasion from members of the selection committee at Carnegie-Mellon University, she became the first woman to head a top-ten graduate school in business education, becoming dean of Carnegie-Mellon's Graduate School of Industrial Management. At Carnegie-Mellon, the fact that Bailey was a woman was a monumental nonissue; her professional and academic credentials made her the right person for the job. The university had long been considered a major center for industrial technology studies, and one of Bailey's goals was to help integrate computer technology into the curriculum. At Carnegie-Mellon, as in all her professional roles, Bailey was able to use both the theoretical and the scientific bases of economics to address real-world problems. She served at Carnegie-Mellon until 1991, when she moved on to the Wharton School of the University of Pennsylvania, where she is now John C. Hower Professor of Public Policy and Management and the chairperson of the Public Policy and Management Department. Her current research areas are economic deregulation; contestability theory; strategic management of economic, environmental, and international regulation; and corporate governance and social responsibility.

Bailey has been cited as a woman who gets things done, and her personal and professional accomplishments illustrate this. When she could not find a special school for her physically handicapped son, she founded one—the Harbor School for Children with Learning Disabilities. She has served on many boards of trustees, including at Princeton University, the Presbyterian University Hospital, the National Bureau of Economic Research, and the Brookings Institution. She also serves on corporate and public-sector boards. She has had leadership roles, including serving as president of the Eastern Economic Association, and has served the economics profession as chair of the Committee on the Status of Women in the Economics Profession. Among her many professional awards are an honorary degree of doctor of engineering at Stevens Institute of Technology, the Directors' Choice Award from the National Women's Economic Alliance Foundation, and a Radcliffe College Alumnae Recognition Award.

CONTRIBUTIONS

In the December 1962 issue of *American Economic Review*, Harvey J. Averch and Leland Johnson published "Behavior of the Firm under Regulatory Constraint." This seminal article extended the traditional theory of the firm to include a regulatory constraint on the behavior of the firm. The Averch/Johnson model inspired many related articles on the theoretical aspects of government regulation of business, but that body of work was not reflected in books on regulation, which remained largely institutional and policy oriented. In her first major publication—*Economic Theory of Regulatory Constraint*—Bailey changed all that. In it, she incorporated the Averch/Johnson model into a full-length treatise, examining in great depth all the theoretical implications of that model on virtually every aspect of regulation, from the fair rate of return to peak-load pricing under regulatory constraint. The book is heavily mathematical and requires a thorough knowledge of calculus for those who would read it for mastery. The more than fifty figures and numerous mathematical models present a challenging read for even the most mathematically gifted professional economists.

In 1977, Bailey teamed with future Nobel laureate William J. Baumol and Robert D. Willig to publish a pathbreaking paper on an important extension of the economic analysis of the theory of the firm: "Weak Invisible Hand Theorems on the Sustainability of Multiproduct Natural Monopoly." This became the opening salvo of a larger effort to extend the traditional analysis of the firm to multiproduct industries, which she did with **Ann Fetter Friedlaender** in a subsequent article. "Traditional economic analysis of the theory of the firm has concentrated on single-product firms. But, in reality, most businesses produce many products, and many regulatory and antitrust issues involve only these enterprises. In recent years, economists and policymakers dealing with antitrust and regulatory issues have increasingly recognized the need for a theory that can be used to evaluate the efficiency of market structures in industries dominated by a few firms operating in a diverse range of markets. For such firms, conventional concepts of structure and performance such as economies of scale, measures of concentration, and barriers to entry do not adequately capture the complexity of market relationships" ("Market Structure," p. 1024). Bailey's articles in the *American Economic Review* and the *Journal of Economic Literature* marked the beginning of the effort to examine the realities of multiproduct, multimarket firms.

Bailey and Friedlaender summarized and interpreted the new theory, tools, and concepts of the emerging field of the economic analysis of multiproduct industries. Their paper examined the empirical implications of multiproduct firms and developed relevant policy considerations for government regulation of such enterprises. While not as mathematical as some of Bailey's previous research in this field, the article showed her ability to put into narrative form many of the new and exotic theories dealing with the regulation of multi-product industries and the companies within them.

Government regulation of economic activity in the United States has had a long and fascinating history. Arguably the most interesting episode of U.S. government-business relations in the twentieth century was that of airline deregulation. A case can be made that deregulating the airlines was the one instance when rational economic policy triumphed over competing rationales for regulation, with the end result being the removal of inefficient rules in favor of the effective discipline of market competition. The real story, however, was much more complicated and interesting. It is described in detail in *Deregulating the Airlines,* a book Bailey coauthored with two economists who were at the CAB during at least a portion of the period when deregulation of the airlines took place. The book provides a valuable insider's look at decision making within the CAB during the critical transition to full deregulation, describing in detail the complex and largely unanticipated problems that the intelligent application of economic theory helped resolve.

Bailey demonstrated her command of the field of government regulation in a 1995 book (*Political Economy*) she coedited with Janet Pack. The book is a collection of classic articles and seminal essays that reflect the evolution of deregulation in the United States and Europe as it transpired over the last quarter of the twentieth century. The articles featured examined the political and economic factors that gave rise to the development of deregulation in the Western world and its growing appeal in Eastern Europe and the Pacific Rim. On the political front, big government became a particular target because growth in the public sector was squeezing private consumption. On the economic front, the combined forces of property rights, private choice, and the evidence that government regulation often distorts efficiency boosted the theory of contestable markets and other alternatives to conventional government regulation of business. The book captured the essence of this deregulation movement, both intellectual and political, and described many of the lessons drawn from the thrust to greater privatization.

As a policy maker at the CAB and as a theoretician in academe, Bailey helped shaped government-business relations as they developed in the last quarter of the twentieth century in the United States. Not content to dwell in the past, in her 1999 Eastern Economic Association Presidential Address ("A Regulatory Framework"), Bailey outlined the future of the government regulation of business. She predicted that a combination of Coasian theory—with its emphasis on incentives and contracts—and contestability theory—with its emphasis on unbundling and free entry—will form the conceptual framework for regulation policy in the twenty-first century. The combination of these two powerful approaches will then be trained on what Bailey described as the three top issues in the new century: (1) global warming as it impacts the desire for sustainable economic growth; (2) the regulation of the high-tech economy, especially the Internet; and (3) societal management of the advances in the biotech and pharmaceutical industries. Bailey believes that policy prescriptions in the twenty-first century will be effective if government regulations can promote social well-being without compromising efficiency, distorting market forces, or destroying incentives, a daunting task if ever there was one.

BIBLIOGRAPHY

Works by Elizabeth Ellery Bailey

Economic Theory of Regulatory Constraint. Lexington, MA: Lexington Books, 1973.

"Weak Invisible Hand Theorems on the Sustainability of Multiproduct Natural Monopoly" (with W. J. Baumol and R. D. Willig). *American Economic Review* 67(3), June 1977: 350–65.

"Market Structure and Multiproduct Industries" (with A. F. Friedlaender). *Journal of Economic Literature* 20(3), September 1982: 1024–48.

Deregulating the Airlines (with D. R. Graham and D. P. Kaplan). Cambridge, MA: MIT Press, 1985.

The Political Economy of Privatization and Deregulation, coedited by J. R. Pack. London: Edward Elgar, 1995.

"A Regulatory Framework for the 21st Century." *Eastern Economic Journal* 25(3), Summer 1999: 253–63.

Works about Elizabeth Ellery Bailey

"Bailey, Elizabeth Ellery." In *Who's Who in Economics,* edited by M. Blaug, 53–54. 3rd ed. Northampton, MA: Edward Elgar, 1999.

"First Woman on Civil Air Panel." *New York Times Biographical Service,* July 1977: 901.

Johnson, K. "Technology's Dean: Elizabeth E. Bailey, Carnegie-Mellon Computer Whiz." *New York Times Biographical Service,* August 1984: 1051.

Carolyn Shaw Bell
(1920–)

• •

In January 1998, the AEA's Committee on the Status of Women in the Economics Profession (CSWEP) created the Carolyn Shaw Bell Award, which is given annually to an individual who has furthered the status of women in the economics profession. Carolyn Shaw Bell, who served as the chair of the CSWEP from 1972 to 1974, in its first two years of existence, is certainly an economist who furthered her profession—through writings, teaching, and research. Indeed, she is much more, having made economics accessible to the general public and worked tirelessly to ensure the acceptance of women into the economics profession. Through her publications in *Newsweek* and similar magazines, Bell has helped the average person understand economic facts and reasoning. For more than twenty-five years, her work and that of other economists on the CSWEP has honored the progress of women in the profession, ensuring that the discipline is open to all.

BIOGRAPHY

Carolyn Shaw Bell was born on June 21, 1920, to Clarence Edward Shaw, an executive at the Dennison Manufacturing Company in Framingham Massachusetts, and Grace (Wellington) Shaw. Events in Framingham during the Great Depression, when many of the workers at Dennison were let go, led her to question economics and may very well have shaped her entire career. Even as a child, Carolyn understood that the unemployment created by the company was a tragic and unavoidable event. Her growing curiosity about her father's company and what the depression really meant inspired her to major in economics at Mount Holyoke College, where she graduated magna cum laude in 1941, during World War II. She went to Washington, D.C., and began another stage of learning about economics, working for the newly formed Office of Price Administration (OPA). At the OPA, she learned that economic theory could be applied in the real world, and she came to appreciate how remarkably efficient the market system can be. Bell worked with John Kenneth Galbraith, whose book *A Theory of Price Control* (1952) discussed the economic issues dealt with during the war, including the market characteristics that shape the success of price controls. Bell worked at the OPA through 1945 and entered the London School of Economics in 1946, where she received a Ph.D. in 1949. Her dissertation discussed how real firms put real technological change into effect and led to her first publication, "A Critique of the Schumpeterian Theory" in the *Quarterly Journal of Economics*.

Bell married Robert Solo, an economist at Harvard University, in 1942, and the couple had a daughter, Tova Marie. In 1951, Bell started teaching economics at Wellesley College. Her marriage had failed, and as a full-time, single parent, she found the salary at Wellesley shamefully low. Bell "was rescued from poverty by Ken Galbraith" ("Thinking about Economics," 25), who helped her find employment working on various projects at Harvard's Social Research Council. There, her training as an economist continued. She taught at Wellesley and did research at Harvard until she married her second husband, Nelson Sibley Bell, on July 26, 1953. Only then was her income sufficient to allow her to quit the Harvard job and concentrate on teaching and her own research agenda. She found that she loved teaching at Wellesley, and she took pride in the students who went on to earn doctorates in economics. Bell became a professor of economics in 1962 and served as chair of the Economics Department from 1962 through 1965 and again from 1979 through 1982. She was named **Katharine Coman** Professor of Economics in 1970, serving in that position until 1989, when she became professor emerita.

In the early years of her career, Bell's research interests were consumer expenditure patterns and the field of marketing and market research. She also began writing for the popular press, penning articles for the *Wall Street Journal*, the *New York Times*, and the *Los Angeles Times*. She frequently appeared before congressional committees because she thought it was important to explain technical aspects of economics so that common people could understand the rationale behind public policies. Bell became known as a woman economist although she herself emphasized that she was a professional economist who happened to be a woman. Realizing the value of clear definitions and accurate data, she became irritated in the late 1960s with the treatment of women's employment in the popular press, economic journals, and policy discussions in Washington. The common assumption was that women's earnings were supplemental to family income, and that public policy should be developed to boost the income of the head of the household—defined as a man supporting his wife and children. This generalization ignored millions of women who had never married and a soaring divorce rate that left women responsible for their own livelihoods. Shaw knew there was evidence to debunk the myth that only men headed households, but it was buried in economic tables and government studies. In 1973, Bell published the first quantitative analysis of the increase of poverty among children, citing the growing economic issues of single women on welfare. She felt that getting these economic facts out could help solve social problems but learned that such was not the case, noting that people continue to believe economic myths long after they have been shattered.

In the early 1970s, the economics reporter for the *New York Times* asked Bell about the typical family, which was assumed to consist of a wage-earning father supporting a wife and two children. Because Bell did not know if this was in fact the typical U.S. family, she proceeded to go through all the published data and proved that the prevailing view was a myth. Even allowing for the incomplete data, she discovered that at most 25 percent of U.S. families fit the "typical" definition ("Let's Get Rid of Families!"). Bell knew that the Bureau of Labor Statistics had actual numbers not reported in its current population survey. She convinced the bureau to present the numbers in a new tabulation highlighting these data. She found that with accurate counting, the typical family was in fact a minority, popular thinking notwithstanding. Realizing that she needed to change the common misconception about this important issue, Bell decided not to publish her findings in a scholarly journal. Instead, she called the editor of *Newsweek* magazine. Her 1977 essay "Let's Get Rid of Families!" got a lot of attention and reached many more people than an article in any economic journal would have. Soon articles about this new research appeared in the scholarly journals without citing Bell, whose work on the typical family had reduced to rubble one of the cornerstones of contemporary economics. Her research in the 1970s and 1980s continued to focus on using the individual as the basis of economic analysis of income rather than the family.

In addition to her writing, teaching, and work on behalf of the CSWEP, Bell served economics in many other ways. She was a member of the Executive Committees of the AEA and the Eastern Economic Association. She was on the editorial boards of *Challenge* magazine, the *Journal of Economic Literature,* the *Journal of Evolutionary Economics*, and the *Journal of Economic Education.* The recipient of many awards for her distinguished teaching, Bell is often cited by women economists in business and academe for the encouragement and help she gave them with their careers.

At its 1971 annual business meeting, the AEA established the CSWEP to investigate sex discrimination among professional economists in all lines of work and to recommend an affirmative action program to rectify the situation. The resolution that established the committee began with the principle that sex discrimination and inequality had no place in the profession. Bell, at that time Katharine Coman Professor of Economics at Wellesley College, was elected to serve as the CSWEP's first chair. The committee was charged with generating a report, which the AEA was to publish in its professional journal, the *American Economic Review.* As chair, Bell was responsible for seeing that the report was published, no easy matter as the journal's editor kept telling her to forget the whole thing, insisting that the issue was divisive and that publishing the report would cause hard feelings among male economists without helping women. Bell reminded the editor that she could not ignore a resolution passed by the AEA, and neither could he. The CSWEP report, "Combating Role Prejudice and Sex Discrimination" was finally published in the December 1973 issue of the *Review.*

Throughout the history of the CSWEP, many prominent economists, including Kenneth Boulding, John Kenneth Galbraith, Barbara Rose Bergmann, **Elizabeth Ellery Bailey**, **Ann Fetter Friedlaender**, Barbara Reagan, **Francine D. Blau**, **Phyllis Ann Wallace**, and Carolyn Shaw Bell, have worked on the committee. Mariam Chamberlain secured a grant from the Ford Foundation that helped finance the CSWEP in its formative years. One of the first items of concern for the committee was to document the problems women faced in the economics profession. Another was to send out questionnaires to Ph.D.-granting institutions to find how many women were economists and where they were employed. This eventually led to the Universal Academic Questionnaire, which provides information on the number of male and female economists employed in Ph.D.-granting institutions. At the urging of the CSWEP, the AEA began publication of *Job Opportunities for Economists*, which appears monthly (except for January and July) and openly advertises job opportunities within the profession. Despite toiling for more than thirty years, the CSWEP still has its work cut out for it, as there continues to be a serious imbalance between the status of men and women in the field of economics. Bell and others who have worked for the CSWEP continue the struggle today.

CONTRIBUTIONS

Bell's scholarly contributions to economics have often involved analyzing the policy implications of faulty models or examining the data deficiencies used to test the validity of theory. Whether reviewing the accuracy of unemployment figures or the theoretical incidence of a tax, she has sought to revise economic reasoning to accommodate institutional change or other realities. This propensity was evident in her first major publication, "A Critique of the Schumpeterian Theory." In it, Bell challenged the Schumpeterian notion that inventing and innovating are extraordinary efforts of uncommon entrepreneurs. For her Ph.D. dissertation, she studied the actual processes of invention and innovation for industrial firms using survey results published in 1947 by the Industrial Research Secretariat of the Federation of British Industries. Bell's observations led her to conclude that investing and innovating are subject to the same costs-and-benefits approach used to evaluate other business activities and hence are normal business processes, not extranormal events.

In the 1960s, Bell published two papers ("Elementary Economics"; "On the Elasticity of Demand") that again questioned conventional economic thinking about ordinary business practices. In the first, Bell showed that most introductory economics textbooks described depreciation accounting in extremely misleading terms that had far-reaching implications for economic policy. In the second paper, she described the actual pricing practices her husband used in his retail business to demonstrate that in at least this one instance: (1) price elasticity measured the effect of price changes on gross margin and not the quantity sold per se; and (2) many factors, such as convenience, and not just price, affect the elasticity of demand.

Bell questioned the appropriateness of Nobel laureate William Baumol's input/output analysis for measuring productivity in the service sector ("Macroeconomics"). Baumol had characterized service industries such as government, education, and the performing arts as a sector wherein productivity increases are sporadic. He reasoned that the lack of economies of scale in service enterprises prevented such businesses from experiencing the kind of technologically progressive productivity growth seen in goods industries. Bell suggested that the slow-growth activities in the service sector "reflect not the technological structure of their own production but the current technology of consumption . . . and . . . the latter has been strikingly neglected in measuring output. Consequently, the input-output ratio used to measure productivity in goods industries in frequently inapplicable to the service industries" (877).

One of Bell's most amazing contributions deals not with economics per se, but rather what it means to be an economist. In a 1998 article ("Thinking about Economics"), she describes her life both in and out of economics. The autobiographical essay is noteworthy for its candor and insights into her philosophy of economics.

> I am not averse to stating my own economic preferences or my value judgments. Every individual has some capacity to produce, to be useful, to do something useful; personal development consists largely in exploring and developing such capacities. It follows that I think each of us should be economically independent, that is able to earn wages by working or being productive in some way. Of course one must allow for temporary difficulties or disabilities, and the emergencies whose burdens should be shared, not individually borne. I believe that no person man or woman, has the right to bring another person into the world unless the parent is financially and emotionally ready and able to support the new human being and raise it alone, if necessary. I think most of us are born with a rich inheritance of human capital although inequalities exist, and I think that each of us has a duty to provide society with a return on the capital it has invested in us. I think more effort can be useful in improving the design of societal and governmental institutions but I hope the basic social culture of my country continues to keep the individual central to its thinking and its policy decisions. (31)

She talks about her years as a student and as a government bureaucrat and her life in higher education. Her comments are sincere, genuine, and heartfelt. Ostensibly a review of her scholarship, the essay offers a glimpse into the soul of an economist, truly a rare and refreshing view.

BIBLIOGRAPHY

Works by Carolyn Shaw Bell

"A Critique of the Schumpeterian Theory" (published under Bell's former name, C. S. Solo). *Quarterly Journal of Economics* 65(3), August 1951: 417–28.

"Macroeconomics of Unbalanced Growth: Comment." *American Economic Review* 58(4), September 1958: 877–84.

"Elementary Economics and Depreciation Accounting." *American Economic Review* 50(1), March 1960: 154–59.

"On the Elasticity of Demand at Retail." *American Journal of Economics and Sociology* 20(1), October 1960: 63–72.

"Let's Get Rid of Families!" My Turn. *Newsweek,* May 9, 1977: 19.

"Thinking about Economics." *American Economist* 42(2), Spring 1998: 18–33.

Works about Carolyn Shaw Bell

"Bell, Carolyn Shaw." In *Contemporary Authors,* edited by A. Evory. Detroit, MI: Gale Research, 1978.

"Bell, Carolyn Shaw." In *Who's Who in Economics,* edited by M. Blaug, 87. 3rd ed. Northampton, MA: Edward Elgar, 1999.

Barbara Rose Bergmann
(1927–   )

A scholar with many interests, Barbara Rose Bergmann has pioneered the study of a variety of topics including the field of sex roles in economic life, the use of computer simulation of economic systems as an alternative to economic theory, and alternative methods for collecting economic data. What unifies these interests is Bergmann's dissatisfaction with the study of economics as usually practiced. She believes that economics suffers from the standard practice of using third-hand government statistics to validate the introspective theories economists develop about the real world while cloistered in their offices. According to Bergmann, the lack of first-hand, data-gathering work is at the root of much of what is nonproductive in economics. To correct this myopia, she has campaigned to bring new methodologies to economics. Her research deals primarily with economic and social policy, including welfare, child care, women's place in the economy and the family, and the labor market problems of women and African Americans.

BIOGRAPHY

Barbara Rose Bergmann was born in New York City to Martin Berman and Nellie (Wallenstein) Berman on July 20, 1927. She received her B.A. in mathematics and economics from Cornell University in 1948, graduating Phi Beta Kappa. She then went to Harvard University, where she earned her M.A. and Ph.D., finishing in 1959. In 1965, she married Fred H. Bergmann; the couple had a son and a daughter.

Bergmann started her economics career at the U.S. Bureau of Labor Statistics in New York City in 1949, staying there until 1953. From 1958 to 1961, she was an economics instructor at Harvard. Then, from 1961 through 1962, she served as senior staff economist on the president's Council of Economic Advisers during the administration of John F. Kennedy. For the next two years, she was an associate professor of economics at Brandeis University. During that time, she also served as a senior member of the staff at the Brookings Institution, where she worked until 1965. In 1966, she began teaching at the University of Maryland, starting as an associate professor and becoming a full professor in 1967. She stayed at Maryland until 1988, when she moved to the American University in Washington, D.C., as a distinguished professor of economics. In 1997, she became professor emerita of economics at both the University of Maryland and the American University.

Bergmann is a prolific author and researcher whose publishing career began in 1960 with her first book, *Projection of a Metropolis*. She would follow up this work with forty years of research, teaching, and writing. Throughout her life, she has published books and articles in economic journals, government publications, and the popular press. In the 1980s, she wrote columns on economic affairs for the *New York Times* and the *Los Angeles Times*. Besides her writings, Bergmann has been actively involved with a number of organizations, having served as president of the Eastern Economic Association, the Society for the Advancement of Socio-Economics, the American Association of University Professors (1990–92), and the International Association for Feminist Economics (2000). She was vice president of the AEA (1976) and has been a member of the editorial boards of the *American Economic Review* (1970–73), *Challenge* magazine, *Signs,* and *Women and Politics.*

CONTRIBUTIONS

Bergmann's interest in using computer simulations to replicate economic systems and her desire to reform the methods of data collection economists use were reflected in her first major publication, *Projection of a Metropolis*. Subtitled *Technical Supplement to the New York Metropolitan Region Study*, the co-authored study, published in 1960, projected economic, demographic, and employment patterns for the New York metropolitan area through 1985. Bergmann wrote the section on the economic projections for the region, and in the process developed and implemented a sophisticated input-output model based on the work of Nobel laureate Wassily Leontief. After the publication of this book, Bergmann turned her research skill to her primary interest, that of sex roles in economic life, a focus reflected in her 1986 book *The Economic Emergence of Women*.

The basic thesis of this book was Bergmann's belief that the sex-role caste system, which had dominated Western economic development since before the time of Adam Smith, was coming asunder: "We are witnessing the breakup of the ancient system of sex roles under which men were assigned a monopoly of access to money-making and the mature women were restricted to the home. The forces behind the release of women from obligatory domesticity are not of recent origin; the move of women into paid work started modestly more than a century ago, and its origins go back at least two centuries. The social and economic forces promoting the emergence of women are far from spent; they continue to reinforce each other and to grow stronger. An economic cataclysm or a wave of religious fanaticism . . . could bring a regression. But barring such upheavals, women are unlikely to retreat back into domesticity. On the contrary, the emergence of women into fuller participation in the economy and in society will probably accelerate" (*Economic Emergence*, 3).

In support of her hypothesis, Bergmann analyzed the economic impetus and social factors behind women's emergence, including but not limited to employment gains in occupations once reserved for men, declining birthrates, and the effects of increasing educational opportunities for women. She also discussed the role of affirmative action in creating job opportunities for women and diminishing wage discrimination.

The value of affirmative action in promoting the advancement of women is a theme that Bergmann has explored repeatedly in her writings: "Title VII of the Civil Rights Act is the basic legal charter of women's rights on the job in the United States. The act was passed by the Congress in 1964 and signed by President Lyndon Johnson. It outlaws virtually all discriminatory employment practices on account of race or sex. Workers who believe they have been injured by sex discrimination of any kind by an employer or a labor union can bring a lawsuit and collect damages if the court decides discrimination has occurred. Class-action suits brought on behalf of groups of employees allow large damage awards in cases where there has been a consistent pattern of discrimination against the group" (*Economic Emergence*, 147–48). Even in the face of conservative attempts during the presidential administrations of Richard Nixon and Ronald Reagan to roll back its effects, the corporate world has pushed the implementation of affirmative action as a way to promote race and sex integration within the labor force ("The Corporation," 284). While noting that affirmative action has produced some negative feedback, especially among white males, Bergmann believes that, on balance, the positives have outweighed the negatives, making affirmative action an important contributor to the economic emergence of women (*In Defense*, 131).

The economic status of children has also been a focal point of Bergmann's research. Always acutely aware of the debilitating effects of poverty, especially on the young, Bergmann has crusaded for programs that can reduce, if not eliminate, the inordinately high number of American children living in poverty. Bergmann's concerns are particularly poignant given that many countries with economies similar to that of the United States have instituted policies that moderate the impact of poverty on young people. As recently as the 1980s, about 23 percent of American children lived in poverty based solely on the wage/income definition of being poor (*Saving Our Children*, 6). This proportion is not materially different than that in other industrialized nations such as Belgium, France, and the United Kingdom, where the percentages of poor children as measured by income were 21, 24, and 29, respectively. When the proportion of children in poverty was adjusted to reflect after-tax income and transfer benefits, 21 percent of children in the United States were poor. By contrast, in Belgium, France, and the United Kingdom, which have aggressive programs to shield children and their families from the effects of poverty, 3 percent, 5 percent, and 7 percent, respectively, of children were poor. Bergmann is convinced that the United States could achieve similar results if only its will to defeat child poverty matched its wherewithal (*America's Childcare Problem*, 238).

Bergmann is noted for her research concerning the economic status of women. This was evident, for instance, in her 1973 critique of the Report of the President's Council of Economic Advisers ("The 1973 Report"). While noting that "the Report recognizes that economic discrimination against women exists and, . . . implies that such discrimination constitutes a serious economic (and social) problem" (509), Bergmann nonetheless took the report to task on several points: "While painting an accurate, reasonably bleak picture of existing reality, the Report tends to underestimate the possibilities and need for social change, and to underemphasize the role of noneconomic forces in having brought about the current situation. Almost absentmindedly, it ignores the transformations in social relations and attitudes, and in economic practices which seem to be occurring and which must accelerate if significant change is to occur. Unfortunately also, the Report suggests very little by way of positive programs" (514).

Hardly a one-dimensional scholar, Bergmann examined the status of other groups whose economic position is as much a product of who they are as it is of their relative productivity. In a 1971 paper ("Effect on White Incomes"), she explored "the economic consequences of discrimination to employers and employees of both races (black and white), and as a corollary to estimate losses which might be suffered by whites if integration of employment were to take place" (295). She concluded that "Discrimination concentrates Negroes into certain occupations while virtually excluding them from others. In the occupations to which Negroes are relegated, marginal productivity may be lowered by the enforced abundance of supply. A model embodying this 'crowding' hypothesis is used to estimate the effects on white incomes of a reduction in discrimination. Whites with only an elementary education might have a once-for-all loss on the order of 10 percent; on all other whites and on national income the effect is estimated to be trivial" (294). Her conclusions were at odds with those of Gary Becker and Lester Thurow, whose research Bergmann respects but whose results she thinks missed the mark.

BIBLIOGRAPHY

Works by Barbara Rose Bergmann

Projection of a Metropolis: Technical Supplement to the New York Metropolitan Region Study (with B. Chinitz and E. Hoover). Cambridge, MA: Harvard University Press, 1960.

"The Effect on White Incomes of Discrimination in Employment." *Journal of Political Economy* 79(2), March–April 1971: 294–313.

"The 1973 Report of the President's Council of Economic Advisers: The Economic Role of Women" (with I[rma]. [Glicman] Adelman). *American Economic Review* 63(4), September 1973: 509–14.

The Economic Emergence of Women. New York: Basic Books, 1986.

"The Corporation Faces Issues of Race and Gender." In *The American Corporation Today*, edited by C. Kaysen, 269-91. New York: Oxford University Press, 1996.

In Defense of Affirmative Action. New York: Basic Books, 1996.

Saving Our Children from Poverty: What the United States Can Learn from France. New York: Russell Sage Foundation, 1996.

America's Childcare Problem: The Way Out (with S. W. Helburn). New York: St. Martin's Press, 2002.

Works about Barbara Rose Bergmann

"Barbara Berman Bergmann." In *Engendering Economics: Conversations with Women Economists in the United States*, edited by P. I. Olson and Z. Emami, 53–72. London: Routledge, 2002.

"Bergmann, Barbara." In *Who's Who in Economics*, edited by M. Blaug, 148–49. 3rd ed. Northampton, MA: Edward Elgar, 1999.

The International Who's Who. 63rd ed. London: Europa Publications, 2000.

Polkinghorn, B., and Thomson, D. L. "Barbara Bergmann (1927–)." In *Adam Smith's Daughters*, 104–17. Northampton, MA: Edward Elgar, 1998.

Trestrail, J. "Answering the Day-Care Question." *Chicago Tribune*, April 7, 2002, section 13.

Rebecca M. Blank
(1955–)

. . . .

Rebecca Blank is an academic with a cause. In this sense, she is a refreshing throwback to the women economists of the nineteenth and early twentieth centuries, economists whose research had a purpose beyond that of winning tenure and getting promoted. Blank wears her progressive principles on her sleeve, writing books and articles that are as compassionate as they are technical.

BIOGRAPHY

Rebecca Margaret Blank was born on September 19, 1955, in Columbia, Missouri. Her father, Oscar Vel Blank, was an extension agent, and her mother, Vernie (Backhaus) Blank, was a homemaker. The family moved several times during Blank's early life because of the nature of her father's work. Blank attended grammar school in East Lansing, Michigan, and junior high and high school in Roseville, Minnesota. She graduated from Alexander Ramsey High School in Roseville in 1973. Blank then attended the University of Minnesota, earning a B.S. in economics in 1976, graduating summa cum laude and Phi Beta Kappa. After receiving her bachelor's degree, she worked from 1976 to 1979 as a consultant and educational coordinator in the Chicago office of Data Resources, Inc. In 1979, she returned to higher education as a graduate student in the economics program at the Massachusetts Institute of Technology, earning her Ph.D. in 1983. While a graduate student, Blank served as president of MIT's Graduate Economics Association for two years.

In 1983, Blank became an assistant professor of economics and public affairs at Princeton University, working in the Department of Economics and the Woodrow Wilson School of Public and International Affairs. She left Princeton in 1989 to become a senior staff economist with the president's Council of Economic Advisers in Washington, D.C. She remained at the council for one year before moving to Northwestern University as an associate professor of economics and an associate professor in the School of Education and Social Policy. While at Northwestern, Blank served as codirector of the Northwestern/University of Chicago Interdisciplinary Training Program in Poverty, Race, and Underclass Issues (1991–96). She was, and continues to be, a member of the research faculty in Northwestern's Center for Urban Affairs and Social Policy. From 1996 to 1967, she directed the Joint Center for Poverty Research at Northwestern while maintaining her affiliation with the Council of Economic Advisers. In 1994, Blank married Johannes Kuttner; the couple has one child. She has been dean of the Gerald R. Ford School of Public Policy at the University of Michigan since 1999. She is also the Henry Carter Adams Collegiate Professor of Public Policy at Michigan, as well as a professor of economics.

Blank has been the recipient of numerous honors and grants. In 1985, she received the Department of Economics Junior Faculty Teaching Award at Princeton University. In 1993, the Association of Public Policy and Management awarded her the David Kershaw Prize. This award is given biannually to a young scholar (under age forty) whose research has had the most important impact on the public policy process. Four years later, Blank received the Richard A. Lester Prize for the Outstanding Book in Labor Economics and Industrial Relations. She has delivered many prestigious lectures, including the Frank Paish Lecture to the Royal Economic Society in 1999, the J. Douglas Gibson Lecture at the School of Policy Studies at Queen's University in Canada, and the Adam Smith Lecture to the European Association of Labour Economists in 2001. Blank also received research grants from the Charles Stewart Mott Foundation (2001) and the Russell Sage Foundation (1997) and has received three from the National Science Foundation.

Blank complements her writing and teaching with professional service related to academe. She was on the board of editors for the *American Economic Review* (1993–97) and served as an executive committee member for the AEA (1995–97). She was coeditor of the *Journal of Human Resources* (1995–97) and has been a member of the advisory boards of *Feminist Economics* (1994–97), the *Journal of Public Economics* (1993–97), and the *Journal of Economic Education* (1992–97 and since 2002). Outside of academe, Blank has been a research adviser for the W. E. Upjohn Institute for Employment Research (1995–96; 2000); has served on the advisory committee of the New Hope Project, a job training and employment program in Milwaukee, Wisconsin (1992–97); and is a member of the Policy Council of the Association for Public Policy and Management (since 2001).

CONTRIBUTIONS

In 1997, Blank published *It Takes a Nation*, and this single work, more than anything else she has written, brought her to the attention of academics and policy makers alike. Funded by the Russell Sage Foundation, the book examined the changing face of poverty in the nineties, considered the effectiveness of previous antipoverty programs, and suggested where the future of the effort to reduce—if not eliminate—poverty in the United States is headed. Blank concluded her investigation with a number of lessons learned; lessons that will surely impact the future of the antipoverty movement:

> Lesson 1. In the last decade, we have consistently misunderstood the nature of poverty in America, believing that it is more behavioral, more ghetto-based, and more a problem experienced by people of color. Hence, for many middle-income Americans, the poor have come to seem alien and less "like us" than they actually are. . . .
>
> Lesson 2. The primary change in the lives of the poor over the past 20 years has been the deteriorating set of economic opportunities available to less-skilled workers. The favorite solution to poverty among most Americans has always been overall growth that creates jobs and helps the poor escape poverty through work and wages. Unfortunately, wage rates have declined steadily on the jobs available to less-skilled workers, which means that employment has become progressively less effective at reducing poverty. . . .
>
> Lesson 3. Out of frustration with persistent poverty, a nihilistic response has emerged that "nothing works" or, perhaps more appropriately "nothing the federal government does to fight poverty works." "Nothing works" seriously misinterprets history and ignores the real successes we have achieved. It also ignores thirty years of knowledge about what works and what does not, accumulated through observation, experience, and program evaluation. . . .
>
> To the extent this book has a single message, that message is to avoid simple explanations for poverty and the false promise of simple solutions. There is no single cause of poverty, and there is no easy way to abolish it. The challenge is to build a balanced system which relies on the contributions of many different groups and programs. . . .
>
> The government has a key ongoing role in public assistance to the poor, but government programs must be buttressed by the behavior of individuals and the involvement of civic institutions, from charities to businesses to community organizations. (5–9)

It Takes a Nation brought Blank acclaim as a public scholar but is by no means the sum total of her research.

Through her academic scholarship and popular writings, Blank has become a recognized expert on just about every aspect of the Personal Responsibility and Work Opportunity Reconciliation Act of 1996, commonly known as welfare reform. Proponents of the act believe the legislation—aimed at reducing welfare usage and increasing work effort—has "been effective beyond anyone's wildest dreams" ("Work, Wages and Welfare," 94). Skeptics of the bill believe that all the success attributed to welfare reform in the late 1990s was entirely dependent on the unprecedented economic boom of the times and the ready availability of jobs (94). Soon after welfare reform became law, Blank posited that "the legislation will produce less dramatic effects than either its supporters or its opponents suggest" ("Policy Watch," 176). She spent the next half-dozen years measuring the effects of welfare reform, including an analysis of its impact on public-assistance caseloads ("What Causes"). Blank has also expressed her views in popular writings for the *Wall Street Journal* ("Unwed

Mothers"), the *Chicago Tribune* ("A Helping Hand"), and the *Washington Post* ("Revisiting Welfare") in an effort to share the insights of her research with the general public.

While noted for her scholarship on welfare and its possible reform, Blank has other research interests. In one of her first major publications, she analyzed how different personal characteristics impact the probability of a worker's choosing public- versus private-sector employment, and within the public sector, choosing between federal versus state/local government jobs ("An Analysis"). Three years later, she combined her choice employment model with her interest in welfare "to calculate the impact of welfare-benefit levels, wages, and tax rates on the location choices of female-headed household" ("The Effect of Welfare and Wage Levels," 186). In the mid-1990s, she published an article debunking the prevailing notion that public-assistance payments were a prime factor in the increase of out-of-wedlock birthrates among teenagers and other women ("Teen Pregnancy"). The article was based on testimony she gave on January 20, 1995, before the House Ways and Means Committee's Subcommittee on Human Resources, which was conducting hearings on welfare reform.

A real change of pace in her research occurred in the late 1980s, when Blank conducted an experiment for the *American Economic Review* to determine the effects of double-blind versus single-blind reviewing on the acceptance of manuscripts submitted for publication in the *Review* ("The Effects of Double-Blind versus Single-Blind Reviewing"). "Double-blind" reviewing is a process in which author(s) and referee(s) are uninformed of each other's identity. "Single-blind" refers to a reviewing process in which the referee(s) knows the name(s) and institutional affiliation(s) of the author(s) but the reverse is not the case. The study, which was quite involved, was truly a change of pace in Blank's research agenda but nonetheless reflective of her eclectic scholarship interests.

BIBLIOGRAPHY

Works by Rebecca M. Blank

"An Analysis of Worker Sectoral Choice: Public vs. Private Employment." *Industrial and Labor Relations Review* 38(2), January 1985: 211–24.

"The Effect of Welfare and Wage Levels on the Location Decisions of Female-Headed Households." *Journal of Urban Economics* 24(2), September 1988: 186–211.

"The Effects of Double-Blind versus Single-Blind Reviewing: Experimental Evidence from the *American Economic Review*." *American Economic Review* 81(5), December 1991: 1041–67.

"Unwed Mothers Need Role Models, Not Roll Backs." *Wall Street Journal*, March 7, 1995: editorial page.

"Teen Pregnancy: Government Programs Are Not the Cause." *Feminist Economics* 1(2), Summer 1995: 47–58.

"A Helping Hand Isn't Enough." *Chicago Tribune*, November 17, 1995: 19.

It Takes a Nation: A New Agenda for Fighting Poverty. Princeton, NJ: Princeton University Press, 1997.

"Policy Watch: The 1996 Welfare Reform." *Journal of Economic Perspectives* 11(1), Winter 1997: 169–77.

"Revisiting Welfare" (with R. Haskins). *Washington Post*, February 14, 2001: A25.

"What Causes Public Assistance Caseloads to Grow?" *Journal of Human Resources* 36(1), Winter 2001: 85–118.

"Work, Wages and Welfare" (with L. Schmidt). In *The New World of Welfare*, edited by R. Blank and R. Haskins, 74–96. Washington, DC: Brookings Institution Press, 2001.

Works about Rebecca M. Blank

Mandel, M. J. ". . . And if it comes, the poor will really take a hit." *Business Week* (3099), April 10, 1989: 20.

Francine D. Blau
(1946–   )

∙∙∙

Francine Blau grew up in a family that considered Franklin Delano Roosevelt a larger-than-life figure. Not surprisingly, Blau took as her personal hero Frances Perkins, FDR's secretary of labor throughout his administration and the first woman to serve in a cabinet position. The choice was incredibly prophetic. As an adult, Blau would honor her hero in a way she could not possibly have imagined when, as a teenager, she decided to attend Cornell University. Since 1994, Blau has been the Frances Perkins Professor of Industrial and Labor Relations at Cornell.

BIOGRAPHY

Francine Dee Blau was born in New York City on August 29, 1946. Her parents, Harold Raymond Blau and Sylvia (Goldberg) Blau, were both teachers. They divorced when she was six years old. For five years following the divorce, Francine and her brother lived with their mother. When their mother became ill, the two children went to live with their father, who was always supportive of Francine's career aspirations. Blau graduated from Forest Hills High School in Queens in 1963. She entered Cornell University and earned a B.S. in industrial and labor relations in 1966. Her decision to study industrial and labor relations was motivated in part by her admiration for Perkins. As an undergraduate, Blau received the Irving M. Ives Award (1964, 1965) and the Daniel Alpern Award (1966) from Cornell's School of Industrial and Labor Relations. At Cornell, Blau was inducted into the Phi Kappa Phi Scholastic Honorary Society, the Pi Gamma Mu Social Science Honorary Society, and Pi Delta Epsilon, a journalism honors society. She married Richard Weisskoff in August 1969; the couple divorced in 1972. On January 1, 1979, Blau married

Lawrence Max Kahn. They have two children, Daniel Blau Kahn and Lisa Blau Kahn.

Blau attended graduate school at Harvard University, receiving an M.A. in economics in 1969 and a Ph.D. in economics in 1975. She began her teaching career in spring 1971 as a visiting lecturer at Yale University. From September 1971 until June 1974, she was an instructor of economics at Trinity College in Hartford, Connecticut. In fall 1974, she became a research associate at Ohio State University's Center for Human Resource Research. She left Ohio State in 1975 for a tenure-track position as an assistant professor of economics and labor and industrial relations at the University of Illinois at Urbana-Champaign. She was an assistant professor there from 1975 until 1978, when she was promoted to associate professor. In 1983, Blau was made professor of economics and labor and industrial relations. While at the University of Illinois, she was named best faculty teacher in undergraduate instruction in 1976. She received the Burlington Northern Faculty Achievement Award, a campuswide honor, for outstanding teaching and research in 1993.

In 1994, Blau left Illinois to become the first Frances Perkins Professor of Industrial and Labor Relations at Cornell, a chair named in honor of her personal hero. In addition to her role as a professor in Cornell's School of Industrial and Labor Relations, Blau is a research associate for the National Bureau of Economic Research (since 1988), a faculty affiliate of the Cornell Employment and Family Careers Institute (since 1996), and a Research Fellow at the Center for Economic Studies/Ifo Institute for Economic Research in Munich, Germany (since 2001). Blau's previous positions include research director of Cornell's School of Industrial and Labor Relations (1995–2001) and research associate with the Canadian International Labour Network (1997–2001). She has served as a visiting scholar with the Russell Sage Foundation in New York City (1999–2000), a visiting fellow at the Australian National University in Canberra (summer 1993), and an associate of the Center for Advanced Study at the University of Illinois (fall 1988).

Blau has been an officer in a number of academic associations. In 1983–84, she served as vice president of the Midwest Economics Association, she was a member of the association's executive board from 1990 to 1993, and she served as the association's president in 1991–92. She was vice president of the AEA in 1993–94 and president of the Industrial Relations Research Association in 1997.

The author or coauthor of nearly 100 articles, books, book chapters, and monographs, Blau is often sought after to serve on the editorial boards of professional journals. Since 1998, she has been on the board of editors of the *American Economic Review*. She is also a member of the advisory board of the *Journal of Economic Perspectives* and was an associate editor of that journal from 1994 until 2001. She serves on the advisory board of the *Journal of Labor Abstracts* (since 1996), and she was coeditor of the *Journal of Labor Economics* from 1992 to 1995. Other editorial boards on which Blau has served include *Industrial Relations* (1989–96), *Feminist Economics* (since 1994), and *Social Science Quarterly* (1978–94).

CONTRIBUTIONS

Francine Blau's scholarly interests were evident in the very first book she published as a sole author, *Equal Pay in the Office*. Dedicated to her parents, the book was meant "to shed . . . light on the causes and consequences of sex segregation in the labor market by going to the level of establishment to examine the relationship of differences in the employment distribution of male and female workers among firms to the male-female pay differential within selected white-collar occupations" (*Equal Pay*, 1). Prior research on male-female pay differentials had focused mainly on the labor market, using aggregate census data for occupational categories that had historically been predominately male or predominately female. Blau examined data "at the level of disaggregation at which many of the employment decisions which produce the observed patterns of employment segregation and pay differences are made" (2). In her study of intraoccupational employment, Blau found a substantial amount of sex segregation by occupation and gender-gap pay differentials. This situation had continued virtually unchanged for twenty years from 1950 to 1970.

Nearly a quarter-century later, Blau revisited the issue of gender differences in pay ("Gender Differences"). This time she and a coauthor found that the world had changed:

> Over the past 25 years, the gender pay gap has narrowed dramatically and women have increasingly entered traditionally male occupations. These two labor market outcomes are closely linked, since considerable research suggests that predominately female occupations pay less, even controlling for measured personal characteristics of workers and a variety of characteristics of occupations, although the interpretation of such results remains in some dispute. (75)

Blau determined that much of the wage-gap narrowing was attributable to the entry of new cohorts of young workers, each faring better than its predecessors. Still, the status of women's pay compared to that of men's had improved, in part, because of a perceptible decrease in occupational segregation by gender. Improvement was measurable but not complete:

> Taking these factors together, it seems plausible that the gender pay gap will continue to decline at least modestly in the next few years. But it seems unlikely to vanish. Women continue to confront discrimination in the labor market, although its extent seems to be decreasing. In addition, at least some of the remaining pay gap is surely tied to the gender division of labor in the home, both directly through its effect on women's labor force attachment and indirectly through its impact on the strength of statistical discrimination against women. Women still retain primary responsibility for housework and childcare in most American families. However, this pattern has been changing as families respond to rising labor market opportunities for women that increase the opportunity cost of such arrangements. Further, policies that facilitate the integration of work and family responsibilities, both voluntary and

government-mandated, have become increasingly prevalent in recent years. Employers are likely to continue to expand such policies as they respond to the shifting composition of the work force and a desire to retain employees in whom they have made substantial investments. In the long run, the increasing availability of such policies will make it easier for women to combine work and family, and also for men to take on a greater share of household tasks. (97)

Blau's decades-long interest in gender differences in labor market outcomes is based on two concerns—equity and efficiency: "One reason for concern over persistent gender differences in labor market outcomes is based on equity or fairness. In this view, the elimination of discrimination against women in the labor market is "a matter of simple justice." Equity concerns over gender pay differentials, regardless of their source, are heightened by the growth in families headed by single women, as well as the increasing dependence of married couples on the wife's earnings. A second reason for concern is based on efficiency. To the extent that the gender gap reflects discrimination, such differential treatment of otherwise equally qualified men and women is wasteful. More broadly, social welfare is maximized if we obtain the greatest possible productivity out of all resources, including human resources" ("Introduction," 3). This sensitivity to fairness, when combined with Blau's appreciation of the importance of productivity in advancing social welfare, gives her scholarship a balance that is sometimes lacking in the writings of others whose good intentions sometimes cloud their analysis.

Obviously, the economic well-being of women is a topic that has dominated Blau's scholarship. She has penned a monumental review article that charts "the trends in well-being of women in the United States" over the last quarter of the twentieth century ("Trends"). Blau has also coauthored a very successful textbook that reviews the research on women, men, and work in the labor market and the household, and includes a chapter titled "Gender Differences in Other Countries" (*The Economics*). It would, however, be an oversimplification to portray her as a one-dimensional scholar. In the mid-1980s, Blau published a paper in applied econometrics challenging the prevailing view "that immigrants constitute a burden on the U.S. transfer payment system" ("The Use of Transfer Payments," 238). She showed that when age and other factors are held constant, immigrant families are less likely to rely on welfare than families native to the United States. Blau also coauthored a detailed examination of black-white earnings trends in the 1970s and 1980s, concluding that while black women fared better than black men in terms of both annual earnings and estimated wages, the two groups experienced stagnating earnings and wages relative to whites of the same sex during the 1980s ("Black-White Earnings"). She has, in short, explored a number of issues in the research-rich field of industrial and labor relations.

Still, Blau's primary research interest, for which she makes no apologies, has been the economics of gender. Actually, she made the commitment to study gender issues at considerable professional risk, for at the time of her decision, women studying women's issues were often perceived as having an agenda:

The decision to work in this area was not, however, without its costs. At the time, research on women was generally not seen as central. For a member of a "marginal group" to work on a "marginal" subject was risky. In addition, a woman working on women, especially one known to have feminist leanings, was suspected of bias. The latter point, the role of values in social-science research, is an interesting and important one. But it has always seemed illogical to assume that, for an issue like gender, women are likely to be ideologues and men neutral, or that an individual, regardless of sex, who favors social change is less objective than one who upholds the status quo. Obviously, either person might be tempted to fit the facts to their views. I have always endeavored to benefit from the insights that concern over gender inequities gives me into problems to study and explanations for observed outcomes, and, at the same time, to be objective as possible in reporting my results, even if they do not accord with what I would have liked to find. Indeed, one quickly learns that a source of great excitement—and great frustration—to the empirical economist is how often the data fail to confirm a priori expectations. ("On Becoming," 24–25)

Blau has always advised other scholars to "follow your interests" without regard to the current fashion in the discipline. Creativity, Blau believes, is optimized when working on what one finds truly fascinating. Clearly, she followed her own advice.

BIBLIOGRAPHY

Works by Francine D. Blau

Equal Pay in the Office, Lexington, MA: D. C. Heath and Company, 1977.

"The Use of Transfer Payments by Immigrants." *Industrial and Labor Relations Review* 37(2), January 1984: 222–29.

"Black-White Earnings over the 1970s and 1980s: Gender Differences in Trends" (with A. H. Beller). *Review of Economics and Statistics* 74(2), May 1992: 276–86.

"Introduction" (with R. G. Ehrenberg). In *Gender and Family Issues in the Workplace*, edited by F. D. Blau and R. G. Ehrenberg, 1–19. New York: Russell Sage Foundation, 1997.

"On Becoming and Being an Economist." In *Passion and Craft: Economists at Work*, edited by M. Szenberg, 20–38. Ann Arbor: University of Michigan Press, 1998.

"Trends in the Well-Being of American Women, 1970–1995." *Journal of Economic Literature* 36, March 1998: 112–65.

"Gender Differences in Pay" (with L. M. Kahn). *Journal of Economic Perspectives* 14(4), Fall 2000: 75–99.

The Economics of Women, Men, and Work (with **M[arianne] A. Ferber** and A. E. Winkler). 4th ed. Upper Saddle River, NJ: Prentice Hall, 2002.

Works about Francine D. Blau

"Blau, Francine." In *Who's Who in Economics*, edited by M. Blaug, 117–18. 3rd ed. Northampton, MA: Edward Elgar, 1999.

Mary Jean Bowman
(1908–2002)

In the second half of the twentieth century, the economics of education emerged as a new and important subdiscipline with the field of economics. Mary Jean Bowman was one of the pioneers leading this movement. She studied how education both affects and responds to economic conditions and economic systems. Bowman was motivated by the belief that there is an ideal congruence between education and economic conditions, so that a good fit between educational and economic systems would accelerate the realization of economic priorities, while a mismatch of the two systems would make the attainment of socially desirable economic outcomes harder to achieve. "She was," said Nobel Prize winner Gary Becker, "one of the leaders in studying the impact of education on occupation, earnings and unemployment" (quoted in Casillas).

BIOGRAPHY

Mary Jean Bowman was born in New York City on October 17, 1908, to Harold M. Bowman and Mary Catherine (Kauffman) Bowman. She graduated Phi Beta Kappa from Vassar College in 1930, winning the Virginia Swinburne Award in Economics. Bowman went on to earn her M.A. in economics at Radcliffe College, where she served as a research fellow from 1932 to 1933. In 1934, she became city supervisor at the U.S. Bureau of Labor Statistics, and from 1935 to 1943 she held the rank of assistant professor of economics at Iowa State University. She received her Ph.D. from Harvard University in 1938. Bowman took a leave from Iowa State in 1935–36 to become director of the Northwest Central Region Consumer Purchases Survey of the U.S. Department of Agriculture, and she was a visiting professor at the University of Minnesota during the summer of 1941. She married Charles A. Anderson on July 18, 1942, and in 1943 the couple had a son. Bowman's husband, Charles

Anderson, was a professor of sociology and education, was director of the Comparative Education Center at the University of Chicago, and occasionally coauthored professional publications (e.g., *Where Colleges*) with her.

In 1944, Bowman became a senior economist with the U.S. Bureau of Labor Statistics. Prior to becoming a research associate and associate professor of economics at the University of Chicago in 1958, she held a number of short-term and honorary positions, including a Fulbright Research Fellowship in Sweden (1956–57) and a contract researcher for Resources for the Future (1957–58). During her time at the University of Chicago, Bowman served on the executive committee of the AEA (1969–71), served on the board of trustees of the Teachers Insurance Annuity Association (1972–76), and was a member of the editorial board of the *Journal of Political Economy* (1959–60). She became professor of economics and education at the University of Chicago in 1969, a position she held until 1974.

Although she retired from full-time teaching at Chicago in 1974, Bowman continued to be active professionally for many years She was a Guggenheim Foundation fellow in 1974, a member of the Ford Foundation's UK-US Exchange Program on the Economics of Education from 1976 to 1982, an editorial board member of the *International Journal of Social Economics* in 1978, and, in 1980, she was appointed to the editorial board of the *Economic Education Review*. During her career, she taught in a visiting capacity at a number of institutions, including the University of Zagreb in the summer of 1973 as a Fulbright distinguished professor, Uppsala University (1974), and the London School of Economics (1975). Bowman served as a consultant to the government of Brazil in 1976 and was associated with the World Bank for several years beginning in 1978. In 1982, she received the Distinguished Service Medal from Teachers College of Columbia University. In the mid-1980s Bowman worked on a study of education in Mexico and, with colleagues from Chile and France, completed a comparative study of the political economy of public support of higher education in those countries (Blaug). Late in her life, Bowman took up painting and wrote poetry. She died on June 24, 2002, at the age of ninety-three in Mongomery Place, a retirement community in the Hyde Park section of Chicago.

CONTRIBUTIONS

Bowman had a long and distinguished career as a scholar. Her first major effort was an undergraduate textbook written for students taking what has subsequently become the principles of economics, both macro- and micro-economics. First published in 1943, *Economic Analysis and Public Policy* was published in a second edition in 1949. Believing that "economic analysis takes on meaning primarily in relation to broad social problems—problems relating to the general level of employment, the allocation of productive resources among different uses, the distribution of income" (v), Bowman wrote a text that emphasized the policy implications of economic theory. The book concentrated on the use of economic analysis in dealing effectively with five generally accepted social ends considered relevant in evaluating the functioning of any economic system: progress in raising real incomes; economic stability and security; allocation of resources in accordance with consumer preferences; freedom in the choice of a job or business; and equity in the distribution of income. Recognizing that at times the simultaneous attainment of these social ends can be at odds, if not mutually exclusive, Bowman still devoted about one-third of the book's chapters to the public policy applications of economic analysis.

Equity of opportunity, if not of income, was always a topic that preoccupied Bowman. This was evident early in her career in a paper she published in the *American Economic Review* ("A Graphical Analysis"). After describing three different kinds of income distribution—by industry, by functional sources (e.g., labor, capital), and by income-receiving units (i.e., personal income)—Bowman developed a detailed graphical analysis of the personal distribution of income in the United States for 1935–36, 1941, and 1942. Her presentation highlighted three graphical approaches to income distribution: those of Vilfredo Pareto, Corrado Gini, and M. C. Lorenz. She noted that the scale of income representation, whether double logarithm or semilogarithm, affected the interpretation of each of the graphical approaches and the policy implications embedded therein. Underlying all analysis was Bowman's belief, when she quoted a remark by the economist Allyn Young, in effect, that highly unequal income distributions reflect the presence of an equally unequal distribution in opportunity (627).

In the early 1960s, there was a flurry of research that sought to measure the contribution of education per member of the labor force to the rate of economic growth. Convinced that education and growth were strongly correlated, Bowman published a review article ("Schultz, Denison") that interpreted the scholarship of Nobel laureate T. W. Schultz and E. F. Denison, each of whom had developed an elaborate and comprehensive model to assess the increasing level of education in the United States as a contributing factor to economic growth. In addition to explaining how the Schultz and Denison models worked, Bowman integrated into her analysis the research of Gary Becker and Kenneth Arrow, two Nobel laureates who made important contributions to what was, in the 1960s, the emerging field of human capital.

Bowman's interest in the nexus of education and economic growth was more than theoretical, as was evident in a massive study she coauthored about the economy of eastern Kentucky (*Resources and People*). Initiated and financed by Resources for the Future, the study sought to shed light on one of the more intractable modern social problems in the United States—the economically depressed area within the country that is easily one of the richest on the planet in terms of natural resources. Divided into two major parts, the study examined the jobs and people of the mountain region of eastern Kentucky, highlighting the availability of natural resources, demographic patterns, the structure and composition of local industry, employment trends, and transportation problems unique to the region. The second part of the study reviewed in depth the eastern Kentucky coal industry, long the backbone of the region's economy. The study concluded that for eastern Kentucky in general and the local coal industry in particular, the search for sustained prosperity would be long and trying and not necessarily successful, a prophecy that has, regrettably, proved largely correct.

While a firm believer in the value of education as a significant—if not a major—factor in determining the rate of a country's economic growth, Bowman was not averse to questioning the wisdom of the unbridled expansion of educational opportunities. The diminishing returns effects of education became evident to her in a study she coauthored for the Carnegie Commission on Higher Education (*Where Colleges*). That study evaluated the basic assumptions propelling the expansion of the community college system in the United States in the 1960s. The two precepts Bowman and her coauthors (one of whom was her husband) reviewed were, first, that geographic proximity of a college to a student's home is an important determinant of attendance, and, second, that the community college experience, especially for the disadvantaged, is one way to ensure more equality of opportunity. Bowman's research indicated that: (1) academic ability and family status are more important determinants of attendance than the geographic proximity of a college; and (2) additional investment in the thirteenth and fourteenth years of education may not be as prudent an expenditure as investment in the earlier years of education, when the real deprivation of opportunity occurs.

As part of the effort in Sweden to design an educational system that would contribute to the achievement of economic priorities, Bowman was asked late in her career to write an essay on the fit, or congruence, between a country's educational and economic systems. Falling back on her ideas concerning the generally accepted social ends considered relevant in evaluating an economy, she discussed at length how an educational system can promote certain goals or ends, particularly economic growth and stability, the formation of human resources, and choice of occupation. While noting that congruence between the educational system and the economy is difficult to attain, Bowman was convinced that the effort, if successful, would appreciably increase the likelihood of achieving socially desirable ends. The belief that matching educational and economic systems maximizes the social good became a fundamental tenet of her philosophy of the economics of education.

BIBLIOGRAPHY

Works by Mary Jean Bowman

Economic Analysis and Public Policy (with G. L. Bach). 2nd ed. New York: Prentice Hall, 1949. Originally published 1943.

"A Graphical Analysis of Personal Income Distribution in the United States." *American Economic Review* 35(4), September 1945: 607–28.

Resources and People in East Kentucky: Problems and Potentials of a Lagging Economy (with W. W. Haynes). Baltimore, MD: Johns Hopkins Press for Resources for the Future, 1963.

"Schultz, Denison, and the Contribution of 'Eds' to National Income Growth." *Journal of Political Economy* 72(5), October 1964: 450–64.

Where Colleges Are and Who Attends (with C. A. Anderson and V. Tinto). New York: McGraw-Hill, 1972.

"Choices by and for People: Processes, Goals, and the Search for Congruence between the Educational System and the Economy." In *Learning and Earning: Three Essays in the Economics of Education*, 9–52. Stockholm, Sweden: National Board of Universities and Colleges, 1978.

Works about Mary Jean Bowman

"Bowman, Mary Jean." In *Who's Who in Economics*, edited by M. Blaug, 148–49. 3rd ed. Northampton, MA: Edward Elgar, 1999.

Casillas, O. "Retired Researcher, Economics Teacher" (obituary). *Chicago Tribune*, July 1, 2002: section 2.

University of Chicago. Biographical information and a curriculum vitae furnished by the University News Office.

Abby Joseph Cohen
(1952–)

Abby Joseph Cohen—partner, managing director, and chief investment strategist for Goldman, Sachs, & Company—has been described as a visionary. She is an unusual economist, one who can explain complex economic analysis in terms that the average person can understand. That ability, along with her penchant for hard work and her record of consistently correct investment advice, earned Cohen acclaim as one of Wall Street's most influential investment strategists during the 1990s. In the male-dominated world of high finance, Cohen had remarkable influence on the buying and selling decisions of millions of stock owners, who would often hang on her every word. On November 16, 1996, for example, the Dow Jones Industrial Average, up 65 points and seemingly headed for another record high close, convulsed when rumors swept Wall Street that Cohen was advising her clients to pull back on their stock allocations. The Dow quickly surrendered 60 points by the time Cohen, using the intercom system that links Goldman offices throughout the world, announced that she had not altered her bullish views. The market immediately began to levitate, and the Dow ended the day up 35 points.

BIOGRAPHY

Abby Joseph Cohen was born on February 29, 1952, in Queens, New York, to Raymond Joseph and Shirley (Silverstein) Joseph. Her father, the son of Polish immigrants, earned a master's degree in finance from New York University and over time developed a specialty in publishing-company accounting. In the late 1960s, he became controller of *Essence,* the African American monthly. Cohen's mother left Poland with her parents in the 1920s and, after graduation from Brooklyn College, worked in the controller's office at General Foods. Both parents encouraged Abby and her older sister to work hard and to be ambitious. Cohen graduated from Martin Van Buren High School in

Queens, New York, and in 1969, she enrolled at Cornell University, one of the few Ivy League colleges that admitted women at the time. She decided on a double major: economics and the then fledging field of computer science. Cohen was discouraged from taking a graduate-level course in computer science by a professor because she was not enrolled in an engineering program, not a graduate student, nor a man. She ignored him, enrolled anyway, and made it her business to finish the class.

She earned her B.A. in 1973. That same year she married her college sweetheart, David M. Cohen, who had majored in labor relations. The couple moved to Washington, D.C., where she worked as a junior economist at the Federal Reserve Board while studying advanced economics at George Washington University, earning her M.S. in 1976. She then accepted a position as an economist/analyst at T. Rowe Price Associates, a mutual-funds company in Baltimore, Maryland. There she focused on economic forecasting and helped construct econometric models to help securities analysts forecast demand in the semiconductor and other high-tech industries.

In 1980, after giving birth to the first of her two daughters, Cohen continued her work in economic and financial forecasting. She noted that the culture had changed since her childhood, when her own mother had left a career to stay at home with her children. "I always wondered how far my mother could have gone," she has said (Bianco, 126). A modest, unassuming woman who works thirteen-hour days, Cohen lives with her husband, the chief labor lawyer for Columbia University, in the same Flushing, Queens, neighborhood where she grew up, close to her widowed father and extended family.

In 1983, after seven years at T. Rowe Price, Cohen answered what she dubbed "the siren call of Wall Street," joining Drexel Burnham Lambert as a portfolio strategist (Bianco, 126). She loved the job right from the start. In 1987, Drexel promoted Cohen to chief strategist, just before "Black Monday"—October 19, 1987—when the Dow Jones Industrial Average fell 508 points, or 22.6 percent, the biggest one-day drop ever, in relative terms. Because Cohen did not foresee the magnitude of the downturn, she failed to alert her clients, but by the next morning she had advised Drexel's clients to use all available cash to buy stocks and bonds, saying that her analysis indicated stocks were a good 15 percent undervalued. This gutsy prophetic call left her both exhilarated and humbled. She learned from this experience, saying she felt the crash had been caused by structural defects in the financial markets (*Current Biography*, 112). Since then, she has paid more attention to this aspect of risk than to other seemingly important but often tangential factors.

In 1990, Drexel collapsed into bankruptcy, and Cohen followed many of her colleagues to Barclays de Zoete Wedd, a London-based merchant bank, but stayed only a few months. She then moved on to what she called the gold standard of the financial world, the New York investment bank Goldman Sachs & Company (*Current Biography*, 112). Hired by Goldman Sachs as chief U.S. equity strategist, Cohen had reached the pinnacle of success in the world of high finance as a chief strategist at one of the most prestigious firms on Wall Street. At Goldman Sachs—a conservative, self-contained firm and one of the last private partnerships in investment banking—she joined with col-

leagues in advising the United States' biggest corporations and world governments on their financial plans. In the ensuing years, as Cohen's bullish
predictions proved consistently correct and the U.S. stock market soared, so
too did her reputation as a financial guru extraordinaire.

Cohen, who has a reassuring and compelling speaking style, became well
known as a spokesperson for her firm, appearing on PBS, CNN, CNBC, and
other television networks. She could present market ideas to varied audiences
without condescending to anyone. Increasingly, small investors based their
decisions on her reports. She became a respected and even beloved figure in
ever-widening investment circles, and by 1996 was probably the most influential analyst on Wall Street. Former *Wall Street Week* host Louis Rukeyser has
described her as the "most consistently correct strategist working for any major firm in the 1990's" (*Current Biography*, 112). In 1997, she was inducted into
Wall Street Week's Hall of Fame. Given Cohen's fame and reputation, many
felt she deserved to be made a partner at Goldman Sachs, which at the time
was making an estimated $5 million annual profit. In 1998, she finally did
make partner at Goldman Sachs, by then a company known to many investors
simply as "Abby Cohen's firm." In December 1999, the New York Stock
Exchange initiated a Bridging the Millennium Series to recognize distinguished leaders of the twentieth century whose achievements continued to
enrich humanity. Individuals selected for recognition were introduced at bell-
sounding ceremonies marking the opening or closing of daily trading. It came
as no surprise when on December 30, 1999, Cohen was so honored.

CONTRIBUTIONS

If nothing else, Cohen proved that you don't need a Ph.D. to tell which
way the economy is headed. Nearly all of the brand-name forecasting gurus
of the 1990s, shackled by the blinders of past experience, kept predicting one
economic downturn after another in the face of an economic expansion without precedent in U.S. history. Only Cohen consistently predicted the unre-
lenting upturn that occurred from the end of 1991 through the beginning of
2001; even her forecasts, while directionally correct, underestimated the
magnitude of growth.

The accuracy of Cohen's forecasts during the 1990s was a direct result of
her willingness to dig deeper in her research than the average economic forecaster. Assisted by Gabrielle Napolitano, a former high school math teacher
turned Wall Street quantitative analyst, Cohen has always based her assess-
ment of the economy on solid projections of corporate earnings, which she
and Napolitano build from scratch. Each quarter, the pair examines in detail
the quarterly earning reports of every Standard and Poor's 500 company. This
enormously laborious and time-consuming task gives Cohen her critical edge
in predicting the movements of an economy in which huge write-offs and
ever-changing accounting rules have complicated earnings forecasts as never
before. Combining these painstakingly developed projections of corporate
earnings with her healthy skepticism of conventional business-cycle theory,
Cohen produced economic forecasts of uncanny accuracy during the 1990s.

She was among the first to argue that prevailing price-earning multiples—perceived by rival forecasters as high by historical standards—were not excessive when "adjusted for low inflation, surging returns on capital, and other unusually favorable economic trends" (Bianco, 127). In the process of being right so often, Cohen earned millions of dollars for her company and its clients and an international reputation as the most influential Wall Street analyst of the 1990s.

Forecasting is a harsh taskmaster. Even the most accurate of gurus is only as good as her last prediction. During the premier of CNBC's *Louis Rukeyser's Wall Street* in April 2002, Cohen called for a 10 percent rise in the Dow Jones Industrial Average and a 15 percent increase in the Standard & Poor's 500. She projected the Dow would reach 11,300 by the end of the year. Three months later, it was hovering in the low 9,000s and seemed destined to drop even further. For this reason, Cohen fell to the bottom of *Fortune* magazine's 2001 list of the fifty "Most Powerful Women in Business," down from her ranking of eighth just one year earlier.

BIBLIOGRAPHY

Works about Abby Joseph Cohen

Bianco, A. "The Prophet of Wall Street." *Business Week,* June 1, 1998.

"Cohen, Abby Joseph." *Current Biography Yearbook 1998*, 111–13. New York: W. W. Wilson, 1998.

"More Women Become Forces in Market Analysis." *Wall Street Journal,* March 10, 1997: 9A.

Truell, P. "Investing IT: The Wall Street Soothsayer Who Never Blinked." *New York Times,* July 27, 1997: sec. 3.

Katharine Coman
(1857–1915)

In one sense, Katharine Coman has achieved a modicum of immortality as the answer to an economics trivia question: Who authored the lead article in the first issue of the *American Economic Review*? Her legacy, however, transcends the publication of a single article. Whereas she created the economics program at Wellesley College, and whereas many of the women profiled in this volume studied and/or taught at Wellesley, Coman, it can be argued, did more to open the economics profession to women, particularly American women, than any other person in the twentieth century. This above all her contributions guarantees Coman a place of significance in the history of economics.

BIOGRAPHY

Katharine Coman was born on November 23, 1857, in Newark, Ohio, to Levi Parsons Coman and Martha (Seymour) Coman. Her father, a graduate of Hamilton College, was a teacher, a shopkeeper, and a lawyer. "He was an abolitionist and led his own company during the Civil War" (Bartlett, 115). Her mother was well educated for the times, having graduated from an Ohio seminary that Mount Holyoke alumnae founded.

Both of Coman's parents believed in the value of educating their daughter as well as their sons. Accordingly, Coman was enrolled in the Steubenville (Ohio) Female Seminary in 1873, though she eventually transferred to the high school at the University of Michigan in search of more advanced work than the seminary would allow her. After graduating from high school, Coman entered the University of Michigan, where she earned a B.Ph. in the spring of 1880. That fall, she accepted a position as an instructor of rhetoric at Wellesley College. Her real interest, however, was economics, and in 1893 she became a professor of political economy at Wellesley. In 1900, Coman organized the

Department of Economics and Sociology at the college, and she was appointed a professor in the new department, a post she held until her retirement in 1913.

As was the case with many progressive women of the late nineteenth and early twentieth centuries, Coman became actively involved in the social-welfare crusades of the time. Although primarily an academic, she was closely associated with the founders of the College Settlement Association (CSA), particularly Katherine Lee Bates. Bates, an English professor at Wellesley, is famous for writing "America the Beautiful," a poem inspired when she was viewing Pikes Peak and the "purple" Rocky Mountains and nearby "fruited" plains (Hogan and Hudson).

Coman and Bates became partners in 1890 and continued their relationship until Coman's death in 1915. Both were deeply committed to the settlement movement and became engaged in a number of related causes such as labor reform, social insurance, and consumer protection. Coman served as president of the electoral board and chair of the standing committee of the CSA from 1900 to 1907. She was also an associate director of the association from 1911 to 1914. Her interest in the labor movement led Coman to become involved in consumer-protection issues. She was a charter member of the National Consumers' League, which lobbied for a number of measures to protect consumers. Coman served as honorary vice president of the league until she died, and her efforts to achieve social justice for laborers, women, and African Americans are as much a part of her legacy as her teaching and publications.

CONTRIBUTIONS

As an economist, Coman produced scholarship that fit the characterization one Nobel laureate used to describe the research of the majority of female economists of her day: "opinionated, tainted with preconceptions of virtue, and devoid of algebraic symbols" (Baumol, 1). Surely a product of its time, Coman's work was, nevertheless, a precursor of the empiricism that would come to be the signature trait of American economic scholarship. In her first major publication ("Wages and Prices in England"), she mined the six quarto volumes of Torold Rogers's *Agriculture and Prices,* published between 1865 and 1887, to produce a table and accompanying graph illustrating the paths of wages and prices in England from 1261 to 1701. Coman took the same institutionalist approach to her second major paper, a statistical profile of African American farmers, the purpose of which was "to test previous conclusions in light of recent statistics, and to indicate the directions of advance so far as our present data warrant prophecy" ("The Negro as a Peasant Farmer," 40).

The publication that gave Coman stature among her contemporaries was the book *The Industrial History of the United States.* An encyclopedic economic history of the United States, the book focused on its industrial development from the discovery of the New World through the economic transformation of the South following the Civil War. In the revised edition, Coman added a chapter on "Contemporary Problems," including tariff policies of the late nineteenth century; currency issues such as the banking crisis of 1907; and the government regulation of business, especially the railroads and the Interstate Commerce Law of 1887. She also wrote a chapter entitled "Conservation," in which she discussed the exploitation of resources and related issues in what amounts to a harbinger of the modern subfield of environmental economics. As if the narrative text of this massive volume were not enough to engage the reader, it has more than 100 illustrations, including maps, numerical tables, diagrams (especially of boats and ships), and photographs of everything from the rice culture in South Carolina to cattle grazing in Oregon's Wallowa National Forest.

During her lifetime, Coman was best known for *The Industrial History of the United States,* but her magnum opus was *Economic Beginnings of the Far West.* This two-volume book had no contemporary rivals; it was unique. Even today, any scholar who wants to understand the how, why, and wherefore of the American West would do well to start by reading Coman's *Economic Beginnings.*

Coman and her partner, Bates, were enamored with the West, which Coman defined as "the vast unknown that lay beyond the Mississippi River" (*Economic Beginnings,* vii). Bates and Coman traveled extensively in the West, as is evident in Coman's dedication of the book:

> To the Trustees of Wellesley College who have generously allowed me four years' leave of absence for the prosecution of research and to the Trustees of the Carnegie Foundation for the Advancement of Teaching who have rendered these *wanderjarhre* financially possible this book is dedicated.

The year *Economic Beginnings* was published, New Mexico and Arizona were admitted to the Union, bringing the number of states to forty-eight. Although Frederick W. Turner had declared the "frontier" closed in 1890, much of the West, especially the Far West, was pristine when Coman and Bates visited it. Recognizing that economic development was inevitable, Coman believed that every effort should be made to conserve the natural beauty of the land. She was especially sensitive to the value of water as a major determinant of economic growth and had an uncanny comprehension of the importance water rights would play in the political economy of the region ("Some Unsettled Problems"). The first of the book's two volumes focused on "Explorers and Colonizers," and the second volume on "American Settlers." Each contained more than 400 pages, and both volumes had extensive bibliographies. The scope and depth of *Economic Beginnings* gives the book a place of honor among the collection of significant works about the American West.

BIBLIOGRAPHY

Works by Katharine Coman

"Wages and Prices in England, 1261–1701." *Journal of Political Economy* 2(1), December 1893: 92–94 plus graph.

"The Negro as a Peasant Farmer." *American Statistical Association*, New series(66), June 1904: 39–54.

The Industrial History of the United States. New York: Macmillan, 1905. New and rev. ed., 1913.

"Some Unsettled Problems of Irrigation." *American Economic Review* 1(1), March 1911: 1–19.

Economic Beginnings of the Far West. 2 vols. in 1. New York: Macmillan, 1912. Reprint, New York: August M. Kelly, 1969.

Works about Katharine Coman

Bartlett, R. L. "Katharine Coman (1857–1915)." In *A Biographical Dictionary of Women Economists*, edited by R. W. Dimand, M. A. Dimand, and E. L. Forget, 115–18. Northampton, MA: Edward Elgar: 2000.

Baumol, W. J. "On Method in U.S. Economics a Century Earlier." *American Economic Review* 75(6), December 1985: 1–2.

Hogan, S., and Hudson, L. *Completely Queer: Gay and Lesbian Encyclopedia*. New York: Henry Holt, 1998: 143.

Kathleen Bell Cooper
(1945–)

• •

Kathleen Bell Cooper is a member of an unofficial cohort of female economists whose hard work, street smarts, and dedication have helped bring a modicum of gender diversity to the world of business economics, a subfield of the economics profession as male-dominated as any in the discipline. What **Beatrice Potter Webb**, **Joan Robinson**, **Elizabeth Ellery Bailey**, and other academic economists did to promote the status of women in the cognitive wing of the field, **Nancy Hays Teeters**, **Marina von Neumann Whitman**, and Cooper did to promote business and policy economics. With little fanfare and even less recognition, Cooper has done as much to advance the status of women in economics as any cognitive economist teaching at a world-class university and publishing regularly in the field's top journals.

BIOGRAPHY

Kathleen Bell was born in Dallas, Texas, on February 3, 1945, to Patrick Joseph Bell and Ferne Elizabeth (McDougle) Bell. On February 6, 1965, she married Ronald James Cooper. The couple had two sons, Michael and Christopher. In 1970, Cooper received her B.A. in mathematics with honors from the University of Texas-Arlington. One year later, she earned her M.A. in economics at the same institution. She was a research assistant in the Economics Department at UT-Arlington until 1971, when she left to become a corporate economist at the United Banks of Colorado, an eighteen-bank holding company in Denver. She continued at the bank as a corporate economist until 1980, when she was promoted to chief economist after completing her Ph.D. in economics at the University of Colorado in Boulder. While working full time at the bank, she taught economics and statistics at the University of Colorado in Denver as a part-time lecturer.

Through her work at United Banks, Cooper began to develop a national reputation as a business economist. In 1981, she took a position at the Security Pacific National Bank in Los Angeles, where she stayed for nine years. She headed the bank's Economics Department, leading a team doing research on national and regional trends, international economics, financial markets, and industry risk. In 1990, Cooper left Security Pacific to become chief economist at Exxon Corporation in Irving, Texas. When Exxon merged with Mobil Oil, she continued as chief economist for the new corporation, Exxon Mobil, where she expanded her scope of responsibilities as manager of the Economics and Energy Division within the Corporate Planning Group.

In addition to her work as a corporate economist, Cooper established herself as a leader in the business economics community. She served as president of the Denver and Los Angeles chapters of the National Association of Business Economists (NABE), and in 1975 she joined the national board of NABE, serving for three years in that capacity. NABE is an organization that provides an opportunity for teaching economists, students, business economists, and corporate leaders to network while furthering the study of economics within the business world. In 1985–86, Cooper served as national president of NABE. She also served on the board of directors of the National Bureau of Economic Research, and she was the vice chair of the bureau's executive committee in 2001. For many years, Cooper was active in the American Banking Association (ABA), serving on the Economics Advisory Council in 1979–81 and again in 1986–90. In 1990, she chaired the ABA. She was a senior fellow in the U.S. Association of Energy Economists, and in 1996 she became its president. Cooper regularly participated in the Conference of Business Economists within the AEA, serving as a technical consultant in 1993–94. In 2001, she was a trustee of the Committee for Economic Development, an independent nonpartisan organization of business and education leaders dedicated to policy research on the major economic and social issues of the day, with the intent of improving the growth and productivity of the U.S. economy. Cooper has also been a trustee of the American Council for Capital Formation and Scripps College.

On March 16, 2001, President George W. Bush nominated Cooper to become undersecretary of commerce for economic affairs at the U.S. Department of Commerce, the crowning achievement of Cooper's long and distinguished career in business economics and community service. Her nomination and those of several others generated some controversy among members of Congress who considered her an advocate for the U.S. oil and natural-gas industry. Despite the fears that Cooper was too close to the oil industry to be an objective decision maker regarding U.S. energy policy, she was readily confirmed, largely because of her obvious abilities, expertise, and extensive business experience in banking, industry, and energy economics.

CONTRIBUTIONS

As a business economist in the banking industry, Cooper was responsible for advising senior managers on a variety of economic phenomena, including trends in the U.S. economy and the status of global economic activity. When she went to work in the energy industry, her principal responsibility was to alert her superiors to variations in demand-and-supply conditions within the world's energy markets, thereby allowing them to assess profit margins and other valuable ratios in the industry.

As a government economist, Cooper oversees the work of the Economics and Statistics Administration (ESA) of the U.S. Department of Commerce; specifically, the activities of the Bureau of Economic Analysis and the Census Bureau. The basic function of these agencies is to provide policy makers with the best data possible upon which to base their decisions. Accurate information about the growth rate of gross domestic product, the number of housing starts, and changes in retail sales also helps businesses and not-for-profit organizations with planning and policy making. As Cooper observed in her nomination statement before the Senate Committee on Commerce, Science, and Transportation in 2001, "The American economy is constantly changing. The makeup of our national output is evolving in ways that make it more challenging to measure. Understanding these changes is a critical function of the economic statistics organization of the U.S. government, as is employing the more sophisticated techniques required." She pledged to maintain and improve the quality of the information that she personally had relied on as a practicing business economist.

Yet of all her contributions to economics, none matches the importance of simply being Kathleen Cooper. In 1980, at the ripe old age of thirty-five, she became one of the few women economists to occupy a corporate top spot in the United States. As she stated at the time, "more and more women are coming into the profession and doing well, but there aren't a lot at the top; I'm a rarity" ("Catch-up"). She parlayed her success in business into a major leadership role in NABE that helped her gain access to other positions of responsibility, culminating with her appointment as undersecretary in the U.S. Department of Commerce. In the process of forging a groundbreaking career as a business and government economist, Cooper led the way for other talented women economists to follow in her footsteps.

BIBLIOGRAPHY

Works by Kathleen Bell Cooper

Prepared statement of Kathleen B. Cooper for nomination to be undersecretary for economic affairs, U.S. Department of Commerce. Presented to the U.S. Senate Committee on Commerce, Science, and Transportation, May 16, 2001.

Works about Kathleen Bell Cooper

"Catch-up for Calculating Women." *Time*, January 8, 1979: 46.

M. Kathryn Eickhoff
(1939–)

The world of economic forecasting is not for the faint of heart. Correctly predicting an important economic event such as the beginning of a recession can bring instant celebrity status in business circles and entitle an economist to charge clients exorbitant fees for future forecasts. Miss the next turning point in the business cycle, however, and the one-time guru is immediately reduced to a has-been. In this viciously competitive environment wherein an economist is only as good as her last predication, M. Kathryn Eickhoff has built a remarkable economics information company widely recognized as one of the most consistently correct forecasting firms in the United States.

BIOGRAPHY

Margaret Kathryn Eickhoff was born in Sedalis, Missouri, on April 11, 1939, to Leo Eickhoff and E. Magdalene (Piatt) Eickhoff. She attended local schools and went on to the University of Missouri-Columbia, where she received her B.A. degree with distinction in 1960. In 1971, she earned an M.A. in economics from New York University. In 1973, she married A. James Smith Jr., owner of the Village Corner jazz club in New York.

Eickhoff's fascination with economics started in her childhood, when her father taught her to save her allowance and lend it back to him through interest-bearing loans. Part of the fun was negotiating the annual interest rates. In 1962, after college and a few inconsequential jobs, she went to work for Alan Greenspan, at Townsend-Greenspan & Company, an economic consulting firm. Eickhoff worked for Greenspan for twenty-three years and became one of his closest associates. In 1966, she became corporate treasurer at Townsend-Greenspan, managing the firm's assets and cash flow, its profit-sharing trust, and the employee's liquid-asset investment fund. She became vice president in 1972 and ran the entire firm from 1974 to 1977 while Greenspan served as the chair of President Gerald Ford's Council of Economic Advisers. In 1980, she became executive vice president of Townsend-Greenspan.

In 1985, Eickhoff was appointed associate director of economic policy within the Office of Management and Budget during the Reagan administration. She served in that capacity for two years. In 1987, Greenspan, then chairman of the Federal Reserve, shut down Townsend-Greenspan because of conflict-of-interest rules. Eickhoff opened her own economic consulting firm, Eickhoff Economics, which she billed as the "intellectual successor" to Townsend-Greenspan. At her own firm, Eickhoff wanted to perpetuate the Townsend-Greenspan approach to economic analysis, rooted in an unblinking faith in free markets. Eickhoff Economics monitors the U.S. economy for its clients, presents new perspectives on economic trends, aids in strategic planning and portfolio analysis, and provides links to macro- and microeconomic data.

Eickhoff has served on the board of directors of AT&T, Fleet Bank, N. A. Pharmacia & Upjohn, Tenneco Automotive, the Manhattan Institute for Public Policy, and the New York Futures Exchange. In 1980, she served as the youngest president of the National Association of Business Economists, and she was named a fellow of NABE in 1982. She was also active in the Economic Club of New York, the New York Association of Business Economists, and the National Association of Female Executives. In 1991, she was chairperson of the Conference of Business Economists. In 1988, the Executive Women of New Jersey named Eickhoff Outstanding Woman Director, and in 1993, she was awarded the Directors' Choice Award from the National Women's Economic Alliance Foundation. When she finds time for recreation, Eickhoff has a passion for sailing on Long Island Sound.

CONTRIBUTIONS

As vice president and treasurer of Townsend-Greenspan & Company, Eickhoff coauthored her first major publication in 1974, a paper that was more prophetic about her career in economics than it was insightful about the topic covered. Her coauthor was Alan Greenspan, who would eventually chair the president's Council of Economic Advisers and the Federal Reserve Board of Governors and with whom Eickhoff developed a long and mutually beneficial professional relationship. In their 1974 essay, the two correctly predicted the bright future awaiting intellectual services in general and economic consulting in particular: "Economic consulting, far from being a narrow specialty, has become an industry in its own right. . . . Moreover, it is one of the newest growth industries in the country. This should not be surprising. Since growth in an industrial society implies an ever-increasing proportion of output coming from intellectual rather than physical components, intellectual services are among the most rapidly growing areas of the economy. Economic consulting is one of these services" ("Economic Consulting," 629). Heeding her own prediction, Eickhoff forged a career in economic forecasting.

The publication that really caught the attention of the business community and catapulted Eickhoff onto the national scene ("Plant and Equipment Considerations") dealt with the pace of capital investment and produced what the *Wall Street Journal* dubbed "The Eickhoff Curve" ("Review and Outlook"). Based on a presentation she gave before the Cleveland Business Economist's Club and the National Association of Business Economists in Cleveland, Ohio, on February 2, 1977, the Eickhoff Curve explains why the expansion of capacity becomes harder in the face of economic uncertainty: "Although other reasons undoubtedly could be thought of, four issues stand out as important contributors to the higher level of uncertainty over the last several years. First, and by far the most important, is the higher rate of inflation and the fear of an increasing rate of inflation in the years ahead. Second is our experience with wage and price controls and the ongoing concern of business that if or when inflation does accelerate in the future, it is only a question of time before controls are once more imposed. The third is the seemingly inexorable rise in the degree of regulatory intrusion into business activity and the rapid acceleration recently in the rate at which changes in the regulatory environment have been occurring. Lastly, is the increasing incidence of injunctions, which temporarily halt projects" ("Plant and Equipment Considerations," 51).

As Eickhoff interpreted events, rising uncertainty would shift the upward-sloping Eickhoff Curve—representing the relationship between capacity expansion and operating rates—downward and to the right. This in turn meant that the business community's willingness to add capacity would only occur when capacity utilization moved to higher and higher levels. Under these conditions, the economic stimulus package President Jimmy Carter proposed in the late 1970s, emphasizing consumer demand rather than investment, would put upward pressure on prices (inflation) without a corresponding increase in output. This is exactly what happened, as Eickhoff had predicted.

As an archetypal representative of the conservative wing of U.S. economics, Eickhoff has always been preoccupied with the alleged deleterious effects of inflation. This was especially evident in her Presidential Address to the Twenty-third Annual Meeting of the National Association of Business Economists on September 24, 1981, in Washington, D.C. The burst of inflation in the United States in the late 1970s and early 1980s was government induced, or so Eickhoff was absolutely convinced: "Our inflation stems from a massive preemption of resources by the government sector at the expense of the private sector. As such, it is the middle stage in a process that began small with 'good' intentions, but in the end can produce a controlled economy and a totalitarian state here as it has elsewhere. A free society cannot coexist indefinitely with inflation because of the instability inflation produces. It must either eliminate inflation and its causes, or institute ever more far-reaching controls" ("Inflation," 18).

She was equally certain that the consequences of inflation would persist indefinitely without structural changes in the way government programs are developed and funded: "With inflation down to tolerable levels and moving in the right direction, complacency could make it difficult to make the changes in government programs that are required if the improvement in inflation is to be anything other than temporary. I see two major problem areas: a potential conflict between defense spending and capital investment, and pressure from fiscal constituencies" (18). She was not particularly optimistic that capital investment initiatives would trump defense spending or that anti-inflation programs would triumph over pro-inflation constituencies.

Her almost pathological fear of inflation moved Eickhoff to embrace a number of proposed policy initiatives originating within the block of conservative economists in the United States. In a 1986 speech to the International Conference on Privatization, Eickhoff, in her capacity of associate director for economic policy in the Office of Management and Budget, gave an unqualified endorsement of President Ronald Reagan's drive to privatize as much of the federal government as politically possible ("Privatization"). Four years later, on October 12, 1990, in a speech before the American Institute for Economic Research in Great Barrington, Massachusetts, Eickhoff, by then president of Eickhoff Economics, called for arbitration as a way to settle fiscal disputes between the executive and legislative branches of government ("The Need"). In the absence of mandatory arbitration, she predicted that in the future, the budget process might break down completely and so jeopardize the day-to-day operations of the federal government, something that actually happened in 1994 when President Bill Clinton took on the Newt Gingrich–led House of Representatives.

Eickhoff has occasionally published professional papers that are clearly works of positive economics. In 1994, she wrote an essay on business anticipation surveys ("Anticipation Surveys, Business"), describing what they are, contrasting them with consumer anticipation surveys, and discussing their importance in the development of government economic policy. For the most part, however, her writings are restricted to the analysis of economic conditions and forecasting the economic outlook for the immediate short term. This is best exemplified by an issue of her newsletter *Eickhoff Economics* that correctly anticipated that the horror of September 11, 2001, would prolong and deepen the economic recession that officially began in March of that year (*Eickhoff Economics*).

BIBLIOGRAPHY

Works by M. Kathryn Eickhoff

"Economic Consulting" (with A. Greenspan). In *Methods and Techniques of Business Forecasting,* edited by W. F. Butler, R. A. Kavesh, and R. B. Platt, 629–35. Englewood Cliffs, NJ: Prentice Hall, 1974.

"Plant and Equipment Considerations in the Capital Goods Outlook." *Business Economics* 12(4), September 1977: 50–54.

"Inflation versus Political Freedom." *Business Economics* 12(8), January 1982: 17–20.

"Privatization: An Idea Whose Time Has Come." Remarks before the International Conference on Privatization, February 17, 1986, Washington, DC. Mimeographed.

"The Need for Arbitration." Remarks before the American Institute for Economic Research, October 12, 1990, Great Barrington, MA. Mimeographed.

"Anticipation Surveys, Business." In *The Encyclopedia of Economics,* edited by D. Green-
    wald, 26–28. New York: McGraw-Hill, 1994.
Eickhoff Economics, October 18, 2001. Mimeographed.

Works about M. Kathryn Eickhoff

"Review and Outlook: The Eickhoff Curve." *Wall Street Journal,* April 4, 1977.

Millicent Garrett Fawcett
(1847–1929)

Millicent Garrett Fawcett was a central figure in the history of the women's suffrage movement in England. Yet, like **Jane Haldimand Marcet** and **Harriet Martineau** before her, she deserves recognition for her contributions to what was, in the mid-1800s, the still-emerging field of economics. Fawcett can be credited with carrying on the educational work of Marcet and Martineau, in that she continued the popularization of economics as an area of study, helping it become comparable in significance to languages, literature, mathematics, and science.

BIOGRAPHY

Millicent Garrett Fawcett was born on June 11, 1847, in Alderburgh, Suffolk, England. She was the fifth daughter of ten children of Newson Garrett and Louisa (Dunnell) Garrett. The close-knit family encouraged intellectual growth and discussion in the six girls of the family as well as the four boys. Her father was a self-made wealthy merchant and shipowner who was involved in politics and community affairs, interests he passed on to all his children, especially Millicent. Fawcett's mother was an intensely religious woman, once described as a "domestic superwoman" ("M. G. Fawcett," 18). According to Millicent Garrett Fawcett, Louisa Garrett's organizational skills would have made her an excellent businesswoman ("M. G. Fawcett," 18). The girls in the Garrett family were encouraged to have careers. Elizabeth Garrett, Millicent's older sister, was the first woman in England to become a doctor, and her success opened the door for other women wishing to enter the medical profession.

From an early age, Fawcett seemed preordained to be an activist in the struggle to secure the vote for women. According to one story, Millicent and Elizabeth and a childhood friend, Emily Harris, were discussing the great issues of the day, trying to decide what role each would play in solving the problems of the world. Emily wanted to devote herself to obtaining a higher education, and the threesome decided that Elizabeth would become a doctor and open the medical profession to women. "After these things are done," Emily said, "we must see about getting the vote." Turning to little Millicent, she continued, "You are younger than we are, Millie, so you must attend to that" ("M. G. Fawcett," 18).

In 1865, at the age of eighteen, Fawcett was fully aware of the political and economic debates of the times. She had read many of the works of **Harriet Hardy Taylor Mill** and her husband, John Stuart Mill, a vocal advocate of women's suffrage. J. S. Mill was then running for Parliament for the City of Westminster, and through his speeches and writings, he introduced the subject of a woman's right to vote into the political arena for the first time. In May 1865, Millicent met thirty-three-year-old Henry Fawcett, a disciple of Mill's and a professor of political economy at Cambridge University. From all accounts, Henry Fawcett, a member of Parliament from Brighton since 1863, and Millicent Garrett were soul mates from the start. They were married in April 1868, when Millicent was twenty years old. A year later, their daughter, Philippa, was born.

Henry Fawcett had been blind since a gunshot accident in 1858. After the marriage, Fawcett acted as her husband's secretary, and in so doing, she added to her own knowledge and understanding of economics, politics, and the nexus of the two. She became a liberal free trader who believed in self-help and individualism. The Fawcetts lived in Cambridge during the fall term and in London when Parliament was in session. Fawcett read to her husband and wrote for him. Together, Henry and Millicent discussed political matters of the day and how they related to his writings. Henry agreed with his wife that women should have the right to vote, and through his seat in Parliament, he worked toward that goal. The Fawcetts became close friends of John Stuart Mill, and their writings, jointly or individually authored, reflected his economic point of view.

In 1867, Millicent Fawcett became a member of the first regular Women's Suffrage Committee in London, and that same year she made her first political speech in favor of the women's vote. Henry Fawcett attended suffrage meetings with his wife and encouraged her political writing on that topic and related women's issues. With her husband's support, Fawcett began submitting essays reflecting her views to the leading journal of the day, *Macmillan's* magazine. This helped established an important relationship for the Fawcetts, as Macmillan became the primary publisher of their books, written together or separately. Besides advocating for women's suffrage, Fawcett was at the center of the movement for higher education for women. A discussion at her house during a tea party in 1869 became the impetus for the creation of Newnham Hall, the first residential institution for the higher education of women. "Millicent Fawcett served as a member of the Council of Newnham College for many years and was made very proud in 1890 when her daughter, Phillipa Fawcett, graduated from Newnham with highest honors in mathematics" (Thomson, 53).

Henry Fawcett had become postmaster general in the cabinet of William Gladstone in 1884, but he often clashed with the prime minister over Gladstone's opposition to women's rights. In November of that year, Fawcett died suddenly from pleurisy, leaving Millicent a widow at thirty-seven. She moved to London to live with her sister, Agnes Garrett, and from that time forward, she identified herself with the cause of women's suffrage. For the next thirty-five years, Fawcett would be a compelling force in the movement she had joined in 1867 at the tender age of twenty. In 1887, she was elected president of the National Union of Women's Suffrage Societies, an umbrella organization for women's suffrage societies in England. Her fight was primarily for the right to vote, but she also championed related causes such as education for women, the opening of the legal profession to women, equal grounds for men and women for divorce, and improvements in the rights of women in the guardianship of their children. She firmly believed that women would get the vote only when their position in society was made equal to that of men.

In an 1899 speech, Fawcett forcefully argued that suffrage for women would give them a chance to play a role equal to that of men in deciding the political future of the nation. She was a nationalist and often centrally involved in the political issues of her day. During the Boer War, the national government sent her to South Africa as the leader of an all-women commission to investigate conditions in British concentration camps. When World War I started, she asked the rank and file of various women's group to suspend their efforts and give their support to the war. Fawcett was sometimes criticized by those urging a more militant approach to women's issues, but as a firm patriot, she was unwavering in her belief that women's rights should only come through legal and constitutional means. In 1918, her faith and determination were partially rewarded when the government gave the right to vote to women over thirty who were property owners. She felt that the fight was not yet over and continued to urge that women be given the vote on an equal basis with men. A year later, at age seventy-two, she retired from active participation in the movement, but she remained spiritually and emotionally involved until the end of her life.

Honors and recognition flowed to this economist and social activist. In January 1899, St. Andrews University gave her an honorary degree for her work to secure higher education for women. In 1924, the British government honored her with the title Dame of the British Empire. Fawcett's most glorious recognition came in 1928, when all women over the age of twenty-one were given the right to vote. That same year, Fawcett was the guest of honor at a public celebration marking the appointment of the first-ever woman cabinet minister and the election of fourteen women to Parliament. "I have had," she said, "extraordinary good luck in having seen the struggle from the beginning" ("M. G. Fawcett," 19). A year later, on August 5, 1929, she died of pneumonia. She was eighty-two years old.

CONTRIBUTIONS

As an economist, Fawcett's greatest contribution was *Political Economy for Beginners*, which first appeared in 1870. Last published in 1911, the book went through ten editions, a record that stood until Paul Samuelson's *Economics* reached its eleventh edition. In the preface to the first edition of *Political Economy for Beginners*, Fawcett wrote: "When I was helping my husband to prepare a third edition of his *Manual of Political Economy,* it occurred to us both that a small book, explaining as briefly as possible the most important principles of the science, would be useful to beginners, and would perhaps be an assistance to those who are desirous of introducing the study of Political Economy into schools. It is mainly with the hope that a short and elementary book might help to make Political Economy a more popular study in boys' and girls' schools that the following pages have been written."

In terms of its purpose, the book was a direct descendent of the works of Jane Haldimand Marcet and Harriet Martineau. In presentation, however, *Political Economy for Beginners,* with its systematic approach to the subject, is more like a modern textbook than the tomes of either Martineau or Marcet. Marcet relied on an "artificial dialogue" to communicate the doctrines of classical economics, Martineau used beguiling tales to deliver her message, and both women were wordy writers. Fawcett was direct, organized, and concise.

An immediate success, *Political Economy for Beginners* was updated with each edition. The tenth edition had four sections, "The Production of Wealth," "On the Exchange of Wealth," "The Distribution of Wealth," and "On Foreign Commerce, Credit, and Taxation." The emphasis was "on microeconomics, but without benefit of diagrams. Such macroeconomic topics as division of labor, population, cooperation, and taxation were treated without any integrating theme" (Thomson, 46). In one sense, the straightforward, no-nonsense approach of *Political Economy for Beginners* was a testimonial to the efforts of Marcet and Martineau in making economics an area of knowledge with which any educated person ought to be familiar.

The only other book on economics that Fawcett wrote as sole author was *Tales in Political Economy* (1874). In content and format, *Tales* was a throwback to the Marcet/Martineau approach "of hiding the powder, Political Economy, in the raspberry jam of a story" (Thomson, 45). In 1872, Fawcett coauthored *Essays and Lectures on Social and Political Subjects*. The book contained fourteen essays, eight of them by Fawcett. She was the sole author of several other books, including *The Women's Victory and After: Personal Reminiscences* and *What I Remember*, and even a novel, *Janet Doncaster* (1875), which enjoyed some success. She published a second novel under a pseudonym to see if it could stand on its own merits; it did not. The author of many essays in the leading magazines of her era, Fawcett is best remembered for using clear and simple writing to continue the Marcet/Martineau tradition of making economics accessible to beginners.

BIBLIOGRAPHY

Works by Millicent Garrett Fawcett

Political Economy for Beginners. 1st ed. London: Macmillan, 1870. 10th ed. published 1911; includes the prefaces to all editions.
Essays and Lectures on Social and Political Subjects (with H. Fawcett). London: Macmillan, 1872.

Tales in Political Economy. London: Macmillan, 1874.

The Women's Victory and After: Personal Reminiscences. London: Sidgwick and Jackson, 1920.

What I Remember. London: T. Fisher Unwin, 1924.

Works about Millicent Garrett Fawcett

The Europa Biographical Dictionary of British Women, edited by A. Crawford et al., 150. Detroit, MI: Gale Research Company, 1983.

"M. G. Fawcett." In *Working for Equity,* edited by F. MacDonald, 18–21. London: Hampstead Press, 1987.

"Millicent Garrett Fawcett." In *Great Lives from History: British and Commonwealth Series,* edited by F. N. Magill. Vol. 2, 984–89. Pasadena, CA: Salem Press.

Thomson, D. L. "Millicent Garrett Fawcett." In *Adam Smith's Daughters,* 43–55. Jericho, NY: Exposition Press, 1973.

Marianne A. Ferber
(1923–   )

In the spring of 1938, Adolf Hitler's Germany annexed Austria, and Marianne A. Ferber's mother correctly predicted that the Sudetenland would be next. The Abeles family prepared to emigrate. In October 1938, immediately after British prime minister Neville Chamberlain's policy of appeasement led to the signing of the Munich Agreement, the Abeleses climbed into the family car with little more than a change of clothes and some personal photographs and headed for the new world. The odyssey changed the lives of just about everyone in the group, but none more so than that of a bright but shy fifteen-year-old girl.

BIOGRAPHY

Marianne Ferber was born in a small farming village in Czechoslovakia on January 30, 1923, the second of two daughters in the Abeles family. The family lived in the Sudetenland, the German-speaking area of western Czechoslovakia. Marianne's father, Karl Abeles, was a farmer, and her mother, Elsa (Ornstein) Abeles, was a full-time homemaker. Both parents were high school graduates. Ferber's father was too full of mischief to be a good student, although she considered him to be a "really . . . brilliant man" (King and Sanders, 83). Her mother, on the other hand, "was the intellectual in the family" who encouraged her daughters to read a variety of books and often took them to Prague to visit museums or take in a play (King and Sanders, 83).

In 1938, Karl and a distant cousin traveled to France, Canada, and the United States in search of a new place for their extended Jewish family to live. They chose Canada as their new home because most of the adults in the group of thirty-nine were farmers, and visas were readily available for agricultural workers. The Abeleses and their extended family immigrated to a farming community near Branford, Ontario, Canada. Marianne Ferber spent the next year working on the farm her father managed for a wealthy insurance broker from Prague. The next year she took a clerical job in Hamilton, Ontario, saving money in anticipation of returning to school. She thought she would have to finish high school but was pleasantly surprised when the registrar at McMaster University, convinced that someone who had studied at a European gymnasium could handle college, allowed her to matriculate at that institution. Four years later, in 1944, Ferber earned her B.A. in economics. She went on to graduate school at the University of Chicago, were she earned her M.A. in 1946 after completing all her course work, but not the dissertation, for the Ph.D.

While at the University of Chicago, she met Robert Ferber, a fellow graduate student. The two were married in 1946. The couple had two children and were married until Robert's death in 1981. Robert took a job in New York City in 1946. Marianne, who put her Ph.D. on hold, went to work full-time as an economist with Standard Oil (N.J.), now part of Exxon Mobil, and taught part-time as a lecturer at Hunter College. In 1948, the Ferbers moved to Champaign, Illinois, where Robert took a position as a research professor of economics and marketing at the University of Illinois, and Marianne was busy raising her children and completing her dissertation. Ferber received her Ph.D. from the University of Chicago in 1954 and began teaching as a lecturer at the University of Illinois, a position she held until 1971. She then became an assistant professor at Illinois and rose to the rank of professor by the time she retired in 1993. After becoming a professor emerita at Illinois, Ferber was appointed Matina S. Horner Distinguished Visiting Professor at Radcliffe College from 1993 to 1995.

During her years at the University of Illinois, Ferber served as director of the Women's Studies Program from 1980 to 1983 and again from 1991 to 1993. She also has served on the editorial boards of a number of important journals, including the *Journal of Consumer Research* (1982–85), *Social Science Quarterly* (since 1987), *Feminist Economics* (since 1993), and the *Review of Social Economics* (since 1994). She was a founding member of the International Association for Feminist Economics and served as president of that organization from 1995 to 1997. Ferber was president of the Midwest Economics Association in 1986–87, and her alma mater, McMaster University, honored her with the Distinguished Alumna Award in 1996.

CONTRIBUTIONS

In a publishing career that spans six decades and includes more than 100 books, articles, and reviews, Ferber has accumulated a body of work and a record of accomplishment few in the discipline can match. Yet she has always remained true to two guiding values: the need to understand the real complexities of any situation, and the desire to see how changing past conditions might improve future outcomes. These values were best articulated in Ferber's coauthored article "The New Home Economics: Retrospects and Prospects," about a branch of economic theory often associated with the career of Nobel laureate Gary Becker.

While commending Becker and others as pathbreakers in the analysis of nonmarket activities in the household, Ferber took exception to the new home economics on two counts. First, the neoclassical approach offers "glimpses of the complex reality of the world only to find that they are totally ignored in the simple, elegant models the authors proceed to construct" ("The New Home Economics," 19). Second, and more important, "is the basic assumption underlying all this work that people always behave rationally, leading to the baffling implication . . . that all outcomes are in some sense optimal. . . . When this approach is combined with exclusive emphasis on analysis of the situation as it is, or even as it has been, it amounts to a tacit endorsement of the status quo and complete neglect of exploration of what might be. Again, examination of the existing situation is a legitimate occupation for social scientists, but some attention to the possibility of changing and improving past performance would greatly increase the relevance of this work to the decisions family members must make" (19).

The desire to learn about the real complexities of a seemly transparent situation was evident early on in Ferber's research. In a study involving men and women faculty members of comparable productivity at the University of Illinois, Ferber went beyond the obvious—"that male and female faculty members are similarly productive, though not always similarly rewarded"—to discover a deeper reality: "[that] current salary and rank are correlated with parental status for men but not women, that salary is higher for married than for single men, and that salary is higher for single than for married women suggest that reward tends to be scaled to perceived financial need" ("Performance," 1000). These subtle differences in treatment, not justified by differential conditions, were still evident more than a decade later when, in a broader study, Ferber learned "that introducing dimensions of work authority," notably the measure of monetary control, "by taking into account the individual's position in the work hierarchy explains more of the variation in earnings than does occupation . . ." ("Work Power," 53). These and similar results convinced Ferber of the need for a feminist economics or—at the very least—the need to inject a feminist perspective into the discipline.

Many economists like to portray their field as a science every bit as objective as chemistry or physics, making it beyond the reach of social movements, politics, or gender bias. Ferber saw things differently. Gender "affects the construction of the discipline in terms of the standpoint from which the world is perceived, and the way the importance and relevance of questions are evaluated" (*Beyond Economic Man,* 2). Given the preponderance of men among its practitioners, economics has to have a masculine perspective. "Feminists raise questions not because economics is too objective but because it is not objective enough. Too many assumptions and methodological ideals have been exempted from critical scrutiny because existing communities of economists have perceived them as universal and impartial" (vii). In an effort to broaden the perspective of economics and give the field an added dimension of reality, Ferber coauthored a textbook with **Francine D. Blau**, *The Economics of Women, Men, and Work.*

Ostensibly a book "that would acquaint students with the findings of recent research on women, men, and work in the labor market and in the household," the text was a refreshing alternative to mainstream analysis, focusing on topics heretofore not found in conventional economics works (*The Economics*, xiii). Using standard neoclassical economics, Ferber explored such topics as "Women and Men: Changing Roles in a Changing Economy," "The Family as an Economic Unit," "Differences in Joblessness: Discouragement, Frictional and Structural Unemployment," and "Sex Differences in Other Countries: What Can We Learn from International Comparisons?" The presentation was rigorous, the contents imaginative, and the results eye-opening. It was as if an archeological dig had uncovered a previously unknown civilization. The discovery was only half as important as its implications, which are still being unearthed today thanks to Ferber and the branch of economics she helped create.

BIBLIOGRAPHY

Works by Marianne A. Ferber

"Performance, Rewards, and Perceptions of Sex Discrimination among Male and Female Faculty" (with J. W. Loeb). *American Journal of Sociology* 78(4), January 1973: 995–1002.

"The New Home Economics: Retrospects and Prospects" (with B. G. Birnbaum). *Journal of Consumer Research* 4(1), June 1977: 19–28.

The Economics of Women, Men, and Work (with F. D. Blau). Englewood Cliffs, NJ: Prentice Hall, 1986.

"Work Power and Earnings of Women and Men" (with C. A. Green and J. L. Spaeth). *American Economic Review, Papers and Proceedings* 76(2), May 1986: 53–56.

Beyond Economic Man: Feminist Theory and Economics (edited with J. A. Nelson). Chicago: University of Chicago Press, 1993.

Works about Marianne A. Ferber

King, M. C., and Sanders, L. F. "An Interview with Marianne Ferber: Founding Feminist Economists." *Review of Political Economy* 11(1), January 1999: 83–98.

"Marianne Abeles Ferber." In *Engendering Economics: Conversations with Women Economists in the United States,* edited by P. I. Olson and Z. Emami, 31–52. London: Routledge, 2002.

Nancy Folbre
(1952–)

• •

In her first major economics publication, Nancy Folbre sought to unravel the impact that the rise of capitalism had on the family in Colonial New England ("Patriarchy"). Twenty years and numerous papers later, her quest to understand how the marketization of familial altruism affects modern life led Folbre to write a provocative book (*The Invisible Heart*) that effectively braided the many strands of her research into a new subfield within the discipline—the economics of caring—and made her one of the more important writers currently active in the field.

BIOGRAPHY

Nancy Folbre was born in San Antonio, Texas, on July 19, 1952. At the time, her father, James P. Folbre, was a financial adviser who managed the business affairs of a slightly eccentric yet well-to-do local oil family. Her mother, Eleanor (Russell) Folbre, was a homemaker. Nancy attended schools in San Antonio, graduating from Alamo Heights High School in 1969. She went to the University of Texas at Austin, earning a B.A. in philosophy in December 1971. Continuing her education at Texas, she received an M.A. in Latin American studies in August 1973. In 1974–75, she was a National Institute of Child Health Care and Development trainee in demography at the University of Texas Population Research Center. From 1975 to 1979, she studied economics as a graduate student at the University of Massachusetts at Amherst, where in 1979 she received a Ph.D. in economics.

In 1979–80, Folbre had a postdoctoral fellowship at the Yale University Economic Growth Center. She landed her first teaching job as an assistant professor of economics at Bowdoin College in Maine in 1980. Folbre remained there until 1983, then moved to the New School of Social Research in New York City as an assistant professor of economics. In September 1984, she became an associate professor of economics at her alma mater, the University of Massachusetts. She has been a full professor of economics there since 1991.

In addition to her career as a teacher and a scholar, Folbre has also been a much-sought-after consultant. In the 1980s, she consulted for the Maine Commission for Women and for the Kenya Fuelwood and the Zimbabwe Energy Planning Projects, both sponsored by the Beijer Institute of the Royal Swedish Academy of Science. In the 1990s, Folbre was a consultant for the Population Council, the World Bank, and the International Labour Office.

As an educator, she has spent most of her time at the University of Massachusetts. She has, nevertheless, held visiting posts at several universities as well as at research organizations. From January through May 1991, Folbre was a visiting associate professor at American University in Washington, D.C. Later that May, she was a visiting lecturer at the University of Wisconsin's Eugene Havens Center. She spent 1992 as a visiting scholar with the Women's Research and Resource Center at the University of California at Davis, and in October 1995, she was a visiting scholar at the Gender Center of the London School of Economics. Her most recent visiting positions were as chair in American studies at the École des Hautes Etudes en Sciences Sociales in Paris (1995–96) and visiting research fellow at the Australian National University (2000).

Like her scholarship and teaching, Folbre's awards and professional service are numerous and significant. Among the recognition she has received are a National Science Foundation grant (1989), a French-American Foundation Fellowship (1995–96), a MacArthur Foundation Fellowship (1998), and the Olivia Schieffelin Nordberg Award for Excellence in Writing and Editing in the Population Sciences (1999). In 2001, Folbre served as president of the International Association for Feminist Economics, and she has been a staff economist with the Center for Popular Economics since 1979. In 2000, she was appointed to the board of the Foundation for Child Development. Her editorial board experience includes *Feminist Economics* (since 1995), *Explorations in Economic History* (since 1995), and the *Journal of Economic Methodology* (since 1997).

CONTRIBUTIONS

Nancy Folbre's first important publication in economics was based on her Ph.D. dissertation at the University of Massachusetts and appeared in a Marxist journal. The article explored "the social relations of production within the rural household of colonial New England" ("Patriarchy," 4) and took dead aim at the prevailing notion of the precapitalist family as a collective and consensual unit. Using historical literature, especially that dealing with the history of Hampshire County, Massachusetts, Folbre argued that the egalitarian vision of precapitalist New England did not square with the facts. The economy of Colonial New England was decidedly patriarchal, and men and their male heirs had a disproportionate share of political economic power compared to women and small children. In and of itself, Folbre's first major publication was not a breakthrough piece of research. Its importance, however, is that it launched her career-long interest in the social, political, and economic consequences of the marketization of caring.

The ascendancy of capitalism as a dominant form of economic organization increasingly reduced many altruistic activities, once given freely, to commodities subject to demand, supply, price, and market analysis: "Much of the economic literature on families is couched within a neo-classical framework based on individual optimization. This framework treats familial altruism, like other tastes and preferences, as exogenously given and focuses on household responses to changes in price and incomes. Altruism is considered rare outside the family, where self-interest undermines the potential for collective action" ("Children," 86). Folbre looked at the commercialization of caring from a different and provocative perspective: "An alternative approach, influenced by feminist theory, places more emphasis on self-interest within the home, and group solidarity outside it. Individuals often engage in forms of collective action that shape the social institutions that govern the distribution of the children. . . . The effects are visible not only in the history of family property rights and law, but also in public policies with disparate impacts on old and young, men and women (as well as upon groups defined by nation, race, and class)" (86). She applied this inspired perspective to research explaining the care and rearing of children ("Children"), the magnitude of nonmarket household output as it affects the pace and size of economic growth in the United States ("Household Services"), and the repercussions of mixing the "realms of 'love' and 'money' for economic analysis, societal well-being, and public policy" ("For Love").

In 2001, Folbre wove the many threads of her research about the economics of caring into a single book that can arguably be considered her magnum opus. *The Invisible Heart*—an obvious reference to Adam Smith's "invisible hand"—is the culmination of more than twenty years of thinking and reflecting on family values. To Folbre, the term *invisible heart* "conveys the ideas of love, obligation, and reciprocity" (xii). "I am an economist who studies the time and effort that people put into taking care of one another. Caring labor is done on a person-to-person basis, in relationships where people generally call each other by their first names, for reasons that include affection and respect. Some of this work is compensated, at least partially, with a paycheck or a share of someone else's paycheck. Some of this work is not compensated by money at all. Economists use the adjective 'nonmarket' to describe work that is not directly paid for and therefore difficult to put a price on. Much of this work is done on behalf of family members—cooking meals, changing diapers, mowing lawns. Much, though not all of it, has an explicitly compassionate dimension. None of it is counted as part of our Gross Domestic Product, and economists generally don't pay it much attention" (xi–xii).

The marketization of caring has some important positive consequences, especially for women, as it means that their work, once valueless when done within the home, now gets counted in national output. "Professional care services are disproportionately provided by women. In 1998, women accounted for about 46 percent of the paid labor force over age sixteen, but 76 percent of those employed in hospitals, 79 percent in other health services, 69 percent in educational services, and 82 percent in social services" (*Invisible Heart*, 55–56).

On the negative side, the increased cost of caring has several undesirable outcomes. Higher costs mean "that more people, especially children, the elderly, and other dependents, cannot always afford the care they need." Additionally, pressures to control or even cut costs may diminish quality, and finally, in a market economy that prizes efficiency and impersonal exchange, those who cannot pay the prevailing rate have to learn to do without (*Invisible Heart*, xv).

In her exploration of the positive and negative ramifications of the relationship between economics and family values, Folbre reviewed the theory and policies for commercializing caring, and she offers some strategies for the future. A section of *The Invisible Heart* is devoted to each of these topics. The theoretical chapters of the book methodically "debunk the conventional economic assumption that we're all automatically better off if we each pursue our own self-interest" (xix–xx). The policy section reviews "the evolution of relationships between family and government, describing both conflicts and complementaries" (xx). It includes a general discussion of various social welfare programs, such as Social Security, public education, and the use of tax incentives and disincentives to alter human behavior. The final section is about what's next and concludes with some guidelines that Folbre believes would "bring the invisible hand of the market into better balance with the invisible heart of care" (231).

The economics of caring has been the main thrust of Folbre's scholarship, but not its only thrust. The author of more than six books and thirty professional articles, nearly twenty book chapters, and numerous op-ed pieces in the *New York Times, Newsweek,* and other periodicals, Folbre has researched a variety of topics in a publishing career noted for its breadth as well as its depth. Two publications—one empirical and one funky—are illustrative of the scope of her work. In 1988, Folbre coauthored a short but information-laden paper, "The Feminization of Inequality." That article mined available income data to show conclusively how "Changes in the distribution of women's earnings . . . reflect both the successes and the shortcomings of feminist political efforts" (56). Greater employment opportunities for women in the 1980s had a positive effect on the incomes of those with the education and training necessary to move into professional-managerial jobs. The flip side of this success was the deterioration of earnings among those women ill prepared for work in the information age, a condition that made them worse off compared to all workers in general and compared to educated women in particular. Folbre and her coauthor noted that class, more than race and gender, was becoming an increasingly significant determinant of the distribution of income.

One of her truly unusual publications is the coauthored book *The Ultimate Field Guide to the U.S. Economy.* Offered as a left-of-center alternative to standard principles of economics textbooks, *Field Guide* is a breezy yet stimulating take on the U.S. economy. Designed as "an accessible, concise reference for answering specific questions" about the economy, "Each page stands alone as a description of an economic fact or trend but also fits into a chapter that systematically covers a particular topic" (10–11). The book offers a refreshing perspective on workers, owners, and other major players in the economic systems of the United States as well as a penetrating discussion of some of the trade-offs with which U.S. society is eternally grappling. Laced with snappy graphs and biting cartoons, *Field Guide* is fun, thoughtful, and always intriguing.

BIBLIOGRAPHY

Works by Nancy Folbre

"Patriarchy in Colonial New England." *Review of Radical Political Economics* 2(2), 1980: 4–13.

"The Feminization of Inequality: Some New Patterns" (with B. Wagman). *Challenge,* November–December 1988: 56–59.

"Children as Public Goods." *American Economic Review* 84(2), May 1994: 86–90.

"Household Services and Economic Growth in the United States, 1870–1930" (with B. Wagman). *Feminist Economics* 2(1), Spring 1996: 43–66.

"For Love or Money—Or Both?" (with J. A. Nelson). *Journal of Economic Perspectives* 14(4), Fall 2000: 23–40.

The Ultimate Field Guide to the U.S. Economy (with J. Heintz et al.). New York: New Press, 2000.

The Invisible Heart. New York: New Press, 2001.

Ann Fetter Friedlaender
(1938–1992)

Ann Fetter Friedlaender literally invented the field of econometric modeling of transport systems. She blended economic theory with econometric analysis in her approach to transportation economics, and her research provided strong support for the movements to deregulate the motor carrier and railroad industries. Sadly, on October 19, 1992, after several years of illness, her life was cut short by cancer when she was only fifty-four years old. Nevertheless, during her remarkably productive career, Friedlaender did groundbreaking research, published eight major books and monographs, and became a recognized authority in her field. More important, she merits recognition for her insightful teaching and mentoring of students as well as her exemplary work on behalf of the economics profession, particularly in bringing more women into the field.

BIOGRAPHY

Born in Philadelphia, Pennsylvania, to Ferdinand Fetter and Elizabeth (Head) Fetter, Ann Fetter graduated from Radcliffe College with a B.A. in economics in 1960. On December 28, 1960, she married Stephan Friedlaender, an architect. The couple had two sons, Lucas Ferdinand and Nathaniel Mark. Friedlaender received a Woodrow Wilson fellowship to the Massachusetts Institute of Technology, where she earned her Ph.D. in 1964. In 1964–65, she served as a Fulbright lecturer in Helsinki, Finland. She taught at Boston College from 1965 to 1974, and she began her distinguished career at MIT in 1974 as a professor. She became a named professor in 1987 and was appointed chair of the Economics Department in 1983, then dean of the School of Humanities and Social Sciences in 1984, serving in that position until 1990. At MIT, Friedlaender held a joint appointment in the Department of Civil and Environmental Engineering and the Department of Economics. She was the first women to head an academic department at MIT and went on to become the first woman to head a school there. At MIT, her course in transportation economics was central to the graduate transportation degree, and she worked to strengthen the economic underpinnings of that program.

Friedlaender served as an associate editor of *Transportation Science* for fourteen years. She was also a director of the Rand Corporation and of Conrail. She was an active member of the AEA, serving as chair of the Committee on the Status of Women in the Economics Profession from 1978 to 1980, where she became a leader in the drive to get more women into graduate school. She also served on the AEA's executive committee for two years, and was AEA vice president in 1987. Friedlaender died in 1992 after battling cancer for several years.

CONTRIBUTIONS

The author of numerous professional articles and eight major books and monographs, Friedlaender was a highly productive scholar whose work dealt with the economics of transportation. She began publishing early in her career. Her first publication started as her doctoral dissertation at MIT and appeared as a book in 1965 when Friedlaender was just twenty-seven years old. Prior to the publication of *The Interstate Highway System*, the only extensive works involving the rigorous evaluation of public-investment projects were confined to water-resource development. Friedlaender changed that with her detailed and technically sophisticated evaluation of the costs and benefits of the U.S. interstate highway system. She concluded that, while suboptimal as an investment, the "Interstate Highway System is a desirable public investment project, for the substantial savings that it creates in resources required for transportation outweigh its considerable costs" (136). This book quickly established Friedlaender as one of the United States' eminent scholars in the field of transportation economics.

In a 1962 message on transportation in the United States, President John F. Kennedy gave official sanction to the desirability of substantially reducing the public regulation of transport. Citing numerous regulatory-induced inefficiencies, Kennedy sent Congress a series of bills recommending a sweeping change in federal transportation regulatory rules. Most of those bills were defeated in committee in 1963, but the effort itself stimulated interest in a major overhaul of transport regulatory policies.

In December 1967, the Brookings Institution, a think tank in Washington, D.C., organized a conference of experts to discuss deregulation in the spirit President Kennedy had proposed. As a prelude to the conference, the Brookings Institution asked Friedlaender, then teaching at Boston College, to prepare a background paper for conference participants on issues in freight transportation policy. The results of her effort—*The Dilemma of Freight Transportation Regulation*—contained an overview of the problem, gave the rationale for regulation, discussed the implications of ending existing practices, and summarized the discussions at the conference. The book and the conference were important precursors of the deregulation movement that took hold in the United States in the late 1970s and early 1980s.

More than a consummate scholar, Friedlaender also invested herself in the teaching and learning process. Beginning in 1973, as a second author of the fifth and later editions of John F. Due's *Government Finance: Economics of the Public Sector*, she helped improve a classic textbook that was published in seven editions from 1954 through 1981. A comprehensive text, the book was concerned with four interrelated issues:

> First: Why is government necessary in a market economy?
>
> Second: What determines the optimal scope and level of government activity?
>
> Third: What criteria should be used in determining how this activity should be financed?
>
> Fourth: What are the consequences of government activity and its financing of the economy? (2)

While concentrating on the topic of public finance as practiced in the United States, the book also included references to Canada as well as to other economies and other countries, giving it an international dimension not readily found in competing texts.

In a particularly dense article about the derived demand for freight (rail and trucking) transportation coauthored with R. H. Spady ("A Derived Demand Function"), Friedlaender made extensive use of a general translog cost function. The purpose of this paper was to improve on the existing specifications and estimations of the demand function for rail and trucking in two ways. First, Friedlaender and her coauthor treated freight transportation as an input in the production process when estimating the derived demand equations. Second, the study recognized that rates and shipment characteristics are jointly dependent, and this interdependence was reflected when estimating demand functions. The result was an important contribution to a small but significant area within the field of transportation economics.

This narrow study was followed up with a comprehensive work, *Freight Transport Regulation: Equity, Efficiency, and Competition in the Rail and Trucking Industries*. Based on research performed in connection with the Center for Transportation Studies at MIT, this study of freight transport regulation, again written with Spady, was a groundbreaking analysis with significant policy implications. Government regulation of business has always been a contentious affair in U.S. economics. "Critics have argued that many regulatory programs produce negative net benefits, while regulation's defenders have pointed to the sound rationales for, and potential gains from many of the same programs" (xvi). The book made important and relevant research available to both scholars and decision makers. Extremely technical, it contains many equations and equation systems, twenty-three figures, and more than eighty tables. The book succeeded in providing new insights into individual regulatory agencies and programs as well as the important economic, political, and administrative aspects of the regulatory process. This 1981 publication was especially timely in light of the trucking deregulation law President Jimmy Carter signed on July 1, 1980.

A busy scholar until the very end of her life, Friedlaender coauthored post-humously an important study on the ability—or, rather, lack thereof—of the U.S. railroad industry to adjust its capital stock to reach a cost-minimizing equilibrium ("Rail Costs"). Under the Staggers Act of 1980, the U.S. railroad industry was granted substantial regulatory freedom to adjust its rates and capital structure through changes in routes and service. Using econometric analysis, Friedlaender and her colleagues studied the size, scale, and capital adjustments within the rail industry in the period 1974–86 to see what adjustment had been made to costs in light of the Staggers Act. Large adjustments were evident in labor as railroads took advantage of the rate freedom and route rationalization allowed under the act. A comparable tendency to economize was not apparent, however, in the adjustment of capital stock. The lumpiness of capital and the demand effects of capital on service and quality were considered possible explanations for the reluctance of the railroad industry to trim capital stock in the same proportions as it had reduced labor requirements.

BIBLIOGRAPHY

Works by Ann Fetter Friedlaender

The Interstate Highway System: A Study in Public Investment. Amsterdam: North-Holland, 1965.

The Dilemma of Freight Transportation Regulation. Washington, DC: Brookings Institution, 1969.

Government Finance: Economics of the Public Sector (with J. F. Due). 6th ed. Homewood, IL: R. D. Irwin, 1977.

"A Derived Demand Function for Freight Transportation" (with R. H. Spady). *Review of Economics and Statistics* 62(3), August 1980: 432–41.

Freight Transport Regulation: Equity, Efficiency, and Competition in the Rail and Trucking Industries (with R. H. Spady). Cambridge, MA: MIT Press, 1981.

"Rail Costs and Capital Adjustments in a Quasi-Regulated Environment" (with E. R. Berndt et al.). *Journal of Transport Economics and Policy* 27(2), May 1993: 131–52.

Works about Ann Fetter Friedlaender

"Ann F. Friedlaender" (obituary). *New York Times,* October 20, 1992.

"In Memoriam: Ann F. Friedlaender." *Transportation Science* 27(2), May 1993: 87.

Selma F. Goldsmith
(1912–1962)

An economic statistician with the federal government, Selma F. Goldsmith "and her successors published before-tax distributions of personal income in current and constant dollars for 20 of the years from 1929 through 1963 and after-tax distributions for 1950–62" (Denison). This work was ultimately suspended, but not before Goldsmith and her colleagues, using a lot of hard work and many ingenious techniques, created accurate estimates of the size and distribution of income in the United States. A relentless attention to detail and an unswerving desire for precision helped Goldsmith produce estimates of income statistics of such high quality that other economists generally accepted her results without question. The degree of confidence professionals expressed in her work was eventually felt by the population at large and is one reason Americans have so much faith in the accuracy of the economic statistics their national government generates.

BIOGRAPHY

Selma F. Goldsmith was born on January 17, 1912, in New York City. The only child of Abraham Fine and Lena (Schwartzman) Fine, she graduated from Morris High School in the city and then attended Cornell University, where she earned a B.A. in 1932, graduating Phi Beta Kappa. After leaving Cornell, Goldsmith went to graduate school at Harvard University, earning a Ph.D. from Radcliffe in 1936 (Denison). Her doctoral dissertation "dealt with business cycles in England in the seventeenth and eighteenth centuries" (Kapuria-Foreman, 188–89), not exactly the ideal preparation for a person destined to become a government economic statistician in the twentieth-century United States.

Goldsmith's first career-oriented jobs were with the U.S. Department of Agriculture and the National Resources Planning Board. While working at the planning board (formerly the National Resources Committee), Goldsmith, still Selma Fine, became involved in the research that would lead to her first major publication ("The Use of Income Tax Data"). Goldsmith married Raymond W. Goldsmith, a long-time professor of economics at Yale University and a distinguished economist in his own right. The couple had three children.

During the 1950s, Goldsmith authored a string of pathbreaking publications on the size distribution of income. In 1955, the originality of her work led the Department of Commerce to honor her with the Distinguished Service Award. A year later, Goldsmith's scholarly efforts were largely responsible for her receiving "a Rockefeller public service award to study the methodology used in developing estimates on the size distribution of income in Great Britain and Canada"; she was the only woman among the sixteen awardees that year (Kapuria-Foreman, 189). Her research career was in full bloom when it came to a tragic and untimely end on April 15, 1962. She died of cancer at her home in Washington, D.C., leaving behind her husband, her children, and a body of scholarship that is still recognized for its innovative approaches in creating high-quality, accurate, and incredibly useful government statistics.

CONTRIBUTIONS

In her first major publication, Goldsmith "explained the adjustments made to income tax data before they could be used for analysis of income distribution" (Kapuria-Foreman, 189). The data were originally collected for the National Resources Committee report *Consumer Incomes in the United States* and needed to be adjusted to yield a true distribution of income for all American families: "The income tax data were to be used only for obtaining the 'tail' of an income distribution, the main body of which was based on extensive primary data on family income collected in the Study of Consumer Purchases. These data, covering the year 1935–36, constituted the largest and most representative body of sample income data ever assembled in this or any other country for the purpose of measuring the distribution of families by size of income. The necessity of using income tax statistics arose solely from an underrepresentation of high income families among the same income schedules actually collected in the Study of Consumer Purchases" ("The Use of Income Tax Data," 149–50). The data adjustments Goldsmith made included modifying the definition of net income through the addition of the value of owner-occupied dwellings, home-produced goods, and certain exclusions from taxable income (Kapuria-Foreman, 189).

During the 1940s, economists accumulated a sizable amount of data on the size distribution of income in the United States, so much so that in 1950 Goldsmith felt it necessary "to appraise some of these statistics and indicate a few conclusions relating to inequality of family income distribution that may be drawn from them" ("Statistical Information," 321). Her review of available data focused on the following: statistics from the 1935–36 Consumer Purchases Study; the jointly administered 1941 survey of the Bureau of Labor Statistics and the Bureau of Human Nutrition and Home Economics; Census Bureau survey data for the years 1944–48; and Federal Reserve Board data gathered in conjunction with the Michigan Survey Research Center for the years 1945–48. Her analysis led Goldsmith to conclude that "the surveys indicate that there was a movement toward greater equality in income distribution from 1935–36 to 1944 which was significant for the low-income groups during the war years and which was arrested after 1945" (337).

In 1954, Goldsmith updated her 1950 paper in a coauthored article ("Size Distribution") that incorporated a new series on family-income distribution, a series that the Department of Commerce's Office of Business Economics (OBE) released in a report titled *Income Distribution in the United States by Size, 1944–1950*. Goldsmith's updating extended the analysis of the size distribution of income in the United States from the 1930s through 1950. This required her to adjust the prewar data to make them comparable with the OBE series in order "to describe the changes in before-tax income distribution that have occurred, and to compare the impact of the federal individual income tax in the prewar and postwar periods" (2).

Toward the end of her regretfully short career, Goldsmith centered her scholarship on summarizing "recent findings concerning changes that have taken place in income distribution in the United States during the past twenty-five years" ("Changes," 504). This shift in emphasis led her to scrutinize closely the income share of the top 5 percent of income earners and relative share of income accruing to low-income families, a topic discussed in a paper published posthumously ("Low-Income Families"). Her examination of the relative shares earned at the high and low ends of the income spectrum led Goldsmith to conclude that (1) the widely reported drop in the share of income of the top 5 percent of families since 1929 was almost certainly overstated ("Changes," 512), and (2) the gain in the share of income of the lowest fifth of families might be greater than thought and "might actually be somewhat higher than in the early postwar years" ("Low-Income Families," 19). Goldsmith always had a healthy respect for the limitations of her findings because of the morass of definitions and conceptual differences involved when integrating survey data with other information from related materials (2). For this reason, she believed that "Future work in the field of income distribution and relative income shares should also be directed towards improving the income definition" (19). For Goldsmith, the hard work of crunching numbers only made sense within the context of good theory.

BIBLIOGRAPHY

Works by Selma F. Goldsmith

"The Use of Income Tax Data in the National Resources Committee Estimates of the Distribution of Income by Size" (with E. Baird). In *Studies in Income and Wealth*, 147–203. Vol. 3. New York: National Bureau of Economic Research, 1939. (Published under the name Selma Fine.)

"Statistical Information on the Distribution of Income by Size in the United States." *American Economic Review* 40(2), May 1950: 321–41.

"Size Distribution of Income since the Mid-Thirties" (with G. Jaszi, H. Kaitz, and M. Liebenberg). *Review of Economics and Statistics* 36(1), February 1954: 1–32.

"Changes in the Size Distribution of Income." *American Economic Review* 47(2), May 1957: 504–18.
"Low-Income Families and Measures of Income Inequality." *Review of Social Economy* 20(1), March 1962: 1–19.

Works about Selma F. Goldsmith

Denison, E. "Goldsmith, Selma." In *The New Palgrave: A Dictionary of Economics*, edited by J. Eatwell, M. Milgate, and P. Newman, 538. New York: Macmillan, 1991.
Kapuria-Foreman, V. "Selma Evelyn Fine Goldsmith (1912–62)." In *A Biographical Dictionary of Women Economists*, edited by R. W. Dimand, M. A. Dimand, and E. L. Forget, 188–93. Northampton, MA: Edward Elgar, 2000.

Heidi I. Hartmann
(1945–)

In 1994, Heidi Hartmann was awarded a MacArthur Fellowship—often referred to as the "genius grant"—in recognition of her pioneering work in the field of women and economics. She is director of the Institute for Women's Policy Research in Washington, D.C., an independent, nonprofit, scientific research organization that she founded in 1987 to meet the need for women-centered, policy-oriented research. A scholar, researcher, and teacher, Hartmann has testified numerous times before Congress and is often interviewed in the media on the issues of comparable worth, family and medical leave, child care, welfare reform, and health care. She also lectures widely on public policy, feminist theory, and the political economy of gender.

BIOGRAPHY

Heidi Irmgard Victoria Hartmann was born in Elizabeth, New Jersey, to Henry Leopold Hartmann and Hedwig (Bercher) Hartmann on August 14, 1945. She received a B.A. in economics with honors from Swarthmore College in 1967. That same year, she married Frank Blair Cochran. The couple, who divorced in 1977, had one daughter, Jessica Lee Cochran. After Swarthmore, Hartmann entered Yale University, where she received an M.Phil. in economics in 1972 and a Ph.D. in economics in 1974. In 1979, Hartmann married John Varick Wells. They have two daughters, Laura Cameron Hartmann Wells, and Katherine Lina Hartmann Wells.

Hartmann worked for the city of New Haven, Connecticut, as a computer programmer and researcher for the city planning department from 1969 until 1972. She then became an acting instructor at Yale University for one year. From 1974 until 1976, she was a visiting assistant professor of economics at the New School for Social Research in New York City. She then worked two years as a senior research economist at the Office of Research of the U.S.

Commission on Civil Rights in Washington, D.C. For eight years, starting in 1978, she was a staff member of the National Academy of Science/National Research Council, also in Washington D.C.; she served as associate executive director of the Commission on Behavioral and Social Sciences and Education. Some of the reports she worked on included: *Women, Work and Wages: Equal Pay for Jobs of Equal Value*; *Women's Work, Men's Work: Sex Segregation on the Job*; and *Computer Chips and Paper Clips: Technology and Women's Employment.*

From 1986 through 1987, Hartmann held an American Statistical Association fellowship at the Census Bureau, where she conducted research on women's poverty. In 1987, she founded the Institute for Women's Policy Research, based in Washington, D.C. In addition to her work at the institute, Hartmann maintains an active role in academe. She is currently a research professor of women's studies at George Washington University. Besides her MacArthur Fellowship, Hartmann has received an honorary doctor of laws degree from Swarthmore College and the Wilbur Cross Medal for Distinguished Alumni of the graduate school of Yale University. She chairs the National Council of Women's Organizations' Task Force on Women and Social Security. She is considered an expert on the issue of Social Security reform and the impact that various plans to change Social Security will have on women; she has spoken widely and given many media interviews on this issue. She serves on the board of the Coalition on Human Needs and the steering committee of the National Committee on Pay Equity. She is also co-chair of the Economists' Policy Group on Women's Issues.

CONTRIBUTIONS

Of the many contributions Hartmann has made to economics, the concept of comparable worth is one of the most significant. She practically invented the notion of equal pay for jobs of equal value. As the National Research Council Committee on Women's Employment and Related Social Issues noted, "The general goal of a comparable worth strategy is pay equity—equitable occupational wage rates that are not influenced by the sex, race, or ethnicity of the incumbents" (*Comparable Worth*, 4). The Equal Pay Act of 1963 had as its goal "equal pay for equal work" and was meant to deal with blatant wage discrimination, which ". . . occurs when one class of people is paid less than another class for doing exactly or substantially the same job: for example, male and female machine assemblers (or truck drivers, secretaries, elementary school teachers, professors, etc.) working side by side, doing jobs that are essentially indistinguishable from one another, producing similar results" (*Women, Work, and Wages*, 9).

The principle of comparable worth is aimed at an insidious form of wage discrimination not specifically addressed in the social legislation of the early 1960s. "A second type of wage discrimination . . . arises when the job structure within a firm is substantially segregated by sex, race, or ethnicity, and workers of one category are paid less than workers of another category when the two groups are performing work that is not the same but that is, in some sense, of comparable worth to their employer" (*Women, Work, and Wages*, 9). Under comparable worth, "jobs ought to be paid according to their intrinsic worth, as measured by such factors as skill required, responsibility entailed, and effort involved . . ." (*Comparable Worth*, 3).

The basis for the comparable worth approach to wage determination is the obvious pay gap between men and women that arises from employment stereotyping and persistent sex segregation of jobs:

> Social science literature has established a correlation between average occupational wage levels and the extent of female representation in the occupation: the more a job is done by women, the lower its average wage level. It is this connection between "femaleness" and lower wage levels that is challenged by the comparable worth strategy. Comparable worth advocates believe that the lower wage rates of female jobs are the result at least partly of discrimination and that wage rates should therefore be realigned. The comparable worth strategy generally involves examination of the relative wage rates of jobs held predominantly by women and those held predominantly by men and study of the bases of these wage rates. Via job evaluation procedures, which attempt to establish objective criteria for such job features as skill, effort, responsibility, and working conditions, the relative value of jobs is established and wage rates are realigned accordingly. (*Comparable Worth*, 4)

One obvious way to close the wage gap between men and women is to have women move in large numbers into job categories traditionally considered men's work. This solution, however, puts the burden of adjustment on women, for while some may welcome the opportunity to move out of segregated job categories, many others who have invested in training or choose to work certain jobs do not want to be penalized for staying put. For comparable worth to become operational, Hartmann has identified two general themes that need further study: the nature and underlying causes of occupational wage differentials and discrimination, and effective ways to implement the strategy and to minimize any potential adverse impact (*Comparable Worth*, 6–7).

Almost of necessity, Hartmann's interest in comparable worth forced her to explore the significance of gender bias in the assignment of work in the labor force (*Women's Work*). The consequences of sex segregation in employment are numerous and involve more than just the obvious gap between the wages of men and women. Occupational choice in the economy as a whole and within and across firms is diminished for both men and women because of preconceptions of what is men's work and what is women's work. Other less-apparent but equally oppressive consequences for women, especially, are lower retirement incomes, greater susceptibility to unemployment, fewer opportunities for on-the-job training, less employment mobility, lower occupational prestige, and increased job stress. The consequences of sex segregation are many, the causes complex, and the solutions involved. "Because the causes of segregation—cultural values, socialization, sex bias and tracking in the educational system and in job training programs, discrimination, and institutionalized and informal barriers in the workplace—interact with each other and operate together to restrict access to education, training, and employment in sex-atypical occupations, remedies are most likely to be effective when they address multiple causes" (130).

While most of Hartmann's research deals with the broad issue of women and work, she has also written on specific issues, as in *Family and Medical Leave,* a pamphlet she coauthored for the Institute for Women's Policy Research. Challenging the assumption "that business or employers are the only group that bears the costs of family and medical leave" (1), Hartmann demonstrated that the absence of a comprehensive national policy on leaves is more costly than not having one. In the late 1980s, the patchwork of state laws and haphazard business practices concerning family and medical leave camouflaged the true cost to workers in particular and to society in general. When these hidden costs were factored in, Hartmann and her coauthors showed that the benefits of a broad program exceeded the costs, contrary to the conclusions of those opposed to an inclusive and consistent national policy.

As head of the Institute for Women's Policy Research, Hartmann takes a panoramic view of the world and women's role in it. She cannot afford the luxury of evaluating circumstances purely from the perspective of a professional economist. This means appreciating the political, social, historical, and psychological aspects of events, and not just their economic implications. This eclectic approach is evident in her coedited book *U. S. Women in Struggle: A Feminist Studies Anthology.* This anthology of twenty-one essays, all of which originally appeared in *Feminist Studies,* "covers the chronology of women's activity in the United States, beginning with the early 1800s" (xiv). The book is inclusive, covering not only intellectual perspectives but also the types of women's movement, both liberal and conservative, that have emerged over time: "Nor have women's activities been only emancipatory, for women have also organized to defend hierarchical, male-dominant families and the 'purity' and supremacy of white, Protestant families" (xv). *U.S. Women in Struggle* presents a collage of women's activism, from their involvement with the Ku Klux Klan in the 1920s to the 1985 strike of clerical and technical employees at Yale University.

BIBLIOGRAPHY

Works by Heidi I. Hartmann

Women, Work, and Wages: Equal Pay for Jobs of Equal Value (edited with D. J. Treiman). Washington, DC: National Academy Press, 1981.

Comparable Worth: New Directions for Research (editor). Washington, DC: National Academy Press, 1985.

Women's Work, Men's Work: Sex Segregation on the Job (edited with B. F. Reskin). Washington, DC: National Academy Press, 1986.

Family and Medical Leave: Who Pays for the Lack of It? (with R. M. Spalter-Roth). Washington, DC: Women's Research and Education Institute, 1989.

U.S. Women in Struggle: A Feminist Studies Anthology (edited with C. G. Moses). Urbana: University of Illinois Press, 1995.

Ann Horowitz
(1936–)

Ann Horowitz received her undergraduate degree in mathematics, and the imprint of that undergraduate education clearly influenced her approach to economics. Whether investigating issues in public finance, aspects of industrial organization, or the implications of a specific social policy, she has consistently trained the analytical power of her mathematical background on the eclectic topics found in her research portfolio. The cumulative output of this effort is a diverse and impressive body of work that began in the 1960s and continues today.

BIOGRAPHY

Ann Horowitz was born in Weymouth, Massachusetts, on August 24, 1936. Her father was Lowell Hoyt Holway, a naval architect, and her mother was Ann (Donohew) Holway. She grew up in Groton, Connecticut, where her father worked at the Electric Boat Company, builders of nuclear submarines. In 1954, she graduated from Robert E. Fitch High School in Groton and then attended the University of Connecticut in Storrs. She graduated summa cum laude in 1958 with a B.A. in mathematics. "Nancy," as most people who know Ann Horowitz well call her, married Ira Horowitz on June 6, 1958. For the next two years, she was a graduate student at the University of Kansas, earning an M.A. in economics in 1960. She then went to Indiana University, where she received her Ph.D. in economics in 1966. While at Indiana, she was the recipient of a Ford Foundation Doctoral Dissertation Fellowship (1965–66).

Horowitz began her teaching career at Indiana University as a teaching associate from 1962 to 1965. She continued teaching at Indiana as an assistant professor of economics after completing her Ph.D. In 1973, she became director of the Florida Econometric Forecasting Project at the University of Florida. Horowitz left Florida in 1975 for Washington, D.C., to become a senior economist on the president's Council on Wage and Price Stability. In September 1976, she returned to the University of Florida as an associate professor of economics and coordinator of graduate studies, the latter a position she held on and off for the next sixteen years. In 1978–79, Horowitz was a visiting associate professor of economics at Michigan State University, and she held visiting fellow positions at the City University of Hong Kong in 1992–94 and again in 1997–98. She retired from the University of Florida as associate professor emerita in July 2000.

Outside of academe, Horowitz was active in a number of government and professional organizations. She served as a consultant to the Florida Department of Administration and worked with the Governor's Economic Advisory Board, helping prepare the Governor's Annual Economic Report from 1973 to 1975. She was a member of the editorial board of Sage Professional Papers in Political Economy (1974–77) and was interim chair of the Industrial Organization Society (1976–77). For six years (1974–80) she was a member of the editorial advisory board of the *Industrial Organization Review.* In spring 2002, Horowitz returned to the City University of Hong Kong as a visiting fellow.

CONTRIBUTIONS

The cumulative output of Horowitz's scholarship—some twenty-plus articles, monographs, books, and contributions to books—is not easily characterized but generally falls into three areas: industrial organization, public finance, and a catch-all category best described as the economics of social welfare. Horowitz and her coauthor husband, Ira, first made their mark writing about the industrial organization of the brewing industry. Their research centered on the declining per capita consumption of beer during the 1960s ("Firms in a Declining Market"), increasing market dominance of megabrewers ("Profiles of the Future"), and the urge to merge in the beer industry ("Concentration"). Horowitz also coauthored a technical paper about the mathematics of entropy-based measures of industrial concentration, concluding that the limitations of entropy analysis almost certainly outweigh its marginal contributions to the field of industrial organization ("Real and Illusory Virtues").

Horowitz's interest in public finance began early in her career and continues today. In 1968, she published an article explaining the interstate differences in state and local government expenditures ("A Simultaneous-Equation Approach"). Her work differed from that of previous studies in two basic ways: "First, simultaneous-equation techniques are used to estimate the more complex models that are developed. Second, the number of state and local governmental employees adjusted to a full-time equivalent basis per 10,000 population *as well as* per capita expenditures are used to measure the amount of goods and services provided by state and local governments. This supplementary employment measure is included because interstate differences in per capita governmental expenditures result not only from interstate differences in the amount of goods and services provided but also from differences in such factors as the level of prices, the amount of transfer payments, the quality of services, and efficiency" (459). Her principal findings were that per capita personal income and per capita state and local governmental expenditures are directly related; income distribution is not a significant determinant of governmental expenditures when the effects of other factors are taken into account; tax effort and public expenditures are directly related; population density is of little value in explaining interstate differences in governmental expenditures; and there is no systematic relationship between income and federal grants-in-aid (475–76).

In a more recent contribution to the field, Horowitz reconsidered the prevailing assumption "that by increasing either the likelihood of an income tax audit or the penalty for underreporting taxable income, the tax authority can reduce the extent to which conscious cheating takes place" ("Tax Audit Uncertainty," 491). She showed that this seemingly safe and innocuous assumption is neither when "the linkage between posttax income and the work-versus-leisure decision is taken into account" (491). Horowitz concluded that the policy implications of her analysis are ambiguous and apologized for this lack of clarity. "Human behavior in our uncertain world is unpredictable, which is what makes this world such an interesting place in which to pass the time and to pay or not pay one's taxes, as the case may be" (509).

With respect to the economics of social welfare, Horowitz has made contributions to the theoretical aspects of the field, such as her paper on the value of using quadratic loss functions to evaluate the effectiveness of macroeconomic policy ("Loss Functions"). The majority of her contributions in this field, however, have been quantitative in nature. An early example of this orientation was a monograph she wrote on auto parts price behavior while she was working for the Council on Wage and Price Stability (*Auto Parts*). In the mid-1970s, she coedited a two-volume work dealing with the racial aspects of economics (*Patterns*). The volumes—one a collection of essays about racial discrimination in housing, and the other about racial discrimination in employment and income—were the outgrowth of a conference on racial discrimination held at Indiana University in May 1973. All the papers included in the work were original contributions to the respective topics and, collectively, represented the best analysis and policy statements of some of the day's leading economists.

Two years prior to the publication of *Patterns*, Horowitz established her credentials in this area with her article on racial differences in income dynamics ("Estimating Racial Differences"). Her effort "to measure the probabilities that families in given income classes will move to different income classes or remain in the same income class over time" (221) differed from other research on the topic in that it used macroeconomic instead of microeconomic data. Using a first-order Markov chain process, Horowitz showed that although the proportion of families in the lowest income class had steadily declined for both races, "low-income black families have a smaller probability than whites of increasing their income, while middle- and high-income black families have a greater chance of a decline in income. The results indicate that the distribution of income for black families does not merely lag behind that of white families. Rather, it would appear that, *ceteris paribus*, the existing disparities will become even greater" (234). Using sophisticated mathematics, Horowitz had investigated a very human condition with insightful clarity and haunting results.

BIBLIOGRAPHY

Works by Ann Horowitz

"Firms in a Declining Market: The Brewing Case" (with I. Horowitz). *Journal of Industrial Economics* 13(2), March 1965: 129–53.

"Profiles of the Future: The Beer Industry" (with I. Horowitz). *Business Horizons* 10(3), Fall 1967: 5–19.

"A Simultaneous-Equation Approach to the Problem of Explaining Interstate Differences in State and Local Government Expenditures." *Southern Economic Journal* 34(4), April 1968: 459–76.

"Concentration, Competition, and Mergers in Brewing" (with I. Horowitz). In *Public Policy toward Mergers,* edited by J. F. Weston and S. Peltzman, 45–56. Pacific Palisades, CA: Goodyear, 1969.

"Estimating Racial Differences in Income Dynamics from Aggregate Data." *Applied Economics* 4(3), September 1972: 221–34.

Patterns of Racial Discrimination. Vol. 1, *Housing;* Vol. 2, *Employment and Income* (editor, with G. v. Furstenberg and B. Harrison). Lexington, MA: Lexington Books, 1974.

"The Real and Illusory Virtues of Entropy-Based Measures for Business and Economic Analysis" (with I. Horowitz). *Decision Sciences* 7(1), January 1976: 121–36.

Auto Parts Price Behavior: 1971–1976. Washington, DC: Executive Office of the President, Council on Wage and Price Stability: May 1977.

"Loss Functions and Public Policy." *Journal of Macroeconomics* 9(40), Fall 1987: 489–504.

"Tax Audit Uncertainty and the Work-versus-Leisure Decision" (with I. Horowitz). *Public Finance Review* 28(6), November 2000: 491–510.

Caroline M. Hoxby
(1966–)

In a research career that began in the mid-1990s, Caroline M. Hoxby has established herself as one of America's foremost experts on the economics of education. Applying sophisticated econometric techniques to mountains of data, she has published numerous papers on a host of interrelated topics such as the efficacy of vouchers, the pros and cons of financing public education with local versus centralized systems, and the impact of teachers' unions on student academic achievement. Her studies are comprehensive, her insights often counterintuitive, and her conclusions usually controversial but never boring. She is one of the brightest stars in the constellation of economists making their mark in the twenty-first century.

BIOGRAPHY

Caroline Minter Hoxby was born in 1966 in Cleveland, Ohio, and grew up in the suburb of Shaker Heights. Her father, Steven A. Minter, is president of the Cleveland Foundation, and her mother, Delores Minter, is a homemaker. Hoxby graduated from Shaker Heights High School in 1984 and went to Harvard University, where she earned a B.A. in economics in 1988, graduating summa cum laude. At Harvard, she was inducted into Phi Beta Kappa and won the Hoopes Prize for Best Thesis in Economics.

After leaving Harvard, Hoxby was a Rhodes Scholar at the Oxford University (1988–90), earning an M.Phil. in economics in 1990. At Oxford, she received the award for Best Master of Philosophy Thesis in Economics. Over the next four years, Hoxby was in the graduate economics program at the Massachusetts Institute of Technology, where she received her Ph.D. in 1994. From 1990 to 1993, she held a National Science Foundation graduate fellowship, and in 1993–94, she received the Spencer Foundation Fellowship for Research Related to Education. Her Ph.D. thesis won the National Tax

Association Award for Best Dissertation in Public Economics in 1994. In May 1993, she married Blair Hoxby, a professor of English literature at Yale University.

Hoxby began her teaching career in 1994 as an assistant professor of economics at Harvard University. She became Morris Kahn Associate Professor of Economics in 1997 and was promoted to full professor at Harvard in 2001. Hoxby serves as a senior adviser to the Brookings Institution's Brown Center for Education Policy. She is also a MacArthur Foundation fellow, a distinguished visiting fellow at the Hoover Institution, and program director of the Economics of Education Program at the National Bureau of Economic Research. She has had a Ford Foundation fellowship (1993–94), a National Science Foundation grant (1995–98), and is working with a National Institute of Child Health and Development grant (1998–2003). In 2000–2001, Hoxby was a Carnegie Scholar. Since 1996, she has advised and/or given testimony for several state legislatures and courts on school finance equalization, charter school legislation, and federal tax policies for higher education.

CONTRIBUTIONS

Hoxby has studied the economics of education at all levels, including higher education ("Tax Incentives"), but the bulk of her research has dealt with primary and secondary education. Her research efforts have been divided between school finances and school efficacy as reflected in student academic achievement. She published her first major paper in 1996, examining the efficiency/equity trade-off associated with local versus centralized financing systems. Prior to her research, the prevailing notion was that the local financing of public education was efficient but not necessarily equitable, while centralized financing was fair but not necessarily efficient. "As this paper will explain, however, equating local finance with efficiency and centralized finance with equity is incorrect and greatly exaggerates the real efficiency-equity tradeoff that faces us" ("Are Efficiency and Equity," 51–52).

In her analysis, Hoxby investigated allocative efficiency, productive efficiency, and equity, where "Allocative efficiency is getting the *amount* of education right. Productive efficiency is getting it at the least cost. Equity is applying this standard of optimality to everyone, regardless of family background or income" ("Are Efficiency and Equity," 54). She argues that the current predicament of school finance is one of productivity (student outcomes) and not the level of spending. From this, she posits that local financing is more likely than centralized financing to improve student achievement, and to do so effectively, efficiently, and fairly. This conclusion was reinforced in her subsequent research that viewed schools as local public goods producers ("Productivity of Schools"). According to Hoxby, the key insight of the paper is that "when the Tiebout process functions with local property tax finance, it can generate verifiable demand information that can be used to manage the productivity of local public goods providers" (28). The "Tiebout process" to which Hoxby refers is associated with a paper by Charles Tiebout that appeared in the *Journal of Political Economy* in 1956.

> The strength of local, property tax-based school finance is its ability to achieve a high level of allocative efficiency, even though schools are publicly provided. This ability is due to the Tiebout ... process in which people move to another school district if, in their district, the marginal utility of school spending gets out of balance with its price. Intuitively, the combination of local finance and the Tiebout process provides a mechanism that, despite using public funding, relinks the marginal costs and marginal benefits of schooling. The most realistic versions of this mechanism that achieve allocative efficiency are those in which public schools are financed by a property tax and the Tiebout process capitalizes the value of local public schools into local house prices. In such models, inequality between the intrinsic value of a district's schools and the per-household cost in property taxes induces movement between districts, until the households within each school district have the same demand for schooling and all households consume the amount of schooling they find (privately) optimal. ("Are Efficiency and Equity," 56)

The Tiebout process coupled with greater parental choice led Hoxby to conclude that competition via charter schools or vouchers, even if the vouchers are limited to use in the public-school system, is likely to enhance student academic achievement ("The Effects of Private School Vouchers"; "Does Competition"). As she puts it, "In general, the results suggest that choice, which would give parents' preferences more relative to those of teachers and administrators, would not undermine academic and disciplinary standards in U.S. schools. On average, parents appear to choose higher academic standards and stricter environments than do school staff. This is not the same as saying the teachers and administrators, as individuals or parents themselves, do not value good academic work or good behavior. The difference in attitude between parents and staff may be due to the fact that it is the staff who have to enforce higher standards in schools, and so they give more weight to the effort that enforcement activities require" ("The Effects of School Choice," 312).

In 1996, Hoxby published a monumental study on school efficacy. The motivation for the study was her desire "to explain why measured school inputs appear to have little effect on student outcomes, particularly for cohorts educated since 1960. ... This study is motivated by two related empirical puzzles. The first is that student-level and school-level data often show little evidence of a relationship between student performance and school inputs, after controlling for the student's background. ... The second is that metropolitan areas with few opportunities for competition among public schools tend to have more generous school inputs—including higher per-pupil spending, higher teacher salaries, and lower student-teacher ratio—but also tend to have worse student performance" ("How Teachers' Unions," 671).

Hoxby considered many candidates to explain this double conundrum in an applied econometric study that used the *Census of Government* and the *Census of Population* for a twenty-year period for some 10,500 school districts in the United States, about 95 percent of the country's total in 1990. Her conclusion: "... the results indicate that teachers' unions succeed in raising school budgets and school inputs but have an overall negative effect on student performance" ("How Teachers' Unions," 708). Among the many reasons for this is Hoxby's assertion, supported by the empirical evidence, that "rent-seeking" and not "efficiency-enhancing" behavior drives teachers' unions; that is, self-interest is more important to teachers' unions than the pure maximization of student achievement (675–76).

As controversial as that conclusion may be, Hoxby has generated other results equally challenging to common myths about primary and secondary education. She has, in another of her signature empirical studies, challenged the notion that student academic achievement is inversely related to class size. She analyzed "the effects of class size on student achievement using longitudinal variation in the population associated with each grade in 649 elementary schools" and concluded "class size does not have a statistically significant effect on student achievement" ("The Effects of Class Size," 1239). In a similar vein, she has shown that, relative to income, spending per pupil in Massachusetts, Illinois, and California remained constant during the twentieth century, rather than being directly related to per-capita income, as is generally assumed ("How Much"). In this and related studies, Hoxby suggests that improvements in student outcomes are not related solely to policy choices. She sees the teaching-learning process as an immensely complicated phenomenon for which no silver bullet or single change—such as smaller classes or greater expenditures per student—will bring immediate and measurable improvements.

BIBLIOGRAPHY

Works by Caroline M. Hoxby

"How Teachers' Unions Affect Education Production." *Quarterly Journal of Economics* 111(3), August 1996: 671–718.

"Are Efficiency and Equity in School Finances Substitutes or Complements?" *Journal of Economic Perspectives* 10(4), Fall 1996: 51–72.

"The Effects of Private School Vouchers on Schools and Students." In *Holding School Accountable: Performance-Based Approaches to School Reform*, edited by H. F. Ladd, 177–208. Washington, DC: Brookings Institution, 1996.

"How Much Does School Spending Depend on Family Income? The Historical Origins of the Current School Finance Dilemma." *American Economic Review* 88(2), May 1998: 309–14.

"Tax Incentives for Higher Education." In *Tax Policy and the Economy*, edited by J. M. Poterba, 49–81. Cambridge, MA: MIT Press/National Bureau of Economic Research, 1998.

"The Effects of School Choice on Curriculum and Atmosphere." In *Earning and Learning: How Schools Matter*, edited by S. E. Mayer and P. E. Peterson, 281–316. Washington, DC: Brookings Institution/Russell Sage Foundation, 1999.

"The Productivity of Schools and Other Local Public Goods Producers." *Journal of Public Economics* 74(1), November 1999: 1–30.

"The Effects of Class Size on Student Achievement: New Evidence from Population Variation." *Quarterly Journal of Economics* 115(4), November 2000: 1239–85.

"Does Competition among Public Schools Benefit Students and Taxpayers?" *American Economic Review* 90(5), December 2000: 1209–38.

Works about Caroline M. Hoxby

Boldt, D. "Economic Effects Are Something Else to Consider about School Choice." *The Philadelphia Enquirer*, November 19, 2000.

Juanita M. Kreps
(1921–)

On January 23, 1977, when Juanita Morris Kreps was sworn in as U.S. secretary of commerce, the occasion was notable for two firsts. Kreps was the first woman appointed to the position, and she was the first professional economist to hold that particular cabinet post. Usually the commerce secretary is an outspoken advocate for the U.S. business community, but Kreps came to the job with a different viewpoint. She was committed to increasing the social consciousness of business professionals while at the same time advancing the interests of the public, including workers and consumers. She worked to promote international trade, a customary role for the secretary of commerce, but she also tried to mitigate the high unemployment rate prevalent during the late 1970s and to combat the stagflation that gripped the U.S. economy during the administration of President Jimmy Carter.

BIOGRAPHY

Juanita Morris was born on January 11, 1921, in the coal-mining town of Lynch, Kentucky. She was the sixth child of Elmer M. Morris, a struggling mine operator, and Larcenia (Blair) Morris. Her parents were divorced when she was four, and Juanita lived with her mother until age twelve, when she was enrolled in a Presbyterian boarding school. In 1938, she entered Berea College in Kentucky. Berea is known for its work-study programs, as most of its students, like Juanita Morris, come from the Southern Appalachian Mountain region and work for the college in lieu of paying tuition, room, and board. These were the years of the Great Depression, and economic conditions took on a special relevance to Morris. She decided after taking her first course in economics that it would be her undergraduate major, hoping this field of study would give her some insight into what was going on in the larger world.

After graduation in 1942, she went on to Duke University, where she received her M.A. in 1944 and her Ph.D. in 1948. On August 11, 1944, she married fellow economist Clifton H. Kreps Jr. The couple would go on to have three children—Sarah, Laura, and Clifton III. While studying at Duke, Kreps also taught there part time, and she worked as a junior economist with the National War Labor Board in 1943 and 1944. For the next ten years, she taught economics at several colleges, including Dennison, Hofstra, and Queens College. In 1955, she returned to Duke University, starting as a visiting assistant professor of economics. In the following years, she would move up through both the academic and administrative ranks at Duke. She became a full professor in 1968, and in 1972, she was named to the James B. Duke Professorship, the university's most prestigious chair. In 1969, she served as dean of the Women's College and as assistant provost, and in 1973 she was appointed university vice president. Four years later, Kreps became U.S. secretary of commerce.

As an economist, Kreps's interest was in labor demographics, with particular attention to the employment issues of women and older workers. She published books, articles, and monographs about labor and related subjects. In terms of women's issues, her economic research highlighted the need for equality of opportunity for women, especially in the marketplace. In 1962, a year before the publication of Betty Friedan's groundbreaking book *The Feminine Mystique,* Kreps pointed out in a speech that women wanted both further education and meaningful work. In 1971, she published *Sex in the Marketplace: American Women at Work,* which gave the current view of the women's labor force and identified problems that needed addressing. She noted that women's participation in the workforce had virtually quadrupled to 31 million from the 1920s to the 1970s, but that women continued to staff the clerical jobs, elementary classrooms, and salesrooms, almost never achieving administrative rank. She recommended that women improve their status through collective bargaining, union membership, and shifting away from the traditional occupations.

Kreps and her collaborator Robert Clark discussed the changing patterns of sex, age, and marriage among workers in their book *Sex, Age, and Work: The Changing Composition of the Labor Force.* Publication of this book coincided with the growing emergence of women into the labor market, and the authors noted that this trend suggested the need for drastically different employment practices in the future. In 1975, Kreps organized a conference called "Women and the American Economy," which produced a document calling for stronger affirmative action programs at universities in recognition of the fact that women would need to be better educated for their full participation in the marketplace. Again ahead of the times, the conference called for public education of preschool children.

During the 1970s, leading corporations, reacting to pressure from women's groups, began to add women to their boards of directors. Because of her economic renown and her position at Duke, Kreps was named to the boards of the New York Stock Exchange, Western Electric, R.J. Reynolds Industries, Eastman Kodak, and J.C. Penney. She recognized that these firsts were a form of tokenism but stated that this tokenism was just a stage that women had to go through. This did not prevent her from feeling that she was obligated to pre-pare extra carefully for board meetings.

In 1976, Kreps was invited to Plains, Georgia, to brief Jimmy Carter after his election as president. She was surprised to learn a little later that she was being considered for the commerce position. When she was sworn in on January 23, 1977, she became the fourth woman in U.S. history to be named to a cabinet post and the first to hold the commerce position. She was joined in the Carter cabinet by Patricia Roberts Harris, who was appointed secretary of housing and urban development.

During her Senate confirmation hearing, Kreps stated that the biggest problem she foresaw was carrying out policies that would create jobs and improve productivity. She further testified that she would give special attention to the job-creating public works program administered by the Commerce Department.

While working in Washington, Kreps lived in an apartment, but on most weekends she commuted to her home in Durham, North Carolina, to be with her husband, who was a professor of banking at the University of North Carolina at the time. In 1979, she returned to Duke University as vice president emerita, a position Kreps has held ever since. Over the next twenty-plus years, she received numerous awards in recognition of her many accomplishments, including the American Association of University Women Achievement Award (1981), the Industry Achievement Award from the National Association of Bank Women (1987), election as a fellow of the American Academy of Arts and Sciences (1988), the EBRI (Employee Benefit Research Institute) Lillywhite Award for Outstanding Lifetime Contribution to Enhancing America's Economic Security (1995), and the Distinguished Women of North Carolina Award (2000).

CONTRIBUTIONS

As an economist, Kreps centered her research on labor-related issues with particular attention to the employment of women and older workers. She was a pioneer in the scholarship devoted to the economics of aging. Her book *Lifetime Allocation of Work and Income* is a collection of essays, most of which Kreps wrote or coauthored. This book called "attention to recent developments affecting the patterns of work and earnings through the life span, recent and projected growth of non-working time, levels of income by age and occupational groups, the impact of economic growth on retirement benefits, the question of optimizing the temporal allocation of work and income, and the growing role of income transfers" (preface, vii). Her work predates by a full generation the issues, research, and related debates that developed in the first decade of the twenty-first century when baby boomers—that demographic surge of individuals born during the years 1946 through 1964—began to retire in appreciable numbers.

Kreps has devoted many of her articles, monographs, and books to the subject of labor, but her primary interest has always been the economics of women. In *Women and the American Economy: A Look to the 1980s,* she assessed the changed status of women in the United States as the last quarter of the twentieth century approached and considered the implications that those changes would have on the future of U.S. society. "At the beginning of this last quarter-century, women make up about forty percent of the nation's labor force. They are going to school longer, marrying later, having fewer children, and living decades beyond the life span of their grandmothers. The forces that shaped these changes in women's lives—industrialization, urbanization, higher levels of learning and a consequent rise in living standards—have left their imprint on the work lives and expectations of men as well, and on the economic potential of the nation" (1).

While much of the prosperity of the 1980s and 1990s was attributed to technology, especially the integration of the computer into the workplace, Kreps and economists of her ilk assign as much significance to the elimination of sex-linked job pools, the impact of affirmative action, and the fair and appropriate employment of human resources in the allocation of people to jobs as to any other factor.

BIBLIOGRAPHY

Works by Juanita M. Kreps

Lifetime Allocation of Work and Income: Essays in the Economics of Aging. Durham, NC: Duke University Press, 1971.

Sex in the Workplace: American Women at Work. Baltimore, MD: Johns Hopkins University Press, 1971.

Sex, Age, and Work: The Changing Composition of the Labor Force (with R. Clark). Baltimore, MD: Johns Hopkins University Press, 1975.

Women and the American Economy: A Look to the 1980s (editor). Englewood Cliffs, NJ: Prentice Hall for the American Assembly, 1976.

Works about Juanita M. Kreps

"Kreps, Juanita M." In *Current Biography,* edited by C. Moritz, 259–61. New York: H. W. Wilson, 1977.

Hazel Kyrk
(1886–1957)

In 1992, University of Chicago professor of economics Gary Becker received the Nobel Memorial Prize for "having extended the domain of economic theory to aspects of human behavior which had previously been dealt with—if at all—by other social science disciplines." Specifically, he had concentrated the power and sophistication of mathematical analysis on the economics of the family, creating a field of study dubbed the "new home economics." Becker's work was an extension of the research of another important but relatively obscure University of Chicago economist, Hazel Kyrk. It was upon her shoulders that Becker stood to achieve the highest recognition conferred on the practitioners of the dismal science.

BIOGRAPHY

A pioneer in the field of consumer economics, Hazel Kyrk was born in Ashley, Ohio, on November 19, 1886, the only child of Elmer Kyrk and Jane (Benedick) Kyrk. Because her mother died when she was a teenager and her father's income was meager, Kyrk had to support herself from an early age. In the early 1900s, she taught school for three years before enrolling at Ohio Wesleyan University in 1904. While at Ohio Wesleyan, she found work as a mother's helper in the home of economics professor Leon Carroll Marshall. When Marshall moved to the University of Chicago in 1906, Kyrk accompanied his family and continued her studies there. The university was then a hotbed of new ideas in the social sciences. In 1910, she earned a Ph.B. in economics and a Phi Beta Kappa key.

Kyrk spent the next year as an instructor at Wellesley College in Massachusetts, then returned to the University of Chicago to pursue a Ph.D. in economics. In 1914, she combined her doctoral studies with a teaching position at Oberlin College in Ohio. After the United States entered World War I four years later, she decided to join the war effort and in 1918 followed her academic adviser, James Alfred North, to London. There, she worked as a statistician for the American Division of the Allied Maritime Transport Council. When the war ended, she returned to her teaching position at Oberlin and resumed work on her doctoral dissertation. It was completed in 1920, making Kyrk one of the first women to receive a Ph.D. in economics at the University of Chicago.

In 1923, her dissertation was published as *A Theory of Consumption*. Shaped by her firsthand observations of regulated consumption in wartime England, the book fused the newly emerging field of social psychology with economics, thereby creating a classic exposition of the social basis of consumer behavior. Kyrk's work analyzed the constraints market conditions place on the consumer's "formal freedom of choice" and drew attention to the changing role of women in the modern economy of the twentieth century. Kyrk noted that production was increasingly moving outside the home, making the housewife more and more a "director of consumption." A distinguished panel of economists awarded *A Theory of Consumption* the prestigious Hart, Schaffer, and Marx Prize for research in economics.

Kyrk left Oberlin in 1923 and spent the next year at the Food Research Institute at Stanford University, where she cowrote *The American Baking Industry, 1849–1923*. The following year, she was a professor at what is now Iowa State University. In 1925, she returned to the University of Chicago, where she remained until her retirement in 1952. During those years, she broadened the economics curriculum to include consumer topics and, in the process, established Chicago as the premier university for the study of family and consumer economics. She trained several generations of graduate students, many of them women, who would go on to distinguish themselves in government and academic careers.

Reflecting her concern for working women, Kyrk taught at the Bryn Mawr College Summer School for Women Workers from 1922 to 1925 and served on the board of the Chicago Women's Trade Union League. Her writing career began to flourish during this period. She became a frequent contributor to the *Journal of Home Economics* and the *American Economic Review* (e.g., "Income Distribution"). In 1940, she coauthored *Food Buying and Our Markets*, a book that truly put the economics in home economics.

Her commitment to the needs of consumers was evident in her various services to federal agencies. In the summers between 1938 and 1941, Kyrk served as principal economist with the Bureau of Home Economics in the Department of Agriculture. There she contributed to the bureau's massive Consumer Purchases Study, a groundbreaking work that became an important economic barometer and, increasingly, a reference point for labor-management negotiations. This massive study was the most comprehensive consumer survey ever attempted. It broke down national consumption patterns by five distinct geographic regions and further subdivided information by urban, village, and farm categories. Published in more than twenty volumes, the study established base-year prices for the cost-of-living index, now called the consumer price index, one of the most widely accepted and re-spected measures of inflation in use today.

Kyrk's work on behalf of consumers continued in 1943 with her appoint-ment as chair of the Consumer Advisory Committee of the Office of Price Administration. During World War II, she represented the consumer's view-point, arguing for standards in consumer goods and for more gradual price decontrols. Later, she joined her colleagues in urging President Harry Truman to establish a permanent consumer service bureau as well as a consumer ad-visory committee in each federal agency. In 1945–46, Kyrk chaired the tech-nical advisory committee for the Bureau of Labor Statistics as it undertook to formulate a "standard family budget." This economic yardstick helped meas-ure the economic health of U.S. families, set levels of income-tax exemption, and ultimately played a role in creating an operational definition of poverty and the poverty line. She was also involved in helping revise the consumer price index to reflect postwar inflation.

When Kyrk retired from the University of Chicago in 1952, she moved to Washington, D.C. There she finished working on her textbook *The Family in the American Economy*. In 1953, her alma mater, Ohio Wesleyan University, honored her with the degree of doctor of humane letters. On August 6, 1957, while vacationing at her summer home in West Dover, Vermont, Kyrk suf-fered a fatal stroke. She was buried in Ashley, Ohio.

CONTRIBUTIONS

During the nineteenth and through the early part of the twentieth centuries, home economics was a subject that emphasized aspects of domestic life, such as meal planning or food selection from the nutritive standpoint. The econom-ics content of the field was minimal and seldom analytical. The 1940 edition of her coauthored book *Food Buying and Our Markets* had its share of standard home-economics fare, such as this passage in the section "Capons, Slips and Stage": "A *capon* is an unsexed male bird, usually 7 to 10 months old, weight-ing over 4 pounds. By caponizing, the effects of maturity are retarded, and the flesh remains tender longer in a capon than a stag. Because of its plump tender breast which carves well and its size, roast capon is popular for com-pany dinner, but is somewhat more expensive than a roaster" (345).

The quoted passage appears in part 2 of the book, "Foods." Part 1—"The Market"—reflects Kyrk's contributions. In it, chapters are focused on the more economic aspects of food buying, including such topics as "The Retail Food Market," "Food Marketing Costs," and "Prices and Price Policies." The anal-ysis in this section of the book is clearly based on applied microeconomics.

In *The Family in the American Economy*, Kyrk aimed the lens of economic analysis on "economic welfare, particularly the economic welfare of American families" (v). In this strain of home economics, the accent was on economics as it pertains to the family. The early chapters of the book established a con-ceptual framework centered on "Forms and Functions of the Family" and "American Families Today." The rest of the book was given to discussions of "Components of Family Income and Wealth," "Social Security," "Income and

Property Rights of Husband and Wife under the Law," and "The Cost of Living." Always the pioneer, Kyrk devoted considerable discussion to the nature, causes, and measurement of poverty. This is a particularly forward-looking portion of the book, considering that a national discussion of systematic indigence, its causes, and its cures would have to wait for another decade and the declaration of President Lyndon Baines Johnson's War on Poverty.

BIBLIOGRAPHY

Works by Hazel Kyrk

The American Baking Industry, 1849–1923 (with J. S. Davis). Stanford, CA: Stanford University Press, 1925.

Food Buying and Our Markets (with D. Monroe and U. B. Stone). New York: M. Barrows, 1940.

"The Income Distribution as a Measure of Economic Welfare." *American Economic Review* 50(2), May 1950: 342–55.

The Family in the American Economy. Chicago, IL: University of Chicago Press, 1953.

Works about Hazel Kyrk

"Hazel Kyrk." In *Notable American Women: The Modern Period,* edited by J. Sickerman and C. H. Greer, 405–6. Cambridge, MA: Belknap Press of Harvard University Press, 1980.

Reid, M. G. "Miss Hazel Kyrk." In *History of the Department of Home Economics, University of Chicago,* edited by M. Dye, 184–86. Chicago, IL: Home Economics Alumni Association, 1972.

Rosa Luxemburg (1870–1919)

Like most intellectuals, economists tend to be long on rhetoric and short on action. Many are quite willing to write, discuss, or otherwise prescribe what should be done to correct a problem or change the pattern of events. Few, however, are inclined to make things happen, especially if even a modicum of personal danger or discomfort is involved. Rosa Luxemburg is a singular exception to this admittedly oversimplified characterization. "She was driven always by the noble dream of socialism" (Shepardson, 2). Consumed by an idealized—if not romantic—view of what could be, Luxemburg believed that democratic socialism would reverse the inherent self-destructive tendencies of market capitalism, rid the world of pogroms and war, and create true equality and harmony among all peoples and nations. She wrote about her dream and worked tirelessly to make it become reality. She lived her dream and, ultimately, died for it.

BIOGRAPHY

The youngest of five children, Rosa (Rozalia) Luxemburg was born in Zamosc in Russian Poland on March 5, 1870, the second daughter of a middle-class, Polish-speaking Jewish family. In 1873, the Luxemburgs moved to Warsaw in search of greater economic and social opportunities as well as a better educational environment for their children. Until she was ten, Luxemburg was educated at home, where her parents, conversant in several European languages and related literature, gave her a cosmopolitan upbringing. In 1880, she entered the Russian Second Gymnasium for Girls, where she encountered prejudice against her heritage and her physical condition.

As a young girl, the dainty (almost tiny) Luxemburg developed a hip ailment, most likely a congenital condition, that caused her to walk with a limp. Luxemburg never let her handicap impede her intellectual development. She graduated at sixteen at the head of her class, "but was denied the gold medal award for her achievement because of her 'oppositional attitude toward the authorities' " (Thomson, 56). After high school, her hatred for Russian authoritarianism combined with her growing zeal for social justice led Luxemburg to join the socialist revolutionary movement. She soon became familiar with the writings of scientific socialists, especially Karl Marx and Friedrich Engels. When she was eighteen, her socialist activities came to the attention of the Russian secret police, and she fled to Switzerland to avoid arrest.

In Switzerland, Luxemburg stayed with Karl and Olympia Lubeck, former German socialists living in Zurich. The Lubecks introduced her to other Russian and Polish exiles and political refugees, whose presence in Zurich helped turn the city into a sanctuary for international revolutionaries. In sharp contrast to the authoritarian sameness and repression that was Warsaw, Zurich offered Luxemburg an intensely stimulating international environment: "to a great extent the next eight years in Switzerland would set the pattern for her for later intellectual, personal and political life" (Shepardson, 8). In 1890, she entered the University of Zurich, ostensibly to study mathematics, natural science, and philosophy, however, she focused on political economy from 1892 until completing her doctorate of laws in 1898.

Her doctoral dissertation, *The Industrial Development of Poland,* was her first contribution to economics. Published commercially, the book was reviewed widely in Germany and Russia. In Poland, the book served as the blueprint for the program of the Social Democracy of the Kingdom of Poland party. During the course of her studies in Zurich, Luxemburg was also busy advancing her political career. Propelled by her relationship with Leo Jogiches, a well-known professional revolutionary of the time, Luxemburg began to establish herself as a leading economic theorist and political activist of the extreme left wing of international socialism. Luxemburg wanted to go to Germany and become part of the large, vital, and well-organized socialist movement in that country. As a citizen of Poland, however, she could not immigrate into Germany. In 1897, through a fictitious marriage to Gustav Lubeck, son of Karl and Olympia, she acquired Prussian citizenship, and in May 1898 she settled in Berlin.

Luxemburg quickly became one of the most effective, respected, and even feared socialist leaders. Her activities so offended the authorities that in 1903 she was sentenced to three months in prison for insulting the kaiser. From 1907 through 1912, she lectured on political economy at the German Social Democratic party training school in Berlin. During this period she wrote her magnum opus, *The Accumulation of Capital* (1913). Because of her prominence, Luxemburg came to know Vladimir Ilyich Lenin and other leading Bolsheviks. When World War I broke out, she was imprisoned again, as much for her revolutionary acquaintances as for her socialist activities.

In 1916, Luxemburg, now dubbed the "Red Rose" by police, and Karl Liebknecht formed the revolutionary Spartacus Union. After the war, and dissatisfied with the failure of socialism in Germany, she helped found the German Communist Party and its newspaper *Die rote fahne* (The red banner). In written word and deed, Luxemburg and Liebknecht urged revolution against the

German government that came to power after the armistice. The two sparked the wave of strikes and riots that swept across the country from the end of 1918 through the middle of 1919.

In January 1919, a particularly violent outbreak occurred in Berlin. Despite fears about their own safety, Luxemburg and Liebknecht stayed in the city to support the workers' revolt. The troops called upon to quell the disturbances were exceptionally brutal, crushing the uprising in a few days. On January 15, the two revolutionaries were arrested and ultimately shot to death by German soldiers—Liebknecht while "trying to escape" and Luxemburg in the back of a car. Her body was driven to a bridge over the Landwehr Canal and dumped into its murky waters, where it remained until the end of May before receiving a proper burial.

CONTRIBUTIONS

In the *Communist Manifesto* (1848), Marx predicted the inevitable collapse of market capitalism as the prelude to socialist revolution. More than fifty years later, capitalist countries were getting stronger, not weaker, and in an attempt to explain why, Luxemburg wrote *The Accumulation of Capital*. With the exception of her doctoral thesis, *Accumulation* was the only Luxemburg work published during her lifetime to deal predominantly with economics. In it, she hypothesized that imperialism—territorial acquisition for the purpose of extending one nation's dominance over others through economic and political hegemony—was delaying the inevitable demise of capitalism Marx had predicted. As Luxemburg saw it, subjugation of third-world countries allowed market-driven developed nations to acquire the resources necessary to sustain economic growth even as domestic supplies of labor and capital in advanced countries were being exploited beyond the point of diminishing returns.

Building on Marx's notion that the accumulation of capital is a necessary and sufficient ingredient for continuous economic expansion, Luxemburg observed that for capitalist accumulation to be successful, "It requires as its prime condition . . . that there should be strata of buyers outside capitalist society" (*Accumulation of Capital*, 351). If, as she hypothesized, "The accumulation of capital as an historical process, depends in every respect upon non-capitalist social strata and forms of social organization," (366) then "advanced" countries had to take advantage of "backward" ones to sustain aggregate demand at levels that permit the continuous accumulation of capital. This was the economic justification of imperialism as practiced by the British in India, the French in Algeria, and Europeans in the American West and Asiatic Turkey.

Luxemburg explained all this in *Accumulation*, a lengthy and difficult book that some would say was not very original. John Hobson (1858–1940), a prolific writer on economics and a contemporary of Luxemburg, published *Imperialism: A Study* in 1902, a decade before *Accumulation* appeared, expounding essentially the same thesis. There is no way of knowing if his work influenced Luxemburg's although both books dealt with imperialism as an inevitable consequence of capitalistic economic growth. One thing is certain, however; of the two books, Luxemburg's has proved more durable.

Originally published in 1913, *Accumulation* has been reissued in numerous English and German editions. **Joan Robinson** used the title for her 1956 work that sought to integrate Luxemburg's ideas about the dynamic development of capitalism with the theories of John Maynard Keynes and modern macro-economics. In so doing, Robinson made Rosa Luxemburg an inexorable part of the link connecting contemporary liberal economics and its nineteenth-century socialist democratic roots.

BIBLIOGRAPHY

Works by Rosa Luxemburg

The Accumulation of Capital (introduction by Joan Robinson). New Haven, CT: Yale University Press, 1951. Originally published 1913.

The Russian Revolution and Leninism or Marxism? (with a new introduction by B. D. Wolfe). Ann Arbor: University of Michigan Press, 1961. Originally published 1922.

The National Question: Selected Writings by Rosa Luxemburg (edited and with an introduction by H. B. Davis). New York: Monthly Review Press, 1976.

The Letters of Rosa Luxemburg (edited and with an introduction by S. E. Bronner; foreword by H. Pachter). Boulder, CO: Westview Press, 1978.

Works about Rosa Luxemburg

Basso, L. *Rosa Luxemburg: A Reappraisal.* New York: Praeger, 1975.

Geras, N. *The Legacy of Rosa Luxemburg.* London: NLB, 1976.

"Luxemburg, Rosa." In *Who's Who in Economics,* edited by M. Blaug, 710–11. 3rd ed. Northampton, MA: Edward Elgar, 1999.

Nettl, J. P. *Rosa Luxemburg* (2 vols.). London: Oxford University Press, 1966.

Shepardson, D. E. *Rosa Luxemburg and the Noble Dream.* New York: Peter Lang, 1996.

Thomson, D. L. "Rosa Luxemburg." In *Adam Smith's Daughters,* 56–72. New York: Exposition Press, 1973.

Jane Haldimand Marcet (1769–1858)

If Adam Smith is the intellectual father of economics, then Jane Haldimand Marcet has to be considered his first daughter. When Marcet was born, Smith was teaching moral philosophy in Scotland and publishing precursors of *The Wealth of Nations,* his magnum opus. When Marcet died some eighty-seven years later, Alfred Marshall was a schoolboy in Merchant Taylors' School in London, amassing the intellectual capital that would eventually help him to become the last of the great classical economists. The entire house of classical economics was essentially built during Marcet's long life, yet she did not contribute one doctrinal brick to its edifice. Her contribution lay in economic education, not economic theory, for Marcet did more to popularize the study of political economy (as economics was called) than perhaps any other person of the nineteenth century.

BIOGRAPHY

Little is known of Marcet's parents, her early life, or her education. Born in London in 1769 to a wealthy Swiss family living in England, Marcet was the only surviving daughter of a prosperous merchant who eventually established a successful bank. Her younger brother, William Haldimand (1784–1862), entered the banking industry through his father's business and went on to become a director of the Bank of England and, ultimately, a member of Parliament. When Jane was a child, girls in England did not receive a formal education. Undoubtedly, tutoring by governesses and frequent household discussions of current economic issues provided a rich environment for her intellectual development.

In 1799, she married Alexander Marcet (1770–1822), a Swiss-born physician who had received his medical degree from the University of Edinburgh. Dr. Marcet practiced medicine and lectured in chemistry at Guy's Hospital in

London. After he retired from his medical practice in 1819, he and Jane moved to Geneva, where he became a professor of chemistry. He died in 1822, leaving Jane Marcet a widow at fifty-three.

Marcet first demonstrated the intellectual prowess that she would become noted for in 1806 when she wrote *Conversations on Chemistry, in which the Elements of that Science are Familiarly Explained, and Illustrated by Experiments*. Published anonymously, the two-volume work was aimed at young women, who seldom received any formal schooling in early nineteenth-century England. Females, even those from upper-class families such as Marcet's, were educated by governesses and tutors, who more often than not relied on books of readings as the primary method of instruction. Marcet began her career in the education of young people by writing about chemistry, which suggests that she drew on her husband's expertise for support and guidance. This could be construed as evidence that her husband had a profound influence on her career. Influence, yes; profound, no. The principal inspiration for Marcet was not her husband but Mary Wollstonecraft, a noted woman of letters in the eighteenth century.

Mary Wollstonecraft (1759–1797), wife of the political philosopher William Godwin and mother of Mary Wollstonecraft Shelley (1797–1851), was an English writer and author of the first great feminist tract, *A Vindication of the Rights of Women* (1792). A champion of coeducational schooling, Wollstonecraft published a number of books in the late 1780s and early 1790s extolling the value of educating women. Wollstonecraft's writings inspired Marcet to take up the cause, which she did in 1806 with the publication of *Conversations on Chemistry*.

Ten years later, in 1816, Marcet applied her intellectual powers to the emerging field of political economy and published anonymously *Conversations on Political Economy, in which the Elements of that Science are Familiarly Explained*. Her goal in writing this book was "to bring within the reach of young persons a science which no English writer has yet presented in any easy and familiar form . . ." (v). Her effort was unexpectedly successful—sixteen editions of the book were published—and was the object of critical acclaim from some of the very scholars—J. R. McCulloch, the popularizer of Ricardian economics, and Jean-Baptiste Say, of Say's Law—whose works she sought to summarize.

CONTRIBUTIONS

Conversations on Political Economy established Marcet's reputation as a writer and educator and made it possible for her to publish a number of books on a variety of topics, all intended to further the education of young people. Besides *Conversations*, she published two other works dealing with economics—*John Hopkins's Notions on Political Economy* and *Rich and Poor*. The former used a collection of stories centered on John Hopkins, a laborer, as the medium for discussing wage and price determination, international trade, and other economic topics. Comparable in coverage to *Conversations*, *John Hopkins's Notions* was intended for the literate working class. *Rich and Poor* was a well-reasoned rationalization of the prevailing social and economic stratification of society. Neither book had the impact or acceptance of *Conversations*.

Using the Socratic form, as suggested by Mary Wollstonecraft, Marcet fashioned her major work on economics as a running conversation between two fictional characters, "the pupil, Caroline—of indeterminable age, sometimes naive, often precocious, always tractable; and her teacher—dogmatic, didactic, loquacious Mrs. B" ("Marcet, Jane Haldimand," 14). Marcet chose Socratic dialogue as the method for explaining the theory and practice of political economy because she believed "it gave her an opportunity of introducing objections, and placing in various points of view questions and answers as they had actually occurred to her own mind,—a plan which would not have suited a more didactic composition" (*Conversations*, viii–ix).

Marcet claimed no originality in her work but acknowledged her debt to Smith, Thomas Malthus, Say, David Ricardo, and the writings of other classical economists as the source of the ideas discussed in *Conversations*. In the twenty-two easy-to-read conversations between Caroline and Mrs. B., Marcet stayed clear of the truly abstruse questions of the era and omitted reference to some of the controversies hotly debated among the classical economists. She fixed her gaze instead on sound and well-established doctrine.

She began her book with an introduction (two conversations) to political economy, then proceeded to discuss the division of labor, the role of prices, and related topics in a series of conversations between teacher and pupil such as this one about the value of exchange:

Caroline: And when the land is occupied by the rich, there seems to be no resource left for the poor?

Mrs. B: What do you suppose the rich do with their wealth?

Caroline: The poor, I am sure, partake, but little of it, for the sums the most charitable give away are but trifling compared to what they spend upon themselves.

Mrs. B: I am far from wishing that the poor should be dependent on the charity of the rich for a subsistence. Is there no other mode of partaking of their wealth but as beggars?

Caroline: Not that I know of, unless by stealth. Oh, no, I guess now—you mean they earn it by their labour?

Mrs. B: Certainly. The poor man may be supposed to say to the rich one, "You have more than you want, whilst I am destitute. Give me some little share of your wealth for a subsistence; I have nothing to offer in exchange but my labour; but with that I will undertake to procure you more than you part with—if you will maintain me, I will work for you."

Caroline: But is it not usual to pay wages to labourers instead of maintaining them?

Mrs. B: It is in effect the same; for the wages purchase a maintenance; the money merely represents the things of which the labourer stands in need, and for which he may exchange it.

Caroline: The labourer may then be supposed to say to the rich man, "Give me food and clothing, and I by my labour will produce for you other things in return."

> *Mrs. B*: Precisely, the rich man exchanges with the labourer the produce or work that is already done, for work that is yet to be done. It is thus that he acquires a command over the labour of the poor, and increases his wealth by the profits he derives from it. (*Conversations*, 91–92)

It is clear from this passage that Marcet did not challenge classical economic thinking but merely accepted it as gospel. She was not there to judge but to communicate; to paraphrase the body of political economy then considered mainstream, translating it into conversational English readily accessible to all. What Marcet lacked in critical analysis, she more than made up for in optimism, ever confident in the goodness of laissez-faire and the liberating characteristics inherent in its social as well as its economic consequences: "Political economy tends to moderate all unjustifiable ambition, by showing that the surest means of increasing national prosperity are peace, security, and justice; that jealousy between nations is as prejudicial as between individuals; that each finds its advantage in reciprocal benefits; and that far from growing rich at each other's expense, they mutually assist each other by a liberal system of commerce. Political economy is particularly inimical to the envious, jealous, and malignant passions; and if ever peace and moderation should flourish in the world, it is to enlightened views of this science that we should be indebted for the miracle" (*Conversations*, 25). Her faith in classical economics was complete, compelling, and utterly convincing.

BIBLIOGRAPHY

Works by Jane Haldimand Marcet

Conversations on Political Economy, in which the Elements of that Science are Familiarly Explained. 4th ed. London: Longman, 1821. Originally published 1816.
John Hopkins's Notions on Political Economy. London: Longman, 1833.
Rich and Poor. London: Longman, 1851.

Works about Jane Haldimand Marcet

"Marcet, Jane Haldimand." In *Who's Who in Economics,* edited by M. Blaug, 732. 3rd ed. Northampton, MA: Edward Elgar, 1999.
Shackleton, J. R. "Why Don't Women Feature in the History of Economics?" *Economics* (24), Autumn 1988: 123–26.
———. "Jane Marcet and Harriet Martineau: Pioneers of Economic Education." *History of Education* 19(4), December 1990: 283–97.
Thomson, D. L. "Jane Haldimand Marcet (1769–1858)." In *Adam Smith's Daughters,* 3–28. New York: Exposition Press, 1973.

Mary Paley Marshall
(1850–1944)

In 1933, John Maynard Keynes, the greatest Western economist of the twentieth century, published *Essays in Biography* (E. Johnson and D. Moggridge). The book consisted of more than twenty-five biographical sketches of notables, mostly British, many of whom Keynes knew personally. These famous people included politicians (David Lloyd George, Winston Churchill); scientists (Albert Einstein); and nine eminent economists, among them Thomas Malthus, William Jevons, and Alfred Marshall. The only female economist—indeed, the only woman whose biography appeared in the book—was Mary Paley Marshall. Keynes held her in the highest regard and considered her an intellectual and thinker every bit as significant to the historical development of economics as her husband or any of the other economists about whom he wrote.

BIOGRAPHY

The story of Mary Paley Marshall is a story of firsts. She was born on October 24, 1850, in Stamford, Lincolnshire, England. Hers was a family of thrifty parsons and scholars; her father was an evangelical clergyman of a very strict Protestant sect. Yet in 1869, he allowed her to do what in those days had never been done before: to become a member of the first cohort of women admitted to Cambridge University. The Cambridge Higher Local Examination for Women had just came into being, and the fact that women would even be allowed to enter Cambridge was an earth-shattering idea to many of that day. It was, Mary Paley Marshall would later write, an outrageous proceeding (*What I Remember*, 12). Her first step was to pass several intellectually rigorous entrance exams. Her father helped her with divinity and mathematics; she was already good at French and German as well as other subjects. On the basis of her scores on the exams, she won a scholarship to the school.

In October 1871, Mary Paley became one of the first five women admitted to Cambridge. She and the others were the first beneficiaries of the efforts of **Millicent Garrett Fawcett** to open higher education to women. Aware that there were many who felt that they did not belong at Cambridge, these young women were closely supervised and kept on a short leash, becoming the nucleus of Newnham College, the women's college at Cambridge University. One of Mary's subjects was economics, which was being taught to the women by Alfred Marshall, who was destined to become the dominant figure in British economics in the late nineteenth and early twentieth centuries. In 1874, after three years of study, there was much excitement as Mary and her classmate, Amy Bulley, became the first women allowed to take what was then regarded as the men's "tripos," or graduate exams, at Cambridge. Mary chose to take the Moral Sciences Tripos of 1874, one part of which examined her knowledge of economics, then called political economy.

Mary passed all her exams. The next year, 1875, she was asked to become the first woman lecturer in economics at Cambridge. By then, there were twenty women students at Newnham, and she took over the teaching of economics from Alfred Marshall. Her supervisor asked her to write a textbook for the lectures, and she undertook that task. Her future as an economist took an unexpected turn when she became engaged to Alfred in 1876. The two were married in July of 1877, and from that time on, she devoted her life entirely to Alfred, submerging her career into his.

Together they completed *The Economics of Industry,* which was published in 1879 under both their names. Mary Paley Marshall started the book for her lecture series, and in the judgment of John Maynard Keynes and others, the book was an excellent text. Alfred Marshall, however, never liked it. In spite of the fact that there was a continuing demand for the text, it was allowed to go out of print without a complaint from Mary.

As the couple moved from Cambridge to the University of Bristol, Oxford, and then back to Cambridge, Mary Paley Marshall continued to lecture on economics. At Cambridge, where they settled in 1885, she resumed her lectureship in economics at Newnham, where she was in charge of the students for many years. The University of Bristol conferred on her the degree of D.Litt. Yet Mary was married to a man who increasingly came to believe that there was nothing useful to be made of women's intellects. In 1896, when there was a proposal to grant women's degrees at Cambridge, Alfred Marshall—in spite of all he had gained from his wife's love, intellect, and encouragement—abandoned friends of a lifetime and came down strictly against the movement, his wife's feeling notwithstanding. Mary, like other women of her time, had been brought up to know, respect, and accept what men thought. Never in her husband's lifetime or afterward did she ask, or expect, anything for herself.

Mary Paley Marshall did not complain when her book was allowed to go out of print. She kept a watchful eye over the proofs and the index of the early editions of her husband's *Principles of Economics,* which replaced it. With her bright mind and charming personality, she could influence the progress of her husband's work without open or direct criticism. It was said that nothing escaped her, and she faced everything in order that her husband, sometimes, need not. From the day they were married until his death in 1924, Mary would devote herself to her husband and his work.

After Alfred Marshall's death, Mary Paley Marshall spent the last twenty years of her life organizing the Marshall Library of Economics at Cambridge. In those days, there were no lending libraries of specialized knowledge. Alfred Marshall had over the years developed an extensive library of economic books, which he lent to his students. He also broke up economic journals, collecting and binding articles according to subject. The preparations of these bound articles and the cataloging of the items by author and subject had been Mary's task over the years. After her husband's death, Mary gave the library, both books and bound articles, to Cambridge. She also established a substantial endowment to support and maintain it. In her seventy-fifth year, she was appointed honorary assistant librarian of the Marshall Library of Economics, a job that allowed her to continue her service to the faculty and students at Cambridge. Through 1941, she spent virtually every morning at the library, and she was there on November 14, 1941, to celebrate the centenary of her husband's birth. On March 7, 1944, she died, and her ashes were scattered in the garden of her beloved home.

CONTRIBUTIONS

Mary Paley Marshall's contributions to economics are embodied in two books: *The Economics of Industry*, which she coauthored with her husband, Alfred, and *Principles of Economics*, on which she worked as long and as hard as her husband but for which he is credited with sole authorship. An obscure volume, *The Economics of Industry* was arguably the best economics textbook written in the nineteenth century. The sequel, *Principles of Economics*, became a recognized classic, a text that was as important to the field of economics in the first half of the twentieth century as Paul Samuelson's *Economics* was to the second half.

The story of *The Economics of Industry* is one of an opportunity lost and an accomplishment unappreciated, largely because of social custom. According to the preface to the book's one and only edition, "This book was undertaken at the request of a meeting of Cambridge University Extension lecturers, and was designed to meet a want which they have felt. It is an attempt to construct on the lines laid down in Mill's *Political Economy* a theory of Value, Wages and Profits, which shall include the chief results of the works of the present generation of Economists" (vi). It was all of that and more. The book was an outgrowth of Mary Paley Marshall's economics lectures at Cambridge and, later, at Bristol. She began working on the book as a single woman in the mid-1870s and published the text in 1879 as the wife of Alfred Marshall, then the principal of University College, Bristol. The book was almost exclusively the work of Mary Paley, but a change in her marital status during its completion led to a coauthored volume. The elevated status (and gender) of Alfred Marshall relative to that of his wife was almost certainly the foremost reason the book never saw a second edition but instead morphed into the sequel, *Principles of Economics*. The same prevailing social customs also explain why the intended companion volume, *The Economics of Trade and Finance*, never saw the light of day. All of this was unfortunate because Mary Paley Marshall had produced an economics text of singular distinctiveness that deserved a better fate than it experienced.

The Economics of Industry is a tightly written textbook that described in terse, direct terms the state of the discipline as it was taught in the leading universities of Great Britain. A mere 231 pages including an index, *Industry* is less than a third the length of its progeny *Principles of Economics*, not counting the latter's 100-plus pages of appendixes. Despite its brevity, *Industry* captured all that was economics in 1879.

Industry consists of three interrelated books: Book I—"Land, Labour, and Capital"; Book II—"Normal Value"; and Book III—"Market Value." The first book is devoted to definitions of economics, economic science, and the principal terms economists use, mainly, *land*, *labor*, *capital*, and *wealth*. The meaning of economics was given a more scientific treatment than was the custom among earlier economists who preferred the rubric "political economy": "This account of Economic science may be summed up in the following definitions: Those portions of human conduct which are directed towards the acquirement of material wealth, and those conditions of human well-being which directly depend on material wealth, are called **Economics. The Science of Economics** collects, examines, arranges and reasons about the facts which are connected with the economic habits and conditions of well-being in various countries at various times" (5).

The second book of *Industry* focuses on the laws of demand and supply and how the interaction of the two determines, along with other factors, the prices of the factors of production, namely, rent (land), wages (labor), interest (capital), and profits (the returns to business management). The third book is an analysis of market value, its determination, and what role customs, monopolies, trade unions, and other factors play in setting and changing prices.

The imprint of *Industry* on *Principles of Economics* is undeniable. The latter book, which went through eight editions from 1890 to 1920 and was regularly reprinted until 1964, was more but was not necessarily better. In the preface to the eighth edition, Alfred Marshall acknowledged his wife's contribution to *Principles:* "My wife has aided and advised me at every stage of successive editions of this volume. Each one of them owes a great deal to her suggestions, her care, and her judgment" (xv). The appearance of Mary Paley Marshall's name on the title page as coauthor would have been a true reflection of the magnitude of her worth.

BIBLIOGRAPHY

Works by Mary Paley Marshall

The Economics of Industry (with A. Marshall). London: Macmillan, 1879.
Marshall, A. *Principles of Economics*. 8th ed. London: Macmillan, 1964. Originally published 1890.
What I Remember. Cambridge: Cambridge University Press, 1947.

Works about Mary Paley Marshall

"Marshall, Mary Paley." In *Who's Who in Economics,* edited by M. Blaug, 741. 3rd ed. Northampton, MA: Edward Elgar, 1999.

"Mary Paley Marshall." In *The Collected Writings of John Maynard Keynes.* Vol. 10, *Essays in Biography*, edited by E. Johnson and D. Moggridge, 232–50. London: St. Martin's Press, 1972. Originally published in John Maynard Keynes, *Essays in Biography*, London: Macmillan, 1933.

Harriet Martineau
(1802–1876)

If **Jane Haldimand Marcet** was Adam Smith's first daughter, then Harriet Martineau was arguably his most famous. Her renown rested on a tripod of scholarship devoted to economic education, moral philosophy, and social commentary. She derived her notoriety in economics from a series of twenty-five monthly issues of *Illustrations of Political Economy* (1832–34), a body of work greatly influenced by Marcet's *Conversations on Political Economy*. Indeed, the popular writings of Martineau and Marcet established the two as the best-selling economists of the first half of the nineteenth century (Thomson, 124). An ardent necessarian—one who believes that only through complete exertion can an individual experience harmony with the natural laws of the universe—Martineau published numerous tracts reflecting her spiritual inclinations and moral sentiments, and in so doing won a sizable readership among those members of Great Britain's emerging middle class alienated by the Industrial Revolution. Martineau was equally famous for her social and political commentaries as exemplified in *Society in America* (1837), a book that ranks with Alexis de Tocqueville's *Democracy in America* (1835), James Bryce's *American Commonwealth* (1888), and Gunnar Myrdal's *American Dilemma* (1945) as classic interpretations of the American way of life. The subject of numerous biographies and the author of an autobiography that is must reading for anyone wishing to understand life and letters in Victorian England, Martineau has a reputation that is broader and deeper than that of any other woman associated with economics.

BIOGRAPHY

The sixth of eight children, Harriet Martineau was born in Norwich, England, on June 12, 1802. Her parents, Thomas Martineau and Elizabeth (Rankin) Martineau, were descendents of Huguenots who had emigrated from France to England in the late sixteenth century to avoid religious persecution. The traditional family vocation was medicine, but Harriet's father became a successful manufacturer of textiles and an importer of wines. Not much is known of Thomas Martineau save that he was a Unitarian and a political radical who imparted these beliefs and values to his children.

Harriet's mother dominated the household and was eager for her children, including her four daughters, to have a good education. The daughter of a wholesale grocer and sugar refiner from Newcastle-on-Tyne, Elizabeth Martineau had a limited formal education, as was the custom for British women of the time. She was nonetheless literate and had a special fondness for poetry. She made sure that her female children learned more than just how to cook and sew, then considered the proper limit of a girl's education.

Harriet Martineau was educated for the most part by her older siblings. Elizabeth, the oldest and nine years' Harriet's senior, taught her French; her brothers, Thomas and Henry, taught her Latin and arithmetic, respectively. She was encouraged to read history, biographies, and literature, and tutors provided guidance in music. Between 1813 and 1815, Harriet and her next-oldest sibling, Rachel, were given an opportunity for fifteen months of formal education with the great Unitarian preacher and teacher Lant Carpenter. The Martineau sisters and a dozen other daughters of Unitarian families were allowed to attend school with boys, and although given comparable but separate instruction, this coeducation instruction was novel for the times.

Martineau's early life was neither happy nor healthy. In her *Autobiography*, she describes how her family attended to her material and educational needs but ignored her emotional wants. She was by her own admission a difficult child, a condition compounded no doubt by her also being a delicate one. She had numerous bouts of indigestion, which a high-strung nervous system often converted into periods of hysteria. In 1814, at the age of twelve, she exhibited the first signs of deafness, a condition that became acute by 1816. Because of her emotional and physical problems, Martineau was sent in 1818 to live with relatives for fifteen months. When she returned home, she had to deal with a series of personal tragedies that made her own problems pale by comparison.

While maturation helped tame the demons inside, Martineau had to confront a number of external events that turned the 1820s into a decade of turmoil for her. In 1824, the eldest Martineau son, Thomas, died after a yearlong illness. One year later, the Martineau business failed in the financial crisis of 1825–26, a contributing factor in the death of her father, who passed away in 1826. During this period, one of the few bright spots in Harriet Martineau's young life, her engagement to John Worthington, became still another source of pain when her fiancé died in 1827 after a long and tortured illness.

With the demise of the family business, Martineau was left to her own resources. To support herself and her mother, she took up needlework by day and writing by night. The needlework provided the wherewithal to keep the family together, but it was her writing that would ultimately make her rich and famous. Her early works were religious compositions, and her first book, *Devotional Exercises*, had been published in 1823. This modicum of success encouraged Martineau to devote even more time and energy to writing, partly as a way to generate some supplemental income but more to escape her personal difficulties.

Like the works of Charles Dickens, Martineau's writings reflect a preoccupation with the subject of unions, factory legislation, and strikes. As an expression of this orientation, she published in 1827 *The Rioters, or a tale of bad times* and *The Turn Out, Patience the best policy*, two tracts that dealt with such topics as worker sabotage, a frequent form of social protest of the times, and the futility of strikes. Her interest in economic issues led her to read Jane Haldimand Marcet's *Conversations on Political Economy*, a seminal event in her life.

In 1829, Martineau moved to London, hoping that propinquity to the publishing world would increase her success. It did not—at least not right away—and she moved back to Norwich. On her return, Martineau decided to enter an essay contest run by the Unitarian magazine *Monthly Repository*. The contest had three categories, and she won all three. Although the prize money was extremely modest, her success convinced Martineau that "authorship was my legitimate career," as she later wrote in her *Autobiography* (198).

Motivated by her winning essays, which described Unitarianism as a viable alternative religion for Catholics, Jews, and Muslims, Martineau returned to London to establish herself in the world of letters. This time, her efforts proved successful. She formulated a plan to write a series of narrative tales to illustrate the basic principles of political economy as developed by Adam Smith, David Ricardo, Thomas Malthus, and the other early writers associated with classical economics. Unlike Marcet's work, which was aimed at children, Martineau's effort sought to provide literate adults with an accurate yet nontechnical analysis of contemporary economic thought. She wanted to sell the *Illustrations of Political Economy* as a single volume, but unable to find a publisher who would commit to a book-length treatise, Martineau sold the project as a subscription series. The initial goal was to sell a thousand copies of the first "illustration" within two weeks of publication. Sales were slow at first until Martineau, on the advice of her mother, sent an advertisement describing her work to all members of Parliament. Sales mushroomed. Good reviews in the general press gave her work further credibility, and by the time she had published the second installment in the series, Martineau was largely freed of financial concerns.

From 1832 through 1834, the twenty-five slim volumes became extremely popular and brought Martineau both fame and fortune. Her next major writing triumph was *Society in America*, published in 1837, the year Queen Victoria ascended to the British throne. This work was followed by a stream of output, for despite repeated encounters with illnesses large and small, Martineau produced a mountain of work—fiction and nonfiction—during her lifetime. As Seymour Martin Lipset put it: "Harriet Martineau was afflicted with many ills, but writer's block was not one of them. She once turned out nine volumes in two years, and in her life time wrote close to fifty books" (*Society*, 39–40).

Her most enduring publication is her *Autobiography*, a work that still commands attention today. Begun in 1854 when Martineau was diagnosed with a terminal illness, the work was not published until 1877, a year after her death. A monumental effort that fills three thick volumes, the *Autobiography* is a window on nineteenth-century England in particular and the Victorian era in general.

CONTRIBUTIONS

Martineau's contribution to economics lay in popularizing the theories of the major classical economists. She embraced Smith's concept of the invisible hand, stressed repeatedly the Malthusian theory that overpopulation is a basic cause of many social ills, and argued persuasively for Ricardo's theory of free trade and the corresponding principle of comparative advantage. Her gift was presentation, as she dispensed the theory of the emerging discipline of economics in synthetic fictionalized treatments suitable for popular consumption. Her stories were naive, their plots mechanical, her characters stereotypes. Yet for all these shortcomings, Martineau's experiment in adult education proved a huge commercial success, propelling her almost overnight into a widely read and recognized celebrity in social, political, and literary circles. She never claimed originality as an economist. Her goal was to transform political economy from a dull and difficult discipline into a practical, understandable subject accessible to all. She sought to create a reader-friendly field of study, an Economics for Dummies, and the results show that she was hugely successful.

BIBLIOGRAPHY

Works by Harriet Martineau

Illustrations of Political Economy. London: Charles Fox, 1834. Originally printed in monthly volumes from 1832 to 1834.
Society in America, edited and abridged, with an introductory essay by S. M. Lipset. Gloucester, MA: Peter Smith, 1968. Originally published 1837.
Chapman, M. W. *Harriet Martineau's Autobiography, with Memorials.* 3 vols. New York: Smith, Elder & Co., 1877.

Works about Harriet Martineau

Hill, M. R. "Harriet Martineau." In *Women in Sociology: A Bio-Bibliographical Sourcebook,* edited by M. J. Deegan, 289–97. Westport, CT: Greenwood Press, 1991.
"Martineau, Harriet." In *Who's Who in Economics,* edited by M. Blaug, 741. Northampton, MA: Edward Elgar, 1999.
Pichanick, V. K. *Harriet Martineau: The Woman and Her Work, 1802–76.* Ann Arbor: University of Michigan Press, 1980.
Rivlin, J. B. *Harriet Martineau: A Bibliography of Her Separately Printed Books.* New York: New York Public Library, 1947.
Thomas, G. *Harriet Martineau.* Boston, MA: Twayne, 1985.
Thomson, D. L. "Harriet Martineau." In *Adam Smith's Daughters,* 29–42. New York: Exposition Press, 1973.
Webb, R. K. *Harriet Martineau: A Radical Victorian.* New York: Columbia University Press: 1960.
Wheatley, V. *The Life and Work of Harriet Martineau.* Fairlawn, NJ: Essential Books, 1957.

Deirdre N. McCloskey
(1942–)

• •

Deirdre N. McCloskey is a second-generation cliometrician and a Chicago School economist. Cliometrics involves the application of econometrics to economic history for the purpose of empirically testing hypotheses that are evaluated within the context of the historical environment in which events transpired. The Chicago School refers to economists who have unabashed confidence in the market system to allocate efficiently scarce resources among competing uses. Chicago economists are especially suspicious of government interventions in the economy, convinced that, despite the best intentions, government meddling usually makes matters worse, not better. McCloskey has produced a body of scholarship that merges the Chicago School with cliometrics in interesting and provocative ways. Her research, particularly that done in the second half of her long and prolific career, has also challenged the official positivism of economics, arguing that this pseudoscientific methodology is as filled with figures of speech as any discipline—all the mathematical modeling and statistical analysis notwithstanding.

BIOGRAPHY

Deirdre McCloskey was born Donald on September 11, 1942, in Ann Arbor, Michigan. Her father, Robert McCloskey, was a professor at Harvard University, and her mother, Helen (Stueland) McCloskey, was a homemaker. Donald graduated from Harvard University in 1964 with a B.A. in economics and stayed at Harvard to earn an M.A. in economics in 1967. Donald became an assistant professor of economics at the University of Chicago in 1968, receiving a Ph.D. in economics from Harvard in 1970. As Donald, McCloskey married Joanne in 1965. The couple had two children and divorced in 1995.

In 1973, McCloskey became an associate professor of economics at the University of Chicago, and in 1979 she earned the title of associate professor of history. She moved to the University of Iowa in 1980, where she was a professor of history and a professor of economics until 1999. While at Iowa, she held the John F. Murray Chair in Economics from 1984 until she left the institution in 1999. That year, McCloskey became a distinguished professor of economics and history at the University of Illinois at Chicago, and in 2001 she added the title of professor of English at Illinois.

In addition to her regular teaching assignments, McCloskey has held numerous temporary or short-term teaching positions, including a visiting assistant professor of economics at Stanford University (spring 1972); a visiting lecturer in the Department of Economics at the University of York in England (1985, 1986); the Tinbergen Visiting Professor of Economics, Philosophy, and Art and Cultural Studies at Erasmus University in Rotterdam (January 1996); and a Distinguished Visiting Faculty Fellow at the University of California-Riverside Center for Ideas and Society (2000). She has also been a fellow at a variety of institutions, including an honorary research fellow in the Department of History at the University of London's Birkbeck College (1976), a fellow in the Research School of Social Sciences at the Australian National University (1982), a fellow at the Institute for Advanced Study at Princeton University (1983–84), and an Honorary Simon Fellow in the Department of History at the University of Manchester in England (1992).

Besides her teaching and research, McCloskey has been involved in service throughout her career. At the University of Chicago, she was the director of graduate studies in economics from 1976 to 1980, and at the University of Iowa, McCloskey was chair of the Economics Department (1981, 1982) and director of the Project on the Rhetoric of Inquiry (1985–99). She has served on the editorial boards of many journals, including the *Journal of History* (1974–79), *Economics and Philosophy* (1983–96), *Feminist Economics* (1994–), and the *American Economic Review* (1997–98). She was coeditor of the University of Chicago Press books on the *New Practice of Inquiry* (1990–99), and she continues as coeditor of the University of Wisconsin Press series of books The Rhetoric of Inquiry (since 1990).

Whatever life has in store for Deirdre McCloskey, nothing will rival what she experienced in making the transition to a woman from a man. The process of changing is chronicled in *Crossing: A Memoir*, a publication as unique and compelling as any article, essay, or book written by the women featured in this volume. The story of her crossing genders is an autobiographical odyssey of McCloskey's life as Donald, as Dee, and finally as Deirdre. The book is remarkable for its openness, insights, revelations, and courage. It reflects the literary side of an economist who is as quantitative as they come.

CONTRIBUTIONS

McCloskey's contributions to economic scholarship are characterized by an eagerness to challenge widely accepted doctrines that, upon close examination, turn out to be more myth than reality. This was evident in her first major publication, *Economic Maturity and Entrepreneurial Decline*. Economic historians had long maintained that from 1870 through 1913, British entrepreneurs lost their innovative edge compared to their own predecessors and their American and German counterparts. This "loss of spirit" was especially evident in the British iron and steel industry, which in the late nineteenth century fell on hard times. Using classic cliometric methods on eclectic and varied pieces of evidence, McCloskey examined the industry's market structure, growth in demand, technological decisions, and comparisons in productivity changes relative to foreign competitors. Her approach was different, even unorthodox, but the conclusion was unambiguous: ". . . entrepreneurs in British iron and steel, from whatever perspective they are viewed, performed well. The history of the industry in the late nineteenth century is one of economic maturity, not of entrepreneurial decline" (vii). This book was based in large measure on McCloskey's Ph.D. dissertation, for which she won the David A. Wells Prize at Harvard University.

Over the next decade, McCloskey published a number of papers and books in which economic history is interpreted through the lens of cliometrics. "Corn at Interest: The Extent and Cost of Grain Storage in Medieval England," in which she describes grain storage as a form of insurance and examines the empirical relationship between the cost of grain storage and the prevailing rate of interest, is typical of these efforts. In the mid-1980s, McCloskey added a new dimension to her scholarship with the publication of *The Rhetoric of Economics*, arguably her most important single work and certainly her most popular.

A literary book about the art of discourse, *Rhetoric* examines how economists use language to influence the thoughts and actions of listeners and readers who are, for the most part, other economists. McCloskey's "purpose of thinking about how economists converse with each other is to help the field mature, not to attack it" (first edition, xix). Often incorrectly perceived as a critique of the role of mathematics and statistics in modern economics, *Rhetoric* is about "how scarce means are allocated to the insatiable desires of people to be heard" (first edition, xviii). Positive empiricism, which is supposedly the rhetoric of economic scholarship, denies the very existence of the literary persuasiveness economists use to convince one another, and this denial has made the discipline less scientific, not more:

> In two usages especially, . . . the field since the 1940s has become so silly that nothing scientific can be expected until it gets over them: blackboard economics and statistical significance. The one is the gift of the Math Department, the other of the Statistics Department. As I have said, no one could reasonably object to mathematics and statistics in economics. But in the Department of Mathematics and the Department of Statistics the outputs are not scientific findings. They are theorems about mathematical objects and statistical tests. Unfortunately the economists have not followed the fields like physics and engineering, which *use* results from the two departments in question without taking over their theorem-proving intellectual values. . . . In physics and engineering people are interested in how a theorem matters in the world, and they have good ways of finding out, chiefly observation and simulation (not statistical significance). By contrast, nothing scientific came from the theorems from the departments of Mathematics or Statistics or Economics, for the good

reasons that (1) the set of theorems is practically unbounded and (2) statistical significance has practically nothing to do with scientific significance. In practical terms what is published in academic journals of economics is so irrelevant to the way real scientific persuasion goes on that I can by now only sit and moan quietly. (second edition, 189)

McCloskey followed the first edition of *Rhetoric* with a series of books and articles about rhetoric in economics. For example, in *The Vices of Economists; The Virtues of the Bourgeoisie*, she added social engineering to statistical significance and blackboard proofs as one of the three great vices of economics. In a coauthored article about economic language, which McCloskey believes consists of orders, information, and persuasion, she estimated that a full one-quarter of gross domestic product is devoted to persuasion, or, as she puts it, the rhetoric of "sweet talk" (One Quarter, 192). Finally, in a coauthored paper about the rhetoric of "significance," McCloskey surveyed all 182 articles appearing in the *American Economic Review* in the 1980s that made use of regression analysis. She determined on the basis of a predetermined set of criteria that "70 percent of the empirical papers . . . did not distinguish statistical significance from economic, policy, or scientific significance" ("Standard Error," 106). This clearly indicated to McCloskey that the authors of these papers did not understand, appreciate, or acknowledge the difference between scientific significance and statistical significance.

BIBLIOGRAPHY

Works by Deirdre (Donald) N. McCloskey

Economic Maturity and Entrepreneurial Decline: British Iron and Steel, 1870–1913. Cambridge, MA: Harvard University Press, 1973.

"Corn at Interest: The Extent and Cost of Grain Storage in Medieval England" (with J. Nash). *American Economic Review* 74(1), March 1984: 174–87.

The Rhetoric of Economics. 1st ed. Madison: University of Wisconsin Press, 1985. 2nd ed. published 1998.

"One Quarter of GDP Is Persuasion" (with A. Klamer). *American Economic Review* 85(2), May 1995: 191–95.

"The Standard Error of Regression." *Journal of Economic Literature* 34(1), March 1996: 97–115.

The Vices of Economists; The Virtues of the Bourgeoisie. Amsterdam: Amsterdam University Press, 1996.

Crossing: A Memoir. Chicago, IL: University of Chicago Press, 1999.

Works about Deirdre (Donald) N. McCloskey

"McCloskey, Deirdre Nansen." *Who's Who in Economics*, edited by M. Blaug, 751–52. Northampton, MA: Edward Elgar, 1999.

Jean Trepp McKelvey
(1908–1998)

• •

Jean Trepp McKelvey was a distinguished labor economist and educator who introduced new and innovative ways of doing and teaching economics. An acknowledged authority on labor relations and arbitration, she taught that there are three essential components of economic discovery: original research, personal observations in the field, and interviews with real human beings who are engaged in the actual practice of earning a living. McKelvey expanded the study of economics through her insistence that fieldwork be an essential tool of economic analysis and discovery.

BIOGRAPHY

Jean Trepp McKelvey was born on February 9, 1908, in Saint Louis, Missouri to Samuel Trepp and Blanche (Goodman) Trepp. She attended high school in East Orange, New Jersey, and then went on to Wellesley College in 1925, where she majored in economics. McKelvey earned many honors at Wellesley, including the prestigious Hart, Shaffner & Marx prize for her undergraduate essay in economics, "Trade-Union Interest in Production." After graduating in 1929 with honors, McKelvey entered Radcliffe College, where she earned her master's degree in 1931 and her Ph.D. in 1933. Her dissertation *Trade Union Interest in Production* expanded on her Wellesley honors essay and was supported by a Wellesley College Trustee Fellowship (1929) and the Fanny Bullock Workman Fellowship (1931–32). Those fellowships made it possible for her to travel to industrial centers throughout the United States to collect firsthand material for her research. This field research furthered her interest in labor economics and taught her the importance of fieldwork in economic research (Lewis).

In 1932, McKelvey joined the faculty at Sarah Lawrence College. This women's college was a good fit for her because it was developing a multidisciplined approach to learning, using experiential studies, fieldwork, and group activities (Lewis). In 1934, she married Bruce McKelvey, but she continued to publish under her maiden name, Trepp, until after World War II. In 1939, she published a pamphlet, *The Uses of Field Work in Teaching Economics,* which was the first of a series based on the unique educational methods she developed for her students involving a systematic use of fieldwork in the economics curriculum. The curriculum included individual or group trips, extended on-location research, and special jobs with community organizations. As she worked to develop a curriculum that served the needs and interests of her students, she realized that her new methods were changing the very scope and content of the field of economics.

In 1944, McKelvey took a leave from Sarah Lawrence and worked as a shop steward at General Motors. She would later say that she learned more from her work at GM than she had ever gained from academic research (*Uses of Field Work,* 37). During the war, she also served as a public panel member, hearing officer, and arbitrator for the National War Labor Board.

In 1946, she resigned from Sarah Lawrence to become the first faculty member of Cornell University's New York State School of Industrial and Labor Relations. She developed the school's first curriculum and taught courses in arbitration, labor practices, and labor law. She achieved the rank of professor in 1951. She published numerous articles and books, including *AFL Attitudes toward Production, 1900–1932* in 1952 and *Dock Disputes in Great Britain: A Study in the Persistence of Unrest* in 1953. Her work at Cornell and her publications helped establish her reputation as an acknowledged authority on labor relations and arbitration. Throughout her career, she was a much sought-after arbitrator, resolving disputes in a number of fields, especially the airline industry. She also edited several books on arbitration.

In the male-dominated field of arbitration, McKelvey broke barriers. A year after she joined Cornell, she became the first woman member of the National Academy of Arbitrators, and in 1970, she was the first woman to be elected president of the academy. She would go on to serve on numerous city, state, and federal mediation panels and would be appointed to several presidential committees on employee-management relations (Lewis). In 1953, the U.S. secretary of labor appointed her as the only woman to a special Labor Department Advisory Committee formed to study changes in the Taft-Hartley Labor Law. In 1955, New York governor William Averell Harriman named her to the New York State Board of Mediation. She was appointed to the Public Review Board of the United Auto Workers in 1960, and she served as its acting chair from 1973 to 1974. In 1970, President Richard Nixon appointed McKelvey to the Federal Services Impasses Panel.

One important issue to McKelvey was the relationship between arbitration and gender. In 1971, as president of the National Academy of Arbitrators, she stated that her study of arbitration decisions since the time of the War Labor Board clearly showed that "the male-dominated world of industrial relations and arbitration wore 'blinders,' when women's jobs were compared with men's jobs" (Lewis, 301). She also argued that if the institution of arbitration was to survive and remain relevant it needed to adapt to the emerging needs of a new social and economic order. She challenged the mindset of the day that arbitrators are born, not made, and developed programs to train arbitrators, including a program especially for women because they were so underrepresented in the field (301).

In 1978, McKelvey was named professor emeritus at Cornell; she continued to teach and work as an arbitrator. She was also actively involved in establishing and coordinating off-campus graduate courses through the school's extensive program throughout New York State. She was the recipient of many awards, including Arbitrator of the Year from the American Arbitration Association (1983), and distinguished-service awards from the Society of Professionals in Dispute Resolution (1989) and the Society of Federal Labor Relations Professionals (1990). She was honored by her high school town of East Orange, New Jersey, which named a housing project after her because of her long service to the United Auto Workers Public Review Board. She had begun working with that board in 1960, and she served on it for the rest of her life. She died in Rochester, New York, on January 5, 1998, at age eighty-nine. She was survived by her husband, Blake, the city historian emerita of Rochester.

CONTRIBUTIONS

McKelvey's publications usually followed a template that helped set her scholarship apart from that of other economists writing in the twentieth century. McKelvey wrote about real issues of current interest to those actively involved with labor-management relations, not about esoteric or arcane matters of little consequence or importance. She put her topics in perspective, discussing the historical, legal, social, and political context that helped elevate the issue in question to a matter of pressing concern to labor-relations professionals. She seldom proposed a solution to the problem or issue but preferred instead to discuss the pros and cons of various options, leaving the readers to decide for themselves which proposed solution made the most sense.

McKelvey's first major publication, "Union-Management Co-operation and the Southern Organizing Campaign," followed this formula almost to the letter. The topic, defined as the participation of trade unions in the task of finding better and more economical methods of production, was an emerging strategy of the American Federation of Labor in the 1920s. To put the question in context, McKelvey reviewed the historical development of the concept, then discussed what role union-management cooperation played in the southern organizing campaign the AFL launched in the late 1920s and early 1930s. She did not reveal her opinion as to the advisability of union-management cooperation, leaving that conclusion open to debate. Her job, as she saw it, was to examine the issue, not resolve it.

She followed the same recipe in a paper she published on the role of state agencies in public-employee labor relations ("The Role"). Originally delivered as an address before a joint meeting of the Association of Labor Mediation Agencies and the National Association of State Labor Relations Agencies on September 1, 1966, the paper discussed "the question of the extent to which public employment labor relations are or should be governed by the same agencies which regulate and help to adjust labor disputes in the private field" (179). After an extensive review of the positions for and against having existing agencies oversee public employee labor relations, McKelvey, true to her way, concluded: "The task of striking a balance between these two positions is left to the reader. Perhaps it is not necessary to reach a judgment one way or the other, for in this field as in so many others, it may be desirable to encourage diversity and experimentation in the laboratories of the fifty states" (196).

In a paper read at the Twenty-first Annual Meeting of the Industrial Relations Research Association in December 1968, she applied her distinctive narrative style to the issue of fact-finding in public-employee relations disputes. McKelvey noted that "Fact finding is regarded as an important method of aiding the resolution of labor disputes involving public employees, serving as a procedural substitute for the strike or lockout" ("Fact Finding," 528). She noted that seventeen states had enacted comprehensive labor relations laws governing public service, which provide for fact-finding when impasses are reached. She examined in detail the experience of four states—Connecticut, Michigan, New York, and Wisconsin—in an effort to determine the factors that influence success or failure in resolving disputes in the public sector. In typical McKelvey fashion, she concluded that ". . . under some circumstances, especially for unsophisticated and inexperienced public bargainers, fact finding has performed both an educational and a dispute-resolving function well beyond what the precepts of orthodox teaching would lead one to expect. In this sense it has shown promise. In another and more profound sense, however, it may prove ultimately to be not only an illusion, but what is worse, an exercise in futility" (543).

In 1971, she applied the McKelvey formula to a timely issue in arbitration: "When conduct sanctioned by a collective bargaining agreement conflicts with the law, what course should the arbitrator take?" ("Sex," 335). In the jargon of labor relations, the issue concerned "the law of the shop" versus "the law of the land" (353). In this paper, delivered as the presidential address at the Twenty-fourth Annual Meeting of the National Academy of Arbitrators in Los Angeles in January 1971, McKelvey presented the pros and cons, placed the issue in perspective, and left it to the audience to answer the question. As always, she was fulfilling her mission: the advancement of arbitration, not the advancement of arbitrators (*Challenges*, 31).

On October 24, 1978, Congress passed the Airline Deregulation Act, ending nearly forty years of government economic regulation of the airlines. The act was one of the most momentous pieces of legislation ever directed at a single industry. Almost nine years later, the New York School of Industrial and Labor Relations at Cornell University, the National Mediation Board, and the Society of Professionals in Dispute Resolution jointly sponsored a national conference to see what a decade of deregulation had wrought. Attendance at the conference was by invitation only. Approximately 300 guests heard presentations from more than 30 academics, executives, and union leaders connected with the airline industry. Papers were given on a number of aspects of deregulation, including collective bargaining, pay and labor markets, the handling of labor disputes, and the future of airline labor relations. Among the distinguished collection of experts presenting papers were Alfred E. Kahn, chair of the Civil Aeronautics Board from 1977 to 1978; Victoria L. Frankovich, president of the Independent Federation of Flight Attendants; and Robert L. Crandall, chief executive officer of American Airlines. Jean McKelvey edited the conference proceedings and papers (*Cleared for Takeoff*). Her biographical tag describes in a nutshell why she was selected for such an honor: "Jean T. McKelvey is an emeritus professor in the New York State School of Industrial and Labor Relations at Cornell University and coordinator of off-campus graduate credit programs. A widely recognized authority on labor relations, she is an arbitrator for many airlines and serves on the Federal Service Impasses Panel and the Public Review Board of the United Automobile Workers" (380).

Perhaps the most revealing of her publications was a pamphlet McKelvey wrote early in her career. *The Uses of Field Work in Teaching Economics* was an outgrowth of a movement at Sarah Lawrence College to introduce students in the social sciences to fieldwork. The goal of this effort was to use practical experience as a teaching device to reinforce and augment classroom learning. As McKelvey wrote: "During the first few years of my teaching at Sarah Lawrence College . . . limited . . . field work was used as a supplement to the classroom instruction in economics. Gradually, however, the program was expanded until field work became not an incidental feature of the curriculum but an integral part of both elementary and advanced courses" (5). The pamphlet was a summary of the field experiences of economics students and how such experiences enhanced the learning process. McKelvey was an enthusiastic proponent of experiential learning:

> The traditional college courses in economics had been largely academic in character, stressing abstract principles and their application to static situations. That economics ought fundamentally to be concerned, not with the behavior of Ricardo's economic man, but with the customs, social habits, beliefs and activities of real human beings engaged in the process of making a living was then a very unorthodox notion which only a few economists, following Veblen, had ventured to develop. Very early in my teaching experience I discarded the classical texts and while I was also engaged in the search for new reading materials I was also casting about for other ways in which the traditional forms of instruction might be modified to serve the needs and interests of the students. I had noted a fear on the part of prospective students that economics would be a dry and statistical subject which only the promptings of parents could lead them to elect. And yet most of these girls were genuinely interested in current events, eager to learn more about the world around them, and almost desperately anxious to find fields of activity which called for their participation in the future. (6)

McKelvey practiced what she preached, fusing book learning with street smarts throughout her professional life, whether teaching, writing or serving as an arbitrator in management/labor disputes.

BIBLIOGRAPHY

Works by Jean Trepp McKelvey

"Union-Management Co-operation and the Southern Organizing Campaign." *Journal of Political Economy* 41(5), October 1933: 602–24. Published under the name Jean Carol Trepp.

The Uses of Field Work in Teaching Economics. Bronxville, NY: Sarah Lawrence College, 1939. Published under the name Jean Carol Trepp.

Challenges to Arbitration (editor). Washington, DC: Bureau of National Affairs, 1960.

"The Role of State Agencies in Public Employee Labor Relations." *Industrial and Labor Relations Review* 20(2), 1967: 179–98.

"Fact Finding in Public Employment Disputes: Promise or Illusion?" *Industrial and Labor Relations Review* 22(4), 1969: 528–43.

"Sex and the Single Arbitrator." *Industrial and Labor Relations Review* 24(3), 1971: 335–53.

Cleared for Takeoff: Airline Labor Relations since Deregulation (editor). Ithaca, NY: ILR Press, 1988.

Works about Jean Trepp McKelvey

"Jean McKelvey." *Cornell University News,* www.news.cornell.edu/ (accessed January 15, 1998).

Lewis, M. "Jean Trepp McKelvey (1908–98)." In *A Biographical Dictionary of Women Economists,* edited by R. W. Dimand, M. A. Dimand, and E. L. Forget, 298–303. Northampton, MA: Edward Elgar, 2000.

Harriet Hardy Taylor Mill (1807–1858)

Harriet Hardy Taylor Mill was a free thinker and a creative intellectual, yet she could not escape the prejudices of her era. For more than twenty years, her writings were merged into the works of John Stuart Mill, and it was his authorship and name that history would remember. He gave his beloved Harriet credit for their intellectual partnership and combined efforts, but his tributes have been largely ignored and forgotten. It is only now that we can recognize and acknowledge Harriet Mill's full contributions to the brilliant and forward-looking nineteenth-century books once attributed only to the renowned British philosopher John Stuart Mill.

BIOGRAPHY

Harriet Hardy Taylor Mill was born on October 8, 1807, in London, England, to Thomas Hardy and Harriet Hurst Hardy. Although her family was upper class and wealthy, Harriet had little formal education. When she was eighteen, her parents arranged a marriage to a well-to-do Londoner, John Taylor, who was eleven years her senior. By the 1830s, she and Taylor had become part of a group of intellectuals supporting William Johnson Fox, a Unitarian preacher who published a radical journal, the *Monthly Repository*. Harriet regularly contributed poetry and reviews to the *Repository* and was one of its major supporters, largely because of its strong feminist orientation.

In 1830, Fox introduced Harriet to another of his supporters, John Stuart Mill. She was then twenty-three and the mother of two sons. In spite of her marriage and family commitments, Harriet Taylor and Mill were instantly attracted to each other, and it was obvious to even the casual observer that the two were hopelessly in love. In the first few years of their relationship, Harriet continued to publish material she wrote in the *Repository*, but after 1832, her work increasingly merged with Mill's. She and John Taylor eventually had three children, and the two remained married until his death in 1849. Nevertheless, during this time, she maintained an intense intellectual and romantic relationship with Mill. This relationship was the cause of scandalous gossip and caused both of them to be estranged from British intellectual society. Still, for the next twenty years Harriet Taylor and Mill worked together, traveled abroad together, and wrote daily love letters when apart.

In 1851, two years after the death of John Taylor, the two were finally married. Both had been in delicate health for many years from tubercles and other assorted ailments, and their married life together lasted only seven years. In 1858, on a trip to Avignon, France, Harriet died. Prior to her death, the couple had been working on the book *On Liberty*. Although it had not yet been completed to the couple's satisfaction, the grief-stricken Mill had it published without any further changes as a memorial to his wife. In the dedication, he wrote "to the beloved and deplored memory of her who was the inspirer and in part author, of all that is best in my writings."

CONTRIBUTIONS

Harriet Mill's contributions are embodied in two major books, *Principles of Political Economy* (1848) and *On Liberty* (1859), although the authorship of each book is attributed solely to her husband, John Stuart Mill. Harriet Mill played a significant role in writing both works. Her husband acknowledged her importance to *Political Economy* in his *Autobiography*:

> The purely scientific part of the *Political Economy* I did not learn from her [Harriet Mill]; but it was chiefly her influence that gave to the book that general tone by which it is distinguished from all previous expositions of political economy that had any pretension to being scientific. . . . The tone consisted chiefly in asking the proper distinction between the laws of the Production of wealth—which are real laws of nature, dependent on the properties of objects—and the modes of its Distribution, which, subject to certain conditions, depend on human will. The common run of political economists confuse these together, under the designation of economic laws, which they deem incapable of being defeated or modified by human effort; . . . The *Principles of Political Economy* yielded to none of its predecessors in aiming at the scientific appreciation of the action of these causes, under the conditions which they presuppose; but it set the example of not treating those conditions as final. The economic generalizations which depend not on necessities of nature but on those combined with the existing arrangements of society, it deals with only as provisional, and as liable to be much altered by the progress of social improvement. I had indeed partially learnt this view of things from the thoughts awakened in me by the speculations of the St. Simonians; but it was made a living principle pervading and animating the book by my wife's promptings. (246)

Political Economy was arguably the last great example of a genre that began with Adam Smith's *Wealth of Nations*. The classical economic tradition from Smith to Mill focused less on the theory of economics and more on its political, social, and cultural aspects. The science of economics, while ever present in the works of the early classical economists, did not become dominant until the 1890 publication of Alfred Marshall's *Principles of Economics*. Even then, the social aspects of the discipline were still important but clearly secondary in significance.

As John Stuart Mill suggests, Harriet Mill framed the tone of *Principles of Political Economy*. She did, however, more than that, writing and/or editing major portions of the book, including "On the Probable Futurity of the Labouring Classes." This chapter reveals her views that the salvation of the working class depended on its mental cultivation, that is, on education and a love of liberty. She was particularly adamant in believing that education would be especially important in promoting the economic well-being and social independence of women:

> It appears to me impossible but that the increase of intelligence, of education, and of the love of independence among the working classes, must be attended with the corresponding growth of the good sense which manifests itself in provident habits of conduct, and that population, therefore, will bear a gradually diminishing ratio to capital and employment. This most desirable result would be much accelerated by another change, which lies in the direct line of the best tendencies of the time; the opening of industrial occupations freely to both sexes. The same reasons which make it no longer necessary that the poor should depend on the rich, make it equally unnecessary that women should depend on men; and the least which justice requires is that law and custom should not enforce dependence . . . by ordaining that a woman, who does not happen to have a provision by inheritance, shall have scarcely any means open to her of gaining a livelihood, except as a wife and a mother. (759)

On Liberty is a book less about economics and more about the importance of freedom as a precondition for the discovery of truth and the full development of the individual. Harriet Mill's contribution to *On Liberty*, while cited in John Stuart Mill's *Autobiography*, is a matter of debate among some writers.

Many commentators believe that *On Liberty* reflects less John Stuart Mill's ideas than those of Harriet Mills. Whether her influence was indeed controlling or essentially peripheral, as others contend; or whether, as Mill himself insisted in his *Autobiography*, the essay was their joint product, is a still-unresolved and much-disputed question (*On Liberty*, viii). What is clear, however, is that a woman was at least as responsible as a man for mapping the terrain of political economy as it was defined in the middle of the nineteenth century.

BIBLIOGRAPHY

Works by Harriet Hardy Taylor Mill

Mill, J. S. *Principles of Political Economy*, edited with an introduction by W. J. Ashey. London: Longmans, Green and Co., 1936. Originally published 1848.

————. *On Liberty*, edited by D. Spitz. New York: W. W. Norton, 1975. Originally published 1859.

Works about Harriet Hardy Taylor Mill

Hayek, F. A. *John Stuart Mill and Harriet Taylor: Their Friendship and Subsequent Marriage.* New York: Augustus M. Kelly, reissued 1969. Originally published in the United States in 1951.

McFadden, M. "Harriet Hardy Taylor Mill." In *Encyclopedia of British Women Writers,* edited by P. Schlueter and J. Schlueter, 325–27. New York: Garland Publishing, 1988.

Mill, J. S. *The Autobiography of John Stuart Mill.* New York: Columbia University Press, 1924.

Selma J. Mushkin
(1913–1979)

A leading writer on health economics in the 1960s, Selma Mushkin gained lasting fame as the coauthor of a 1971 report on lead poisoning in children. A decidedly non-economic study, the report is about children living in the District of Columbia. Among its major findings were that 30–50 percent of the city's poor children might be suffering from lead poisoning, the effects of which could range from mild nervous disorders to severe brain damage and death. The study was instrumental in the technological search for interior paints that used other substances—water or latex—than lead as a base.

BIOGRAPHY

Born in Centerville, New Jersey, in 1913, Selma Mushkin worked professionally under her maiden name. She was married to Israel S. Weissbrodt, and the couple had three children—two daughters and a son. Mushkin received her B.A. at Brooklyn College in 1934 and an M.A. at Columbia University a year later. She then immersed herself in a career in government and, while pursuing her education, eventually earning a doctoral degree from the New School of Social Research in New York City in 1956.

Mushkin came to Washington, D.C., in 1937 to be chief of financial studies in the Social Security Administration. In 1949, Mushkin switched jobs, becoming an economist with the U.S. Public Health Service, a position she held until 1960. She then served as a research professor at Johns Hopkins University in Baltimore, Maryland, in the early 1960s, and from 1963 through 1968, she held a comparable position at George Washington University in Washington, D.C. From 1968 until 1970, Mushkin was director of research at the Urban Institute in Washington, D.C., focusing her efforts on the study of state and local finances. She returned to teaching in 1970, serving as director of the Public

Service Laboratory at Georgetown University until her death from cancer on December 2, 1979.

During the 1960s and 1970s, Mushkin held a variety of advisory and service positions. She was an adviser to the Commission of Intergovernmental Relations, worked as an economist with the U.S. Office of Management and Budget and with the Organization for Economic Cooperation and Development in Paris, and was the executive secretary of the New Coalition of Mayors, Governors, and County Officials. Mushkin was a fellow of the Woodrow Wilson International Center for Scholars at the Smithsonian Institution, the American Public Health Association, and the Institute of Medicine of the National Academy of Sciences.

CONTRIBUTIONS

Mushkin's published scholarship can generally be divided into two separate yet related subtopics within the field of human capital: the economics of health and the economics of education. In the late 1950s and early 1960s, the study of human capital was emerging in response to the question, "What is the contribution of changes in the quality of people to economic growth?" ("Health," 129). Early pioneers in the economics of human capital placed considerable emphasis on investment in human beings through education. Mushkin argued persuasively that health was as important a factor in improving the quality of life as education. She ultimately concluded that improvements in health care were at least as significant as improvements in education in raising the rate of economic growth.

In a seminal article in the *Journal of Political Economy*, she noted that "Health and education are joint investments made in the same individual. The individual is more effective in society as a producer and as a consumer because of these investments. And often the return on investment in health is attributed to education" ("Health," 130). Mushkin observed that even though health and education are complementary investments, they are, nevertheless, different: "Health programs increase the numbers in the working force as well as the quality of labor's product. Education chiefly affects quality of the producers." Even though health-induced human capital formation cannot be defined as neatly as units of education embodied in the workforce, she called for research that would do just that. Nearly a decade later, Mushkin responded to her own call to action with a coauthored article ("Investment") that estimated the lifetime health expenditures on the 1960 U.S. workforce.

One of Mushkin's genuine insights into the economics of health came from her documentation of the large share of the nation's health-care resources devoted to the care of the terminally ill ("Mushkin, Selma"). She estimated that more than 20 percent of all nonpsychiatric hospital and nursing-home expenditures were spent on the terminally ill.

The impetus for this came from a combination of the medical profession's desire to play god and the willingness of families to save a loved one regardless of the low prospects for success. "The fragmentary research that exists suggests that services for terminal illness are technically medical team responses to illnesses that cannot be cured. And the resulting heroic efforts of the health professionals are reinforced by family decisions made out of fear, guilt, and love" ("Terminal Illness," 183).

In response to this enormous concentration of health-care resources in a futile attempt to extend life, Mushkin became one of the first health economists to reason that changes were needed in the distribution of health-care resources if the country were to maximize the return on its investment in health. "An incremental upping of price for the patient and his family will not significantly reduce use. What is required is a reassessment of ethical and legal principles, along with a restructuring of institutions that are contributing to anguish and suffering while diverting health resources that could be used to prevent disease or effect cures" ("Terminal Illness," 184).

The second branch of Mushkin's research was devoted to the economics of education. In 1962, she edited a book on higher education *(Economics)* that included her articles on projected enrollments and facilities needs in higher education by the 1970s and the options available for the states to finance the expansion in public higher education needed to accommodate the baby-boom bubble. In the mid-1960s, she focused her scholarship on the economics of education on the financing of the ongoing expansion of secondary education in the United States ("Financing") and on the program development necessary for raising the educational attainments of children from low-income and/or culturally deprived groups ("Educational Policies"). Mushkin also wrote about the need to expand educational opportunities for "groups who completed their formal school years earlier and are engaged in active participation in the work force and in research" ("Resource Requirements," 464). This made her a forerunner in the call for lifelong learning for working adults, a facet of education now taken for granted but once considered novel.

BIBLIOGRAPHY

Works by Selma J. Mushkin

Economics of Higher Education (editor). Washington, DC: U.S. Department of Health, Education, and Welfare, 1962.

"Health as an Investment." *Journal of Political Economy* 70(5, pt. 2), October 1962: 129–57.

"Financing Secondary School Expansion." In *Financing of Education for Economic Growth*, edited by L. Reifman, 267–98. Paris: Organization for Economic Co-operation and Development, 1966.

"Resource Requirements and Educational Obsolescense." In *The Economics of Education*, edited by E. A. G. Robinson and J. E. Vaizey, 463–78. London: St. Martin's Press, 1966.

"Educational Policies for the Culturally Disadvantaged Child." In *Social Objectives in Educational Planning*, 287–302. Paris: Organization for Economic Co-operation and Development, 1967.

"Investment in Health: Lifetime Health Expenditures on the 1960 Work Force" (with B. A. Weisbrod). In *Human Capital Formation and Manpower Development*, edited by R. W. Wykstra, 296–308. New York: Free Press, 1971.

"Terminal Illness and Incentives for Health Care Use." In *Consumer Incentives for Health Care,* edited by S. J. Mushkin, 183–216. New York: Podist, 1974.

Works about Selma J. Mushkin

"Lead Poisoning Expert Selma Mushkin" (obituary). *Washington Post,* December 4, 1979: Metro section.

"Mushkin, Selma." *Who's Who in Economics,* edited by M. Blaug, 812. Northampton, MA: Edward Elgar, 1999.

Margaret Gilpin Reid
(1896–1991)

In an active career that lasted fifty years, Margaret Gilpin Reid published dozens of articles, books, and essays. In doing so, she became internationally recognized as a leading scholar in the economics of the home and the analysis of consumer behavior (Bowman). With her contemporaries **Hazel Kyrk** and **Mary Jean Bowman**, Reid helped to create at the University of Chicago the intellectual environment that natured three future Nobel laureates in economics—Theodore Schultz, Gary Becker, and Milton Friedman: "Reid inspired . . . Theodore Schultz, whom she first met" at Iowa State University (Forget, 358); "Gary Decker's new home economics is, while distinct in many respects, an extension of work she conceptualized" (Bowman, 134); and Milton Friedman drew on her "concepts of 'permanent' and 'transitory' income . . . in his 1957 application of the permanent income hypothesis to short-term shifts in consumption and saving" (Bowman, 134). In recognition of her many contributions to economics and other economists, the AEA made Reid a distinguished fellow in 1980, the first woman in the history of the association so honored.

BIOGRAPHY

Margaret Gilpin Reid was born on a farm near Winnipeg, Canada, on January 27, 1896. Her father was John Clements Reid and her mother was Martha Louise (Sparling) Reid. Little is known about her early life. "She trained as a schoolteacher and taught in rural schools until 1916, when she seized the opportunity to begin a five-year course of study in home economics at a new degree programme established at the Manitoba Agricultural College" (Forget, 357). Reid graduated in 1921 and decided to pursue an academic life instead of teaching high school. She was a lecturer in home management at the MacDonald Institute of the Ontario Agricultural College from 1921 until 1927. In 1927, she went to the United States and entered graduate school at the University of Chicago as a doctoral student working under Professor Hazel Kyrk (Forget). After completing her course work, Reid began a doctoral dissertation in the late 1920s that would become the basis of her classic work *Economics of Household Production*.

In 1929, she accepted a one-year appointment to Connecticut College in New London. A year later, she moved to Iowa State College (now Iowa State University), where she lectured on consumption economics in the Departments of Economics and Home Economics (Forget, 357). Reid became a naturalized U.S. citizen in 1939 and remained at Iowa State until 1943, working her way to a full professorship in 1940. In the mid-1940s, she worked as a government economist in Washington, D.C. From 1943 through 1944, Reid was an economist in the Division of Statistical Standards in the Executive Office of the President. A critic of the "assessments of the war-time cost-of-living index that neglected effects of changing incomes on the quality of goods traded," she directed the technical analysis for a report to the President's Committee on the Cost of Living (Bowman). Reid's analysis was appended to the full *Report of the President's Committee on the Cost of Living* published in 1945. For the next three years, she headed the Family Economics Division of the Department of Agriculture (Forget, 357).

In 1948, Reid became a professor of economics at the University of Illinois at Urbana-Champaign, and in 1951, she moved to the University of Chicago as a full professor of economics. She stayed there until retiring in 1961, the same year she received an honorary doctor of law degree from the University of Manitoba. Reid then devoted her time and energy to research, particularly her studies on various aspects of poverty and the relationship between income and health. She died in 1991.

CONTRIBUTIONS

Reid's magnum opus, *Economics of Household Production*, was one of a series of textbooks John Wiley & Sons published in the field of home economics. Other titles in the series are *Household Equipment, Experimental Cookery from the Chemical and Physical Standpoint*, and *Food Preparation Recipes*. Reid's work was obviously different. She was *in* home economics but not *of* home economics. With her book, she transformed home economics into the economics of the home: "The household is our most important economic institution. Yet economics of household production is a neglected field of study. With few exceptions the interest of economists has been concentrated on that part of our economic system which is organized on a price basis. The productive work of the household has been overlooked, even though more workers are engaged in it than in any other single industry" (*Economics*, v). For Reid, the household was in essence a microcosm of the economy, in that it produces, consumes, and allocates scarce resources (its labor) among competing uses. In her analysis of household production and the role of the household manager, Reid devoted whole chapters to such topics as the effects of gainful work on the household productivity of wives and mothers, the cost and value of goods produced at home, family consumption, the household labor pool, and scientific management in the household.

Above all, Reid was painfully aware that the status of women was directly related to the value of their work. She reasoned that if household production were deemed to have little or no economic value, then women's status would always be second class.

> From time immemorial women have been the principal household workers. In spite of the fact that household tasks have declined, and the majority of unmarried and some married women are engaged in specialized gainful occupations, the position of every woman is influenced by the status of household production. In early childhood, sex discrimination, in toys and type of activity encouraged, is based on the fact that girls are likely to be housekeepers so should play with dolls and learn to be sweet and attractive. It is thus that their livelihood is assured. Thoroughness of education is not deemed so necessary for girls as for boys; and girls tend to enter gainful occupations where the period of training is short. Women in gainful work everywhere find themselves handicapped in certain respects by the general attitude concerning the ability of women and their probable permanence in an occupation. (*Economics*, 317)

Reid devoted her professional life trying to change the attitude economists had of household work, and thus of women.

In 1947, she published a paper ("The Economic Contribution") that described in detail several methods that could be used to measure the economic value of homemakers' contributions to the well-being of the family. Four years later, Reid argued for a systematic approach to measuring the magnitude and distribution of nonmoney income, including the contributions of housewives ("Distribution"). In 1959, at a special general session at the annual meeting of the American Home Economics Association, Reid correctly predicted several important changes that would take place in family life over the next fifty years, changes that would necessitate a reevaluation of the economics of the household, that is, of the status of women. Among her almost clairvoyant forecasts were the rise of the nuclear family (and the corresponding isolation of the elderly); a significant increase in the number of working women, especially married women; and the increasing need for consumer-protection legislation as families purchase more ready-made products instead of producing them at home ("Families").

Her research invariably spilled over into other areas related to the economics of households. In 1938, she published *Consumers and the Market*, which "raised the consciousness of consumers about such issues as advertising, labelling, credit, legal protection and the responsibility of the state for ensuring consumer protection" (Forget, 359). She also wrote about farm families (e.g., "Effect") and even penned a defense of Friedman's permanent-income hypothesis ("Consumption"), an idea that originated with her. By the end of her career, Reid had morphed from a home economist into a respected theoretician whose writing, once confined to home-economics journals, regularly appeared in major economics publications (Forget, 359). She transformed the study of household activity into a major topic in the field of economics, and she contributed to the ascendancy of women and their work as legitimate topics for academic study.

BIBLIOGRAPHY

Works by Margaret Gilpin Reid

Economics of Household Production. New York: John Wiley & Sons, 1934.

Consumers and the Market. New York: Crofts and Co., 1938.

Report of the President's Committee on the Cost of Living. Washington, DC: 1945.

"The Economic Contribution of Homemakers." *Annals of the American Academy of Political and Social Science.* May 1947: 61–69.

"Distribution of Nonmoney Income." In *Studies in Income and Wealth.* Vol. 13. New York: National Bureau of Economic Research, 1951.

"Effect of Variability of Incomes on Level of Income-Expenditure Curves of Farm Families" (with M. Dunsing). *Review of Economics and Statistics* 38(1), February 1956: 90–95.

"Families in a Changing Economy." *Journal of Home Economics* 51(3), September 1959: 569–72.

"Consumption, Savings, and Windfall Gains." *American Economic Review* 52(4), September 1962: 728–37.

Works about Margaret Gilpin Reid

Bowman, M. J. "Reid, Margaret Gilpin." In *The New Palgrave: A Dictionary of Economics,* edited by J. Eatwell, M. Milgate, and P. Newman, 134. New York: Macmillan, 1991.

Folbre, N[ancy]. "For Margaret, with Thanks." *Feminist Economics* 2(3), Fall 1996: xi–xii.

Forget, E. L. "Margaret Gilpin Reid (1896–1991)." In *A Biographical Dictionary of Women Economists,* edited by R. W. Dimand, M. A. Dimand, and E. L. Forget, 357–61. Northampton, MA: Edward Elgar, 2000.

Jennifer F. Reinganum
(1955–)

· ·

Mathematical economics might not seem to have much, if anything, to contribute to the analysis of the legal system as it has evolved in the United States. Jennifer Reinganum's research not only disproves this misconception, however, but also shows that the application of mathematics to the law can yield new and provocative insights into why the U.S. legal system operates the way it does.

BIOGRAPHY

Jennifer F. Reinganum was born on January 10, 1955, in Columbus, Wisconsin, and grew up in Marshall, Wisconsin, a small town outside of Madison. Her father, Philip H. Freidel, was a dairy farmer and realtor, and her mother, Shirley (Koch) Freidel, was a sales consultant. In 1973, Reinganum graduated from Marshall High School and enrolled in Oberlin College in Oberlin, Ohio. She graduated from Oberlin in 1976 with a B.A. in economics and a B.A. in mathematics. She then attended Northwestern University in Evanston, Illinois, where she earned an M.S. in quantitative methods in 1978 and a Ph.D. in managerial economics and decision sciences in 1979. At Northwestern, she was co-winner of the 1980 Irving Fisher Award for her doctoral dissertation, "Dynamic Games of R&D with Rivalry." She is married to Andrew F. Daughety, a professor of economics at Vanderbilt University. The couple has four children: Samuel, Katherine, Daniel, and Michael.

Reinganum began her teaching career in 1979 as an assistant professor of economics at the California Institute of Technology. She stayed at Cal Tech until 1987 except for one year (1985–86) as a visiting associate professor of business economics at the University of Chicago. At Cal Tech, she was director of graduate studies for the Social Sciences Program and advanced to the rank of full professor of economics. In 1987, she became a professor of economics and management at the University of Iowa. She served as a visiting faculty member at the Centre d'Économie et de Finances Internationales at the Université d'Aix-Marseille II in Aix-en-Provence, France, during May 1992. Reinganum left Iowa in 1995 to become the Bronson Ingram Professor of Economics at Vanderbilt University, her current position.

Since 1981, she has had seven National Science Foundation grants. Reinganum has also been an Alfred P. Sloan research fellow (1985–87), a fellow of the Econometric Society (1989), and a faculty scholar at the University of Iowa (1992–94). She received the Regents' Award for Faculty Excellence at the University of Iowa in 1990. A reviewer for more than a dozen of the most prestigious journals in economics, she has been coeditor of the *Journal of Economics and Management Strategy* (1991–98) and editor (one of six) of the *RAND Journal of Economics* (1998–). Since 1998, she has been a member of the editorial boards of the *American Law and Economics Review* and the *Journal of Economic Literature*, and in 1995–2001 she was a member of the editorial board of the *American Economic Review.*

Besides her teaching and research, Reinganum has been active in service to the academic community. She was a member of the board of the AEA's Committee on the Status of Women in the Economics Profession (1991–93), has been a member of the Southern Economic Association's board of trustees (1996–2000), and was a member of the board of directors of the American Law and Economics Association (1999–2002).

CONTRIBUTIONS

At the beginning of her career, Reinganum mined her Ph.D. dissertation and published several articles that applied a game-theory approach to the diffusion of technology (e.g., "On the Diffusion"). She also wrote a number of papers involving the use of mathematical analysis to examine problems and issues in industrial organization. In her first major professional article, Reinganum investigated the "optimal search strategies for agents facing stochastic prices, wages, or demand conditions" ("A Simple Model" 851). Her specific goal was to demonstrate "that price dispersion can exist even within the context of a very simple model," and she accomplished her objective through the use of highly sophisticated mathematics on a world made manageable via simplifying assumptions. Two years later, she followed that paper with one that showed that "if the value of adopting a cost-reducing, capital-embodied process innovation declines with the number of firms which have already adopted it, then the firms adopt the new technology in sequence so that it is 'diffused' into the industry over time" ("Market Structure," 618). Again, her approach involved the application of powerful mathematical analysis to an assumption-simplified industry. She continued in this vein in a third paper, about a "long-standing interest in industrial organization" on "the effect of monopoly power upon incentives to engage in innovative activity" ("Uncertain Innovation," 741). The pattern of exploration was the same; high-powered mathematics applied to a market structure rendered sterile by unrealistic assumptions.

In the mid-1980s, as Reinganum put some time and distance between herself and her education at Northwestern University, her research emphasis began to change. The influence of **Nancy L. Schwartz** and Morton Kamien, the two economists who literally invented the field of mathematical industrial organization, waned, and Reinganum found her voice. Her scholarship remained as analytical as ever, but the focus of her interests shifted to the application of economics to the law and away from industrial organization. In 1986, for instance, she coauthored an article in which a model of settlement and litigation is developed and then examined to see how such factors as the likelihood of a settlement and the allocation of litigation costs affect the equilibrium probability of a trial ("Settlement"). Having shifted the object of her research interest, Reinganum began to explore the relatively new and exciting world of theoretical legal economics.

Symbolic of the many articles wherein Reinganum applied economics to the law is one she published on law enforcement and criminal choice.

> The purpose of this paper has been to integrate a model of plea-bargaining with a model of criminal choice and crime detection. It was shown that, for each possible outcome of the first stage (in which people decide whether or not to commit a crime and the police allocate resources to crime detection), there is a unique sequential equilibrium (surviving appropriate refinement) for the plea bargaining subgame in which defendants make settlement offers that may be accepted or rejected by the prosecutor. In equilibrium, a group of defendants with sufficiently low conviction probabilities will refuse to plead guilty for any positive sentence; that is, they "pool" together at the offer $S = 0$; the remaining defendants, who have higher conviction probabilities, make plea offers that perfectly reveal their private information. All defendants face a positive probability of trial, and low-probability types suffer a negative externality due to the existence of high-probability types for whom they could be mistaken. ("The Law Enforcement Process," 127)

In this and subsequent research, Reinganum combines her knowledge of game theory, mathematics, and economics in an analysis of law and the criminal-justice system with refreshing originality, generating unanticipated conclusions.

Although Reinganum was quickly establishing a reputation as one of the leading scholars applying economic reasoning to legal questions, she did not forsake her interest in industrial organization. This was clear in 1995, when she published an article on market structure, product safety, and liability ("Product Safety"). Still, her focus and fame is clearly in the field of economics and law. A particularly interesting application of this fusion is her coauthored paper about the implications of relaxing the current practice of prohibiting the use of pretrial settlement negotiations in the litigation process ("Keeping Society in the Dark"). The article focused "on the issue of making (currently) inadmissible settlement demands admissible in court, both as an interesting question in its own right and as an example of the larger issue of analyzing institutional rules that restrict the flow of information" (204). Reinganum noted that despite reducing the flow of information—generally considered a source of market inefficiency—making settlement negotiations admissible would increase the expected number of trials and all the associated costs. "Thus, we can conclude that, although keeping settlement demands inadmissible as evidence may contribute to the public interest, such a policy cannot be construed as contributing to the (private) interests of all the individual litigants" (215).

A particularly unique expression of Reinganum's current scholarship is evident in her coauthored paper "On the Economics of Trials: Adversarial Process, Evidence, and Equilibrium Bias." Prior to this publication, Reinganum researched relatively narrow aspects of the intersection of law and economics. In exploring the economics of trials, Reinganum took a broad look at a generally held legal assumption "that while legal processes are costly, agents should expect that (at least on average) legal processes are fundamentally unbiased" (365). The rationale for this assumption is the bedrock of the legal world: "After all, if a trial occurs, each participant can hire competent counsel, access the same quality of expert testimony, and so forth. In short, we expect the adversarial process embodied by the legal system to generate (at least, on average) unbiased estimates of liability and damages, and therefore agents in the economy should not anticipate significant relative distortions due to the legal process: a deadweight loss, yes, but one that is not systematically influencing different sides of the market differently" (365–66).

Using a strategic sequential search model—a method Reinganum employed in her analysis of research and development by firms in a duopoly—she showed that, contrary to popular legal beliefs, bias is possible in the trial process. The sources of this bias can be "differences in evidence sampling cost," divergence of plaintiff and defendant estimates of liability, and "asymmetry in the sampling distribution of evidence" ("On the Economics of Trials," 367). The nonapparent conclusion of this analysis is that ". . . there is reason to expect that adversarial processes are not unbiased and may create inefficiencies in the economic relationships that depend on them for enforcement or compensation. The source of such inefficiencies is the now familiar combination of incomplete information and sequential choice by self-interested agents. If agents in economic relationships anticipate a systematic bias in enforcement or compensation, then prediction of the outcome of those relationships (prices charged, units sold, investments made, bargains struck) must also account for this bias" (389–90). The real significance of this paper is its comprehensive scope and the implication that Reinganum is capable of producing truly profound breakthroughs in the economics of the legal system.

BIBLIOGRAPHY

Works by Jennifer F. Reinganum

"A Simple Model of Equilibrium Price Dispersion." *Journal of Political Economy* 87(4), August 1979: 851–58.

"Market Structure and the Diffusion of New Technology." *Bell Journal of Economics* 12, 1981: 618–24.

"On the Diffusion of New Technology: A Game Theoretic Approach." *Review of Economic Studies* 48, 1981: 395–406.

"Uncertain Innovation and the Persistence of Monopoly." *American Economic Review* 73(4), September 1983: 741–48.

"Settlement, Litigation, and the Allocation of Litigation Costs" (with L. L. Wilde). *RAND Journal of Economics* 17(4), Winter 1986: 557–66.

"The Law Enforcement Process and Criminal Choice." *International Review of Law and Economics* 13, 1993: 115–34.

"Keeping Society in the Dark: On the Admissibility of Pretrial Negotiations as Evidence in Court" (with A. F. Daughety). *RAND Journal of Economics* 26(2), Summer 1995: 203–21.

"Product Safety: Liability, R&D, and Signaling" (with A. F. Daughety). *American Economic Review* 85(5), December 1995: 1187–1206.

"On the Economics of Trials: Adversarial Process, Evidence, and Equilibrium Bias" (with A. F. Daughety). *Journal of Law, Economics and Organization* 16(1), 2000: 365–94.

Works about Jennifer F. Reinganum

"Reinganum, Jennifer F." In *Who's Who in Economics,* edited by M. Blaug, 935. 3rd ed. Northampton, MA: Edward Elgar, 1999.

Ingrid H. Rima
(1925–)

• •

The quintessential survivor, Ingrid Rima fled the pending doom of Adolf
Hitler's Germany with her family. She later navigated the stifling male chauvinism of economics to establish a distinguished fifty-plus-year career of teaching, scholarship, and service in a profession that has a history of marginalizing
women.

BIOGRAPHY

The oldest of three children, Ingrid Hahne Rima was born to Max F. Hahne
and Hertha (Grunsfeld) Hahne in 1925 in Barmen, Germany, not far from
Cologne. Because this was a time of political and economic instability in Germany, her parents decided to immigrate to the United States. Ingrid was born
in Germany only because her mother did not want to make a weeklong sea
voyage while pregnant. One year prior to her birth, Ingrid's father had settled
in Patterson, New Jersey, where he ran a textile mill. Both her parents were
well educated and spoke several languages. Her mother had studied literature
and languages, and before her marriage she had worked as a purchasing agent
for a large iron and steel manufacturer. Her father had an engineering degree
and worked as a textile engineer.

In the early 1930s, the family settled in Brooklyn, New York, and Ingrid
and her siblings went to the neighborhood public schools. Rima's experiences
in her Irish/Italian Catholic neighborhood were something of a cultural ad-
venture, as her family had come from a part of Germany that was historically
Protestant, with Lutheranism the state religion. She enjoyed talking about different aspects of religion and neighborhood life with her family. Her early
experiences led her to believe that all Americans were Catholic; only when
she later ventured a few blocks from home did she realize that there were
other Protestant and Jewish families living nearby. Hers was a family of talk-

ers, and her parents encouraged discussions about daily experiences. Both parents expected their three children to be high achievers, and for Ingrid this meant piano and ballet lessons in addition to regular schoolwork. The family moved almost every other year because Rima's mother was always in search of a better school for the children. One of Rima's favorite schools allowed students to advance according to ability, not age. She entered the school as a second grader, quickly moved into a combined second and third grade, and by June of that year was in the fourth grade.

In the 1930s, most female high school students were encouraged to pursue commercial programs that would prepare them for secretarial jobs until they got married. Rima's parents did not subscribe to this view. They encouraged her to do anything she thought she would enjoy, as long as she showed a natural talent and was willing to work hard. Rima was one of only a few girls from her grade school to go on to Brooklyn's Erasmas Hall High School to pursue a college preparatory program. The college prep program required students to take at least three years of one language and two years of another, as well as science and mathematics.

In 1941, Rima finished high school and entered Hunter College, then a women's college within the City University of New York system. She was still studying ballet and thinking seriously of a career as a ballerina when she took her first economics course. In it, she was introduced to price theory: she loved all those beautiful and orderly graphs, thought market equilibrium was an extraordinary phenomenon, and regarded marginal cost and marginal revenue as the most exquisite concepts in the world. She was enchanted with the geometry of economics and the possibility for economic planning in a politically democratic country and decided to major in economics. Studying Alfred Marshall's *Principles of Economics* and **Joan Robinson**'s *Economics of Imperfect Competition* in honors economics, she knew she had made the right career decision. Keynes's *General Theory* and the notion of involuntary equilibrium at less than full employment were just so much frosting on the cake. In 1945, she graduated from Hunter with a B.A. with honors and Phi Beta Kappa.

At Hunter, Dorothy Lampen (later Thomson), the author of *Adam Smith's Daughters*, was Rima's mentor and her honors supervisor. Another influential role model was Hazel Roberts, whose work on Marshall Vauban is still recognized among economic historians. Rima has always valued the role that women's colleges play in the higher education of women, believing that they help women realize that they can succeed in virtually any environment. Her education at Hunter gave her confidence in her abilities, and she felt she was far better prepared for graduate school than many men of her generation.

In 1945, Rima was awarded a scholarship to the Ph.D. program in economics at the University of Pennsylvania. Her areas of study there were monetary and international theory and labor economics. There were no women faculty members in the economics department and only a few women graduate students; Rima was the only woman taking economic theory. Her master's thesis, "The Bretton Woods Agreement and International Exchange Rates," concerned the question of the relative fixity of exchange rates. While working on her master's, she helped Raymond Bye, one of her professors, with revisions to his popular principles of economics textbook. She received her M.A. in 1946 and was offered a tenure-track position as an instructor of economics at Temple University in Philadelphia. Except for visiting appointments, she would spend her entire career in the Economics Department of the Fox School of Business and Management at Temple.

While teaching at Temple, Rima was working on her Ph.D. dissertation, "The Pricing of Public Sector Goods." She received her Ph.D. from the University of Pennsylvania in 1951 and became an assistant professor of economics at Temple in 1952. Over the years, she frequently taught a course in the history of economic thought. Because of her interest in theory, she found the approach used in most history-of-thought textbooks of the day not analytical enough, and so she developed a more theoretical approach to the course. Her lecture notes became handouts, and her handouts eventually became a textbook. *Development of Economic Analysis* was published in 1967 and is now in its sixth edition and a leading seller in the field. In the late 1940s and early 1950s, Rima devoted most of her time to her teaching, her writings, and to earning tenure at Temple University. She did not have time for a personal life, as she felt that even dating briefly would sidetrack her career. In 1954, however, she met her future husband Philip, then an instructor at the naval advanced electronics school in Memphis, Tennessee. They were married on June 19, 1957, and had two sons—David, born in 1958, and Eric, born in 1962. Not until 1967, when a new business dean and former labor economist familiar with her work came to Temple and asked her to chair the Economics Department, did Rima feel comfortable in her career.

Aware of salary differentials at the school, Rima agreed to become chair only if she was promoted to full professor and received an appropriate raise. In 1967, she became the first woman chair and the first woman professor in Temple University's School of Business. Rima chaired the Department of Economics from 1968 to 1970 and found that she did not like administrative work. In the summers of 1972 and 1973, she was a visiting professor at the University of Pennsylvania, and in the summer of 1974, she was a visiting lecturer at the University of Bremen in Germany.

Over the years, Rima has won many academic awards and honors. In 1990, she received the Distinguished Scholar Award by the International Society for New Ideas at the Sorbonne in Paris. In 1997, she was given the Fox School Leadership Award for Excellence in Teaching and the Lindback Teaching Award. In 2000, she became a Fulbright Distinguished Professor of Economics, serving in Guangzhou, China, where she taught economics at Zhongshan University's Lingam College. She was the first Fulbright scholar to be designated a distinguished lecturer in China, and in that capacity gave guest lectures throughout the country.

CONTRIBUTIONS

Rima has provided over a quarter-century of valuable service to the economics profession, most of it with the Eastern Economic Association (EEA) since its inception in 1974. She served as the editor of the *Eastern Economic*

Journal from 1979 to 1992. From the very beginning, one of the objectives of the EEA was to be inclusive, which meant having annual meetings where new members to the profession could give papers and presentations representative of a broad array of viewpoints and approaches to economics. This was seen as an alternative to the AEA, whose annual meetings are dominated by established scholars or their protégés giving papers in line with the prevailing neoclassical tradition. In her twelve years as the editor of the *Eastern Economic Journal,* Rima helped serve the needs of the rapidly growing economics profession, making journal space available to emerging scholars teaching at up-and-coming universities trying to establish themselves as research institutions. To negate the common and largely correct impression that papers are often accepted or rejected because of institutional affiliation or professional connections, Rima instituted a double-blind reviewing process. This gave credibility to the *Eastern Economic Journal* and set a precedent that other journals in the discipline later followed.

Rima's scholarly contributions can be divided into two general areas: labor economics and the history of economic thought. Her work in labor economics has centered on resurrecting the Keynesian perspective on the nature and causes of unemployment. She is convinced that contemporary economists have all but forgotten the phenomenon of involuntary unemployment: "Neglect of Keynes' concept was understandable during the prosperous 1950s and early 1960s but its neglect since that time reflects the persuasiveness of the marriage which has been effected between the job search models of household behaviour and models of rational expectations responses to inflation" ("Whatever Happened," 62). To introduce a new generation of economists to Keynesian thinking on unemployment, Rima has taken it on herself to respecify the labor-supply curve, believing that "Respecification . . . provides a basis for demonstrating that the unemployment which accompanies stagflation or slumpflation is involuntary in the sense in which Keynes used the term" ("Involuntary Unemployment," 541).

Her respecified labor-supply schedule "provides an alternative to the neoclassical interpretation of the unemployment associated with stagflation or slumpflation as simply reflecting a reallocation of time to non-market or search activities in consequence of the real wage reduction associated with rising wage goods prices. Real wages do, of course, fall when wage goods prices rise. Instead of inducing workers to offer less labor when real wages fall, the respecified labor supply curve implies that the real wage effect of inflation is necessarily *positive*. If the rightward shift it engenders (together with a possible real asset effect) is not accompanied by a corresponding increase in job opportunities, the resulting unemployment is involuntary in the Keynes sense" (549). Rima has also applied her analysis to sectoral changes in employment in an attempt to explain the destruction of "good" jobs in the goods-producing sectors (manufacturing) and the creation of "poor" jobs in the service sector ("Sectoral Changes").

As important as Rima's work in labor economics may be, her significant contributions to the scholarship of economics have come in the analysis of the historical development of economic thought. Her classic text in the field, *De-*

velopment of Economic Analysis, first published in 1967 and now in its sixth edition, is her most widely recognized work. The book "traces the development of economic theory from its pre-analytical stage to modern micro-macro analysis" (i). The six chronological epochs essential to Rima's telling of the story of economics are: preclassical; classical; critics of classicism such as Karl Marx; the neoclassical school; the alternatives to neoclassicism including Keynesian economics; and contemporary (since 1945) economics including the post-Keynesian movement but not, curiously, supply-side economics. Although sensitive to the status of women in the profession, or, rather, the lack thereof, Rima falls victim nevertheless to her own education. The sixth edition of *Development of Economic Analysis* has a name index that includes 5 entries of ambiguous gender, 6 entries that are clearly women, and more than 240 entries (more than 96 percent of the total) that are men.

Rima's history-of-economic-thought research also includes several smaller works that focus on the contributions of individual economists. She is one of a small number of writers who have authored or edited a book about the incomparable Joan Robinson *(The Joan Robinson Legacy)*. Rima published a sensitive essay in memory of Alfred S. Eichner, a post-Keynesian economist who attracted considerable attention with his book *The Megacorp and Oligopoly: Micro Foundations of Macro Dynamics* (1976). She has also written about Adolph Lowe's political economics ("Adolph Lowe's"). Rima was so taken with Lowe and his idea of "instrumentalism as enlightened intervention" that she even dedicated a two-volume book she edited to him, writing, "For Adolph Lowe as a tribute to his pioneering and inspirational intellectual leadership in understanding political economy" *(The Political Economy,* v).

One of Rima's most original books is a volume she edited about numeracy in economics. Contrary to the current impression that the mathematical and quantitative sides of economics are relatively recent developments, she shows in *Measurement, Quantification, and Economic Analysis* that economists "have long relied on measurement and quantification as essential tools" (i). The volume features twenty-four essays, two of them by Rima, that examine the use of numeracy in economics from William Petty's political arithmetic to the mathematics of rational expectations.

BIBLIOGRAPHY

Works by Ingrid H. Rima

Development of Economic Analysis. 6th ed. New York: Routledge, 2001. Originally published Homewood, IL: Irwin, 1967.

"Involuntary Unemployment and the Respecified Labor Supply Curve." *Journal of Post Keynesian Economics* 6(4), Summer 1984: 540–50.

"Whatever Happened to the Concept of Involuntary Unemployment?" *International Journal of Social Economics* 4(3/4), 1984: 62–71.

The Joan Robinson Legacy (editor). Armonk, NY: M. E. Sharpe, 1991.

The Political Economy of Global Restructuring, vols. 1 and 2 (editor). Brookfield, VT: Edward Elgar, 1993.

"The Megacorp and Macrodynamics: Essays in Memory of Alfred Eichner." *Journal of Post Keynesian Economics* 16(2), Winter 1993–94: 189–95.

Measurement, Quantification, and Economic Analysis: Numeracy in Economics (editor). New York: Routledge, 1995.

"Adolph Lowe's Political Economics: Instrumentalism as Enlightened Intervention." *American Journal of Economics and Sociology* 56(3), July 1997: 303–19.

"Sectoral Changes in Employment: An Eclectic Perspective on 'Good' Jobs and 'Poor' Jobs." *Review of Political Economy* 12(2), April 2000: 171–91.

Works about Ingrid H. Rima

"Ingrid Hahne Rima." In *Engendering Economics: Conversations with Women Economists in the United States,* edited by P. I. Olson and Z. Emami, 14–30. London: Routledge, 2002.

Rima, I. H. "My Trip through Life as I Recall." Autobiographical essays provided by the subject to the authors; n.d.; 27 pp.

Alice M. Rivlin
(1931–   )

• •

In 1975, after having distinguished herself as a staff economist at the Brookings Institution, a liberal research and public policy organization in Washington, D.C., and after serving as assistant secretary at the Department of Health, Education, and Welfare during the administration of Lyndon Baines Johnson, Alice Rivlin was appointed the founding head of the newly formed Congressional Budget Office (CBO). A liberal Democrat and the author of numerous books and articles on national policies, Rivlin found herself at the center of a conflict as Congress revamped its budgeting procedures during the Gerald Ford administration. Prior to her appointment, the congressional budgeting process was at best inefficient and at worst chaotic. Put together on a piecemeal basis and usually based on inadequate and inaccurate information, the congressional budget was generally a reflection of the biases of the political party in control of Congress and not the product of reasoned judgment based on hard evidence. Rivlin changed all that. In the process, she established herself as one of the most influential policy makers to work in Washington in the last thirty years.

BIOGRAPHY

Alice Mitchell Rivlin was born Georgianna Alice Mitchell on March 4, 1931, in Philadelphia, Pennsylvania. Her mother was Georgianna (Fales) Mitchell and her father was Allan C. G. Mitchell, a professor of nuclear physics. Given her mother's first name, Rivlin dropped it in favor of her second name, Alice. She grew up in Bloomington, Indiana, where her father taught at Indiana University. Alice returned to Pennsylvania to attend Bryn Mawr College, graduating magna cum laude in 1952 with a bachelor's degree in economics. In 1955 she earned an M.A. in economics from Radcliffe College of Harvard University. That same year, she married Lewis A. Rivlin, a lawyer in private practice in Washington, D.C. The couple had three children and were divorced in 1977. While at Radcliffe, Rivlin was a teaching fellow and tutor in economics at Harvard University. She received her Ph.D. in economics from Radcliffe in 1958.

In 1957, Rivlin began a long association with the Brookings Institution, a well-respected liberal think tank noted for independent research, education, and publications on social issues. Except for one four-year interval when she held various positions in Johnson's Great Society program, Rivlin remained with Brookings until 1975, serving as a staff member of its Economic Studies Division from 1958 to 1966, a senior staff economist in 1963, and a Brookings Senior Fellow in 1969. Brookings was the perfect outlet for her many publications dealing with economic analysis and the development of public policies designed "to perpetuate the rapid productivity growth that creates personal and national wealth" while using "that income and wealth wisely to build a strong and just society that does not dissolve in decadence and disunity" ("The Challenges of Affluence").

While at Brookings, Rivlin served as a consultant to the federal government, working for the House Committee on Education and Labor in 1961–62 and the secretary of the treasury from 1964 to 1966. In 1966, she entered government service full-time when she joined the Johnson administration's newly created Department of Health, Education, and Welfare (HEW) as a deputy assistant secretary for program coordination. Impressed with her insights and work ethic, President Johnson promoted Rivlin in 1968 to the post of assistant secretary of HEW in charge of planning and evaluation. In this capacity, she implemented a system of budgeting and programming and brought economic reasoning to bear on the agency's policy making.

In 1969, Rivlin returned to the Brookings Institution, where she was a senior fellow in the Economic Studies Program until 1975. At Brookings, she cowrote three noteworthy volumes under the title *Setting National Priorities,* which were published by the institution in 1971, 1972, and 1973. Each book was an intensive analysis of the Nixon administration's budget for the subsequent fiscal year and suggested alternatives to the White House's budget priorities. In addition to her work for Brookings, Rivlin published articles in *The New York Times Magazine, Current, Science,* and *The New Republic* on a variety of topics including social experimentation, national health insurance, income distribution, and federal taxation.

As a result of the Congressional Budget and Impoundment Control Act of 1974, Congress established the Congressional Budget Office (CBO) in July of that year. A landmark piece of federal budget reform legislation, the act was a backlash to the excessive domination by the executive branch of the budget process during the Nixon years. By law, the CBO was designed to monitor the national economy and its impact on the federal budget, to provide budgetary statistics for Congress, and to propose alternative budgeting policies. The Speaker of the House and the president pro tem of the Senate were to select the director of the CBO on the recommendations of the budget committees. By virtue of her vast experience and knowledge of the federal budget process, Rivlin became a leading candidate for the job. In November 1974,

Senator Edmund Muskie of Maine and Representative Brock Adams of Washington, each the chair of his respective budget committee, agreed on Rivlin as their choice to head the CBO. On February 24, 1975, she was sworn in as director by House Speaker Carl Albert and Senate president pro tem James Eastland.

For the next eight years, Rivlin revamped the way Congress went about preparing a budget. She put an end to Congress's piecemeal budgetary decision-making process in favor of budgetary planning based on three-year projections instead of on the former year-to-year basis. Rivlin was conscientious about communicating her results to the general public as well as to elected officials, giving the budgetary process a transparency that it did not previously have. She irritated Presidents Jimmy Carter and Ronald Reagan with reports from the CBO that routinely supplied Congress with sober and sometimes pessimistic budget information, economic forecasts, and policy analyses. Rivlin believed that one of her functions was to offset the unbridled optimism of the forecasts and projections that regularly came from the executive branch, whether the president was a Democrat or a Republican. In 1983, Rivlin returned to the Brookings Institution as director of its Economic Studies Program.

A long-time member of the AEA, Rivlin served as the association's president in 1986, the first woman to do so. In 1987, she became a senior fellow at the Brookings Institution, and in the spring of 1988, she was a visiting professor at the John F. Kennedy School of Government at Harvard University. Two years later, she married Sidney Graham Winter, a fellow economist. Rivlin left the Brookings Institution in December 1992 to become Hirst Professor of Public Policy at George Mason University in Virginia, a post she held for one year until January 1993. She then returned to public life as deputy director of the White House Office of Management and Budget during Bill Clinton's first term. There she honed the budgeting and policy skills she had learned as director of the CBO. In October 1994, Rivlin was promoted to director of the Office of Management and Budget, making her one of President Clinton's most important advisers. In June 1996, she left the White House to become the vice chair of the Board of Governors of the Federal Reserve System, then headed by Alan Greenspan. Rivlin stayed at the Federal Reserve until 1999, returning to Brookings as a senior fellow in the Economic Studies Program while also serving as chair of the District of Columbia Financial Management Assistance Authority. In 2001, Rivlin left Brookings to become a professor of urban management and policy at the New School University in New York City.

CONTRIBUTIONS

In 1975, Rivlin gave the prestigious Richard T. Ely Lecture at the annual meeting of the AEA. She used the occasion to discuss her views on household income and the role economists should play in the development and implementation of policies aimed at altering its distribution. To Rivlin, the traditional approach of economists to the age-old debate on the optimal distribution of income was too theoretical and arcane. She wanted to encourage a more proactive stance among professional economists, and she said so in clear and emphatic terms: "In my own view, discussions of optimum distributions of income or opportunity are fascinating intellectual parlor games unlikely to make any contribution to the policy debate on income shares. Economists who want to make themselves useful would be better advised to put their effort into defining some real policy alternatives, estimating their costs and effects and explaining what they are talking about to the public and its political representatives so that the political process, for all its faults, can at least operate with more knowledge of what is possible than it has at present" ("Income Distribution," 8).

This attitude exemplified three personal biases evident throughout Rivlin's career. "All authors have their biases. One of mine is optimism" (*Reviving,* 3). Rivlin has always believed "that America's current economic and political problems are serious but not insurmountable . . . ," as long as pragmatic, results-oriented solutions are brought to bear. She did not pursue a liberal or conservative agenda and never played to the ideological purists of either the left or the right. The policies she recommended to the four presidents she served reflected a strong belief in the efficacy of private markets and a conviction that public action is often necessary and constructive. A third bias, against "magic wands and painless solutions," complemented her pragmatic inclinations, giving Rivlin a philosophy about public economic policy that set her apart from others in Washington practicing the same trade without nearly the same level of success. This was especially evident in the 1990s in her campaign to reduce the national debt, which she believed was "the biggest single impediment to revitalizing the American economy" (13).

Rivlin came to this conclusion after studying the Swedish economy. While impressed with Sweden's high standard of living and absence of poverty, she nonetheless came to the conclusion that high budget deficits had reduced national savings and capital formation. These, in turn, would jeopardize Sweden's ability to sustain economic growth over the long term. Not wishing a similar fate for the U.S. economy, Rivlin was a tireless advocate during the Clinton administration for a combination of policies that would raise government revenues and stimulate economic growth, the dual impact of which would reduce the national debt and promote prosperity. President Clinton got the message, and the U.S. economy in the late 1990s responded much as Rivlin had predicted.

BIBLIOGRAPHY

Works by Alice M. Rivlin

"Income Distribution: Can Economists Help?" *American Economic Review* 65(2), May 1975: 1–15. Also available as "General Reprint Series 307," Washington, DC: Brookings Institution, 1975.

"Overview." In *The Swedish Economy* (coeditor with B. P. Bosworth), 1–21. Washington, DC: Brookings Institution, 1987.

Reviving the American Dream. Washington, DC: Brookings Institution, 1992.

"The Challenges of Affluence." Adam Smith Award Lecture, National Association of Business Economists, Chicago, IL, September 11, 2000.

Works about Alice M. Rivlin

"Alice Mitchell Rivlin." In *Engendering Economics: Conversations with Women Economists in the United States,* edited by P. I. Olson and Z. Emami, 73–87. London: Routledge, 2002.

Levy, D. "Interview with Alice M. Rivlin." *The Region.* Minneapolis, MN: Federal Reserve Bank of Minneapolis, June 1997.

"Rivlin, Alice." In *Who's Who in Economics,* edited by M. Blaug, 939. Northampton, MA: Edward Elgar, 1999.

Smith, A. M. "Clinton's Top Women: Who They Are, How They Got There, What They're Like." *Executive Female* 16, March/April 1993: 38–43.

Joan Robinson
(1903–1983)

• •

In 1975, the year the United Nations proclaimed the International Year of the Woman, virtually everyone in economics thought Joan Robinson, arguably the greatest woman economist ever, would be chosen for the Nobel Memorial Prize in Economics. Indeed, expecting Robinson to win the award, "The American magazine *Business Week*, after sounding out the American economics profession, felt so sure of the choice as to anticipate the event by publishing a long article on her, presenting her explicitly as being on everyone's list for this year's Nobel Prize in Economics" (Pasinetti, 212). Characterizing her as a "socialist who sounds like a conservative," the *Business Week* article noted that her views on wages and prices "are what American businessmen talk about at board meetings," even though among American economists "she has been more ignored than adored." Still, the magazine, citing "her work on the relationship between capital accumulation and growth, as well as her 1933 classic *The Economics of Imperfect Competition*," considered her a prime candidate for the prize.

Prime candidate or not, Robinson did not receive the award then or in any subsequent year. The 1975 prize was shared by Tjalling C. Koopmans, a pioneer in the mathematical technique of linear programming, and Leonid Kantorovich, a Russian economist virtually unknown outside the then Soviet Union. That the Royal Swedish Academy of Science—the awarding authority for the prizes in physics, chemistry, and economics—missed a golden opportunity to recognize one of the truly great economists of the twentieth century in no way diminishes Joan Robinson and her significance to the discipline. On the contrary, not winning the award had a perverse effect on Robinson's reputation: "Ever since, in shoptalk among economists all over the world, Joan Robinson has become the greatest Nobel Prize winner that never was" (Pasinetti, 212).

BIOGRAPHY

Joan Robinson was born Joan Violet Maurice on October 31, 1903, in Camberley, Surrey, England. Her parents were Helen Margaret (Marsh) Maurice and Major General Sir Frederick Maurice, both members of prominent and distinguished British families noted for their Christian Socialist religious beliefs and independent thinking. Robinson's paternal forebears included Frederick Denison Maurice, a noted Christian Socialist who was forced from his professorship at Cambridge University because of his controversial views on eternal damnation. Her maternal great-great-grandfather Spencer Perceval became prime minister but was tragically assassinated while in office. Her maternal grandmother, Jane Perceval Marsh, founded the Alexander Hospital for Children with Hip Diseases in London. Robinson's father was regarded as one of the ablest officers in the British army. One of four girls in a family of five children, Robinson displayed from early on the keen mind and seriousness of purpose that characterized her remarkable family.

In 1918, during World War I, Robinson learned from her father the importance of doing and saying what is right, no matter the consequences. Robinson's father, then director of military operations, alleged publicly that Prime Minister David Lloyd George's government had deceived Parliament and the country about the strength of the British army prior to Britain's entrance into the war. Sir Frederick Maurice felt that this deception had left British troops unnecessarily exposed to German military might along the Western Front. In what is still known in British history as the Maurice debate, Robinson's father wrote an unprecedented letter to the London *Times* accusing the government of a deception that had tragic consequences for British soldiers. Although the letter resulted in the end of Sir Maurice's promising military career, he was always sure that he had done the right thing. Robinson was fourteen when her father resigned, but his example would stay with her throughout her lifetime.

Being a bright member of a wealthy family, Robinson was able to attend the respected St. Paul's School for Girls in London. While there, this extremely conscientious student found time to volunteer at a settlement house for the underprivileged, an experience that helped cultivate her lifelong interest in the problems of the poor. In 1921, she left St. Paul's and entered Girton College, a women's college associated with Cambridge University. At Cambridge, she studied economics from 1922 through 1925 as a Gilchrist Scholar. In 1925, Robinson graduated from Girton with second-class honors in economics despite being regarded as one of the best economics students at the university, having been "the only person to place Class I in the Intercollegiate Examination in Economics" (Turner, 17) in June 1923. Whatever dismay Robinson experienced as a result of her second-class honors was short-lived, for within the year she married Austin Robinson, a Cambridge economist and teacher, and the two left for India, where Austin served as a tutor to the Maharajah of Gwalior until 1929.

In India, Joan Robinson had her first look at the overwhelming poverty prevalent in an economically underdeveloped country, an experience that would shape her view of political economics forever. In 1929, the Robinsons returned to Cambridge as the Western world lapsed into the decade-long Great Depression. At Cambridge, Robinson earned her master's degree and then began her research, professional publishing, and the tutoring of students. By 1930, her first publication, a book review, appeared, and in 1931 she became an assistant lecturer in economics at Cambridge. Her husband's position as a lecturer in economics may have given Robinson an advantage in securing an entry-level position in the male-dominated world of Cambridge University, but it was her own work as a tutor and scholar that earned her a regular faculty position.

In 1931, Cambridge was at the center of an important revolution in economic thinking led by John Maynard Keynes, who would go on to become the most famous Western economist of the twentieth century. Robinson was in the center of this revolution because of her involvement in a group of economists dubbed the "Circus," which met regularly to discuss the new economics that Keynes was advancing. She was also hard at work on what would become her major contribution to economic theory, her groundbreaking book *The Economics of Imperfect Competition*. Robinson was thirty when the book was published in 1933, and it established her reputation as a first-rate economist. The book became a classic that was reprinted ten times through 1959 and reissued in a new edition in 1969. Her pioneering theories of imperfect competition are now an integral part of mainstream economic thinking and are taught in basic economic courses throughout the world.

If Robinson had done nothing after publishing *Imperfect Competition*, her reputation as a brilliant economist would still have been firmly established. She was, however, not one to rest on her laurels. In addition to her teaching and writing, Robinson raised a family. Her daughter Ann was born in May 1934 and her second daughter, Barbara, was born in October 1936. In 1937, she published *Introduction to the Theory of Employment*, and she would go on writing, teaching, and publishing for the next forty years. During this period, she published numerous articles, professional essays, and books, the most notable being *The Accumulation of Capital* (1956). Beginning in 1951, the first volume in the five-volume set of her *Collected Economic Papers* appeared. In 1965, upon her husband's retirement from teaching, Robinson was made a professor at Cambridge University. She retired in 1971 but continued publishing through the early 1980s. In August 1983, after a lengthy illness, she died in Cambridge, England.

CONTRIBUTIONS

Robinson authored more than 300 articles, books, book reviews, essays, pamphlets, and op-ed pieces, so it is virtually impossible to summarize briefly her contributions to economics. There are, however, two works that deserve special recognition: *The Economics of Imperfect Competition* and *The Accumulation of Capital*. In the latter book, Robinson described the dynamic long-term consequences of the accumulation of capital, blending the works of the four economists who had the most profound impact on her own thinking: Alfred Marshall, the last of the great classical economists; Karl Marx, the father of scientific socialism; John Maynard Keynes, the creator of modern macroeconomics; and Michal Kalecki, an obscure Polish economist whose ideas paralleled those of Keynes but were, in Robinson's judgment, superior.

The thrust of *Accumulation* is that economic growth depends on the interplay of capital accumulation and technological progress. Robinson concluded that the success of capitalism rests on technical progress as reflected in increases in productivity, most frequently embodied in new types of equipment, which in turn requires the accumulation of capital. The proper balance between capital accumulation, growing productivity, and the acquisition of new equipment would ensure a steady state of economic growth. If, however, the interaction between accumulation and technical progress was not optimal, economic development would move in fits and starts, and the resulting surges and lapses in economic activity could have political and social consequences as well as economic ones. The real significance of *Accumulation* is that it gave rise to a new school of economics called post-Keynesian economics, which holds that unemployment, inflation, and other so-called macroeconomic problems really have their origins in the microeconomic foundations of an economy.

For post-Keynesian economists, *Accumulation* is Robinson's most important work, but for mainstream economists it is *Imperfect Competition*. In that book, Robinson developed a theoretical explanation of the pricing behavior and related practices of oligopolies, defined as industries dominated by a small number of large firms. Prior to the appearance of *Imperfect Competition*, economists treated oligopolies as aberrations and concentrated their analysis on the behavior of perfectly competitive markets, which are markets with such large numbers of buyers and sellers that no individual participant could set price or in any way shape or influence market conditions. Such a model of economic behavior did not ring true in the real world, and Robinson's *Imperfect Competition* sought to explain how companies actually operated, not how economists thought they should operate. Robinson's work was the embodiment of the expression "there is nothing so practical as a good theory." The kinked demand curve, the concept of marginal revenue, and other ideas developed in *Imperfect Competition* are today an integral part of contemporary microeconomics and among the many reasons Robinson is considered one of the foremost economists in the history of the discipline.

BIBLIOGRAPHY

Works by Joan Robinson

The Economics of Imperfect Competition. London: Macmillan, 1969. Originally published 1933.

Introduction to the Theory of Employment. London: Macmillan, 1969. Originally published 1937.

An Essay on Marxian Economics. London: Macmillan, 1966. Originally published 1942.

"The Production Function and the Theory of Capital." *Review of Economic Studies* 21(2), 1953: 81–106. Reprinted in *Collected Economic Papers*, vol. 2.

The Accumulation of Capital. London: Macmillan, 1969. Originally published 1956.

Economic Philosophy. London: Watts and Company, 1962.

Economic Heresies: Some Old-Fashioned Questions in Economic Theory. New York: Basic Books, 1971.

Collected Economic Papers. London: Basil Blackwell. Reprint Cambridge, MA: MIT Press, 1980.

Works about Joan Robinson

Cicarelli, J., and Cicarelli, J. *Joan Robinson: A Bio-Bibliography*. Westport, CT: Greenwood Press, 1996.

Eichner, A. S., and Kregel, J. A. "An Essay on Post-Keynesian Theory: A New Paradigm in Economics." *Journal of Economic Literature* 13(4), December 1975: 1293–1314.

Feiwel, G. R., ed. *The Economics of Imperfect Competition and Employment: Joan Robinson and Beyond*. New York: New York University Press, 1989.

———. *Joan Robinson and Modern Economic Theory*. New York: New York University Press, 1989.

Gram, H., and Walsh, V. "Joan Robinson's Economics in Retrospective." *Journal of Economic Literature* 21(2), June 1983: 518–50.

Harcourt, G. C. "Joan Robinson." In *International Encyclopedia of Social Sciences, Biographical Supplement*, edited by D. S. Stills, 663–71. New York: Free Press, 1979.

Marcuzzo, M. C., Pasinetti, L. L., and Roncaglia, A., eds. *The Economics of Joan Robinson*. New York: Routledge, 1996.

Pasinetti, L. L. "Joan Violet Robinson." In *The New Palgrave: A Dictionary of Economics*, edited by J. Eatwell M. Milgate, and P. Newman, 212–17. New York: Stockton Press, 1987.

Rima, I[ngrid]. H., ed. *The Joan Robinson Legacy*. Armonk, NY: M. E. Sharpe, 1991.

"Robinson, Joan." In *Who's Who in Economics*, edited by M. Blaug, 944. Northampton, MA: Edward Elgar, 1999.

"A Socialist Who Sounds Like a Conservative," *Business Week*, (2403), October 20, 1975.

Thomson, D.L. "Joan Robinson." In *Adam Smith's Daughters*, 105–33. New York: Exposition Press: 1973.

Turner, M[arjorie]. S[hepherd]. *Joan Robinson and the Americans*. Armonk, NY: M. E. Sharpe, 1989.

Isabel V. Sawhill
(1937–)

Isabel Sawhill was one of a group of women economists, including **Alice M. Rivlin**, **Nancy Hays Teeters**, and **Juanita M. Kreps**, who came to prominence through their careers in government service. Sawhill recognized that she faced discrimination as a woman in the field of economics, but fortuitously, she started her career at a time when the increasing government regulation of business created a demand for trained economists, particularly as policy makers in the public sector. Sawhill became a noted economist through her government service, but she has served the discipline well as a college teacher and administrator, researcher, editor, and writer.

BIOGRAPHY

Isabel Van Devanter Sawhill was born on April 2, 1937, in Washington, D.C., to Winslow B. Van Devanter and Isabel E. Van Devanter. She attended Wellesley College from 1955 to 1958 and then went on to New York University, where she earned her B.A. in 1962 and her Ph.D. in 1968. At NYU, she was often the only woman in her classes. On September 13, 1958, she married John Sawhill, who would become energy czar under President Richard Nixon and, later, president of NYU. The couple has one son, James.

Sawhill started her economics career as a policy analyst in the U.S. Department of Health, Education, and Welfare in 1968 and by 1970 had moved on to the U.S. Office of Management and Budget. In 1970, she began teaching at Goucher College, where she stayed until 1973, serving as chair of the Economics Department from 1971 to 1973. In 1973, she became a senior research associate at the Urban Institute, a Washington think tank, serving as the director of the Women and Family Policy Program in 1975.

By 1977, Sawhill was back in government service as director of what then was called the National Commission for Manpower Policy, which advised

Congress and the president on employment issues. At the urging of Sawhill and others, the agency was renamed the National Commission on Employment Policy. Her chief concern as director was how to achieve price stability with full employment. She has described herself as ideologically middle-of-the-road, understanding that government intervention cannot solve all problems.

In 1979, Sawhill returned to the Urban Institute, serving as program director for Employment and Labor Policy. In 1980, she became a codirector of the institute's Changing Domestic Priorities Project. The Urban Institute remains one of her professional homes. She also serves as a member of the board of editors of the *Journal of Economic Literature* and *Land Economics*. She has contributed articles to economic journals, magazines, and newspapers, including *Daedalus* and *Newsday*.

In addition to her research and publishing work, Sawhill has served on the board of trustees of American Assembly; as a member of the Committee on Developing American Capitalism, the National Council on Employment Policy, and the National Committee for Research on the 1980 Census; and on the advisory board of the General Accounting Office study of the 1981 welfare amendments. She is currently affiliated with the Brookings Institution in Washington, D.C.

CONTRIBUTIONS

Sawhill has published a significant volume of scholarship in the general area of employment and labor policy, with special emphasis on the economic circumstances of women and the poor. Building on previous research and mining the data available in the 1970 census, she published in 1975 an important book about the single-parent family. *Time of Transition: The Growth of Families Headed by Women* is an extensive empirical analysis of what was then an emerging concern of families headed by a single parent, usually a woman. As William Gorham, then president of the Urban Institute wrote in the foreword to that book: "This book performs an especially timely service, dealing as it does with the single-parent family, a phenomenon that has grown at a very rapid rate in recent years. As the authors point out, the single-parent family . . . is transitional in two senses. For a large proportion of the individuals involved, it is a transitional stage between marriages. At the overall societal level, it is a symptom of the transition from what the authors call the 'distributive' family of the 19th and early 20th centuries, in which a man working outside of the home provided resources for financially dependent women and children, and a form adapted to the less specialized marital roles we seem to be moving toward, in which both husbands and wives will share more equally in the physical care and financial support of their children" (xi).

Sawhill's work is particularly important because she devoted an entire chapter to a new and an increasingly significant topic, "What Happens to Children in Female-Headed Families?" As Sawhill noted, "The rise in family headship by women has been mirrored by an even more dramatic shift in the living arrangements of children. Children living with only one parent increased twelve times as rapidly as children living with both parents between 1960 and 1970. Indeed, over that period, the absolute increase in numbers of children in single-parent homes exceeded the increase in children in two-parent homes" (*Time of Transition,* 129). Sawhill and her coauthor analyzed the consequences for children in the female-headed family, including the incidence of juvenile delinquency, scholastic and occupational achievement, and family stability later in life.

Sawhill was perceptive enough to see that while "for most women, single parenthood is a 'time of transition' between living in one nuclear family and another" (*Time of Transition,* 159), the explosion in the number of female-headed families would have long-term repercussions on the social, cultural, and economic fabric of U.S. society for years to come. She came back to this theme in one of her most recent publications, noting, as she had predicted a quarter-century earlier, that "The absence of fathers in the home has profound consequences for children. Almost 75 percent of American children living in single-parent families will experience poverty before they turn 11 years old, but only 20 percent of children in two-person families. . . . Indeed, virtually all of the increase in child poverty between 1970 and 1996 was due to growth in the number of single-parent families. . . . Children who grow up absent their fathers are also more likely to fail at school or drop out, experience behavioral or emotional problems requiring psychiatric treatment, engage in early sexual activity, and develop drug and alcohol problems" ("Fathers," 422).

In the 1980s, Sawhill turned the focus of her research on the matter of economic growth. The stagflation that gripped the U.S. economy during much of the 1970s made reviving economic growth, reducing unemployment, and controlling inflation the three most important items on the nation's agenda. Sawhill's analysis of the status of the U.S. economy in the early 1980s led her to offer the following formula for stimulating and sustaining growth without inflation:

> First, barriers and disincentives to full participation in the labor force can reduce the proportion of the population that works. . . . In terms of sheer numbers as well as sensitivity to public and private policies that encourage or discourage work, two groups stand out: adult women and older Americans. In particular, the Social Security System and institutional arrangements that make combining parenthood and work difficult bear scrutiny.
>
> Second, the job opportunities of the future will be predominantly and increasingly in white-collar or service occupations. . . . [G]ood secondary school preparation seems essential.
>
> Third, fears that a new industrial revolution is going to produce widespread technological unemployed seem unjustified. The benefits of maintaining technological preeminence are many. . . .
>
> Fourth, . . . a continuing federal commitment to assist the disadvantaged to become more economically independent seems like a worthwhile investment of federal funds.
>
> Fifth, federal leadership in assuring the availability of privately financed mid-career training opportunities may be desirable; . . .
>
> Finally, more innovative ways of managing and rewarding workers have

considerable potential to improve productivity, humanize work, and make fighting inflation less painful. ("Human Resources," 123–24)

As the prosperity of the 1980s all but obliterated the national memory of the economic malaise of the 1970s, Sawhill once again centered her scholarship on those being left behind. She was particularly taken by the persistence of poverty in the face of plenty, especially the level of poverty in the United States compared to other industrialized countries. The presence of an underclass located in the nation's urban areas and composed mostly of African Americans was, in Sawhill's judgment, a major source of the problem. This hard core of poverty was the result of numerous factors—racism, illegal drugs, the continuous deterioration of the urban infrastructure—the amelioration of which would require a redoubling of the antipoverty movement. In addition to the customary poverty-reduction measures, Sawhill thought that success would require several new approaches, including the reestablishment of parents' responsibility for their children, the prevention of early childbearing, better daycare and other child support programs, and expecting welfare mothers to work ("Poverty").

Ten years later, Sawhill was sending out the same message but with a slightly different spin. While always conscious of the relationship between race and economic mobility, she came to put increasing importance on class as a determinant of upward mobility, a change of perspective that recognized that status as well as skin color affects the incidence of poverty. "Opportunity is here defined as the extent to which an individual's economic and social status is determined by his or her own skills and effort rather than by class of origin. It is typically measured as the relationship between parents and their offspring on various indicators of class—occupational status and income are common ones. The more closely the status of individuals reflects the status of their parents, the less opportunity exists in a society and the more class matters. Conversely, the more independent the overall parent-offspring relationship, the less class matters" (*Getting Ahead*, 46).

To uncouple the economic and social status of parents and offspring, Sawhill advocates a set of policy initiatives that she has championed for the better part of her adult life: improved schooling at the primary and secondary levels; early childhood education and support of families; affirmative action; and government tax, benefits, and welfare policies that incentivize individuals to work.

BIBLIOGRAPHY

Works by Isabel V. Sawhill

Time of Transition: The Growth of Families Headed by Women (with H. L. Ross). Washington, DC: Urban Institute, 1975.

"Human Resources." In *Regrowing the American Economy*, 100–124. Englewood Cliffs, NJ: Prentice Hall for the American Assembly, 1983.

"Poverty and the Underclass." In *Challenge to Leadership: Economic and Social Issues for the Next Decade* (editor), 215–52. Washington, DC: Urban Institute, 1988.

Getting Ahead: Economic and Social Mobility in America (with D. P. McMurrer). Washington, DC: Urban Institute, 1998.

"Fathers, Marriage, and Welfare Reform" (with W. F. Horn). In *The New World of Welfare*, edited by **R[ebecca]. M. Blank** and R. Haskins, 421–35. Washington, DC: Brookings Institution Press, 2001.

Works about Isabel V. Sawhill

"Catch-up for Calculating Women." *Time*, January 8, 1979, 45–46.

"Sawhill, Isabel V(an Devanter) 1937–." In *Contemporary Authors*, 416. Vol. 130. Detroit, MI: Gale Research, 1990.

Anna J. Schwartz
(1915–   )

In 1976, the American economist Milton Friedman won the Nobel Memorial Prize in Economics. Half that award belonged to Anna J. Schwartz. For more than thirty years, Schwartz and Friedman formed one of the most famous and influential research teams in the history of economics, producing three monumental books and many seminal articles on monetary economics (Lipsey). Friedman once observed that their relationship was "... an almost perfect collaboration. Anna did all the work and I got a lot of the credit" (Fettig). This gallant remark contained more than an element of truth. In a career that spanned more than sixty years and saw the publication of more than 125 books, contributions to books, book reviews, and articles in the most prestigious economics journals, Schwartz has earned the professional respect of her peers but not the public recognition accorded her intellectual partner.

BIOGRAPHY

Anna Jacobson Schwartz was born in New York City on November 11, 1915, into a family with two daughters and three sons. Her father, Hillel Joseph Jacobson, was a rabbi, and her mother, Pauline (Shainmark) Jacobson, was a housewife. In 1934, Schwartz graduated Phi Beta Kappa with a B.A. degree from Barnard College. She earned her M.A. in 1935 from Columbia University and, almost thirty years later, in 1964, received her Ph.D., also from Columbia. She married Isaac Schwartz, a businessman, in October 1936. The couple, who had been married nearly sixty-three years at the time of Isaac's death in January 1999, had four children. In 1936, Schwartz worked briefly for the U.S. Department of Agriculture, then, in the same year, she became a research associate at the Social Science Research Council at Columbia University (Lipsey).

In 1941, she moved to the National Bureau of Economic Research (NBER) as a senior research staffer. Located in New York City, the NBER is a private, nonprofit research organization founded by the American economist Wesley Clair Mitchell of Columbia University to study business cycles. Except for a stint as staff director of the U.S. Commission on the Role of Gold in the Domestic and International Monetary Systems in 1981–82, Schwartz has been associated with the NBER since 1941.

She has supplemented her duties as a research economist with a variety of teaching assignments over the years. In 1952, Schwartz was an instructor of economics at Brooklyn College, and she held a similar post at Baruch College in 1959–60. She served as an adjunct professor of economics at the City University of New York (CUNY), Graduate Division of Hunter College, from 1967 to 1969, and held the same title at New York University's Graduate School of Arts and Science in 1969–70. Since 1986, she has been an adjunct professor of economics at the Graduate School of CUNY.

A prolific writer, Schwartz published her first professional article in the May 1940 issue of the *Review of Economics and Statistics.* Her first book, coauthored with A. D. Gayer and W. W. Rostow, appeared in 1953 and dealt with the growth and fluctuations of the British economy during the first half of the nineteenth century. Most of her early works focused on financial history, especially the accumulation and analysis of monetary data. When in the early 1960s Schwartz was assigned to work with Friedman on the NBER's long-term project on the money supply and its effects on the economy, her skills complemented his perfectly (Friedman and Friedman, 232). He was the theorist, she the empirical whiz who found the data to support his hypotheses. Their collaboration produced three books that became the foundation for the revival of the monetarist school of economics, moving monetary theory, according to one journalist, "from what was once regarded as practically the lunatic fringe of the economics profession to a position in center stage, with great influence on the conduct of national economic policy" (Heinemann). The two also coauthored several articles in prestigious journals, the first appearing in the *Review of Economics and Statistics* in 1963 and the last published in the *American Economic Review* in 1991.

In additional to her research with Friedman, Schwartz published numerous articles on her own or in concert with other distinguished economists including Phillip Cagan, Michael Bordo, and Karl Brunner. Her prodigious scholarly output led to several appointments on the editorial boards of a number of important journals. From 1972 to 1978, she served on the editorial board of the *American Economic Review,* and Schwartz has been a continuous member of the editorial boards of the *Journal of Money, Credit, and Banking* since 1984, the *Journal of Monetary Economics* since 1975, and the *Journal of Financial Services Research* since 1993.

Her long and distinguished career has been recognized with many awards and honors, including the presidency of the Western Economic Association (1987–88), and honorary degrees from the University of Florida, Rutgers University, and Emory University, among others. In 1993, she was designated a distinguished fellow of the AEA, and in 1997, she was named an honorary fellow of the Institute of Economic Affairs.

CONTRIBUTIONS

Of her many contributions to the field of economics, the three books that Schwartz coauthored with Friedman are clearly the most significant. In 1950, Arthur Burns, then director of research at the NBER, invited Friedman to participate in a bureau-inspired project concerning the quantity of money in the United States and its role in business cycles. Schwartz and Friedman were paired as a writing team. The two worked long distance, relying primarily on the mail, which Friedman claimed had its advantages because it "meant that everything had to be written down, avoiding the inevitable misunderstandings that arise from verbal communications" (Friedman and Friedman, 165). The first major output of that collaboration was *A Monetary History of the United States, 1867–1960*.

The book—the first of a quartet of works that the NBER sponsored as part of its long-term project on the quantity of money—was about "the stock of money in the United States." It traced "changes in the stock of money for nearly a century, from just after the Civil War to 1960," examining "the factors that accounted for changes," and analyzed "the reflex influence that the stock of money exerted on the course of events" (*Monetary History*, 3). A massive volume of more than 800 pages, the book offered four basic conclusions about the relationship between the quantity of money and the state of the economy.

1. Changes in the behavior of the money stock have been closely associated with changes in economic activity, money income, and prices.
2. The interrelation between monetary and economic change has been highly stable.
3. Monetary changes have often had an independent origin; they have not been simply a reflection of changes in economic activity. . . .
4. In monetary matters, appearances are deceiving; the important relationships are often precisely the reverse of those that strike the eye. (676)

This book and its conclusions became the principal force behind the revival of monetarism in the 1960s and 1970s.

The second book in the Friedman-Schwartz trilogy was *Monetary Statistics of the United States*. In reality, this book was a giant footnote to *Monetary History*. Subtitled *Estimates, Sources, Methods*, the volume describes in great detail the sources of data and methods of analysis Schwartz and Friedman used to compile their estimates of the U.S. money supply. As the authors noted, the book was intended for "the monetary statistician who is interested in basic data on the quantity of money. It provides raw material for analysis but little economic analysis" (3). Of the work's 600-plus pages, more than one-third are devoted to the presentation of elaborate tables and charts.

In between Schwartz and Friedman's first two books, Phillip Cagan published *Determinants and Effects of Changes in the Stock of Money, 1875–1960*, the second volume in the NBER's quartet of texts on the U.S. money supply. The fourth book in the NBER series and the third and final volume Schwartz and

Friedman coauthored was *Monetary Trends in the United States and the United Kingdom: Their Relation to Income, Prices, and Interest Rates, 1867–1975.* This book extended the statistical analysis of *Monetary History* through 1975 and applied it to estimates of the money supply in the United Kingdom. The conclusions reached in *Monetary Trends* tended to reinforce those Schwartz and Friedman arrived at in *Monetary History.* Taken in toto, the books Schwartz and Friedman wrote became the pedestal on which the bust of monetarism rests to this day.

Schwartz was also the sole author of many works, including an important essay on foreign exchange market intervention ("The Rise and Fall"). Foreign exchange market intervention denotes a process in which a central bank tries to manipulate market forces so that the international value of its currency remains at some predetermined, normative level. Schwartz notes that, with the exception of Japan, monetary authorities in most advanced countries, particularly in Europe and the United States, have abandoned exchange-rate intervention as a policy objective. She reached this conclusion after analyzing the equivocal record of past episodes of intervention, reviewing the inconclusive results of empirical research, and examining the many problems of implementation that intervention advocates have ignored. She published the results of this research in her eighty-fifth year.

BIBLIOGRAPHY

Works by Anna J. Schwartz

A Monetary History of the United States, 1867–1960 (with M. Friedman). Princeton, NJ: Princeton University Press for the National Bureau of Economic Research, 1963.
Monetary Statistics of the United States: Estimates, Sources, Methods (with M. Friedman). New York: National Bureau of Economic Research, 1970.
Monetary Trends in the United States and the United Kingdom: Their Relation to Income, Prices, and Interest Rates, 1867–1975 (with M. Friedman). Chicago: University of Chicago Press for the National Bureau of Economic Research, 1982.
"The Rise and Fall of Foreign Exchange Market Intervention as a Policy Tool." *Journal of Financial Services Research* 18(2/3), 2000: 319–39.

Works about Anna J. Schwartz

Bordo, M. D., ed. *Money, History and International Finance: Essays in Honor of Anna J. Schwartz.* Chicago: University of Chicago Press, 1989.
Fettig, D. "Anna Schwartz." *The Region.* Minneapolis, MN: Federal Reserve Bank of Minneapolis, September 1993.
Friedman, M., and Friedman, R. D. *Two Lucky People.* Chicago: University of Chicago Press, 1998.
Heinemann, H. E. "Milton and Anna: Book Two." *New York Times,* July 12, 1970, business and finance section.
Lipsey, R. "Anna Jacobson Schwartz." In *The New Palgrave: A Dictionary of Economics,* edited by J. Eatwell, M. Milgate, and P. Newman, 267. New York: Macmillan, 1991.
"Schwartz, Anna." In *Who's Who in Economics,* edited by M. Blaug, 1005–6. Northampton, MA: Edward Elgar, 1999.

Nancy L. Schwartz
(1939–1981)

Few lights in economics burned brighter than that of Nancy Schwartz, and fewer still burned briefer. In a distinguished career that was over all too soon, she established herself as one of the most prolific and important scholars in the field of economics, leaving a mark that is still a source of inspiration for those women and men following in her footsteps.

BIOGRAPHY

Nancy Lou Schwartz was born in Fort Wayne, Indiana, on March 27, 1939, to Helen (Dessaur) Schwartz and Richard Schwartz, an orthopedic surgeon. Her father's occupation took the family to Pittsburgh, Pennsylvania, and Albany, New York, during Schwartz's formative years. After high school, she attended Oberlin College in Ohio, graduating Phi Beta Kappa with a B.A. in economics in 1960. Schwartz then enrolled in the graduate economics program at Purdue University, where she earned her M.S. in 1962 and her Ph.D. in 1964. Her dissertation involving finding the optimal scheduling of towboats and barges along a river with multiple branches required elaborate and complex computation to solve (Kamien, 387), and was a precursor to the analytical research she would produce during her brief but productive career.

After receiving her Ph.D., Schwartz began her academic career teaching in the Graduate School of Industrial Administration at Carnegie-Mellon University in Pittsburgh. Friends described her as a shy scholar who, while too polite to point out a logical flaw in an argument directly, had the uncanny ability to find the weakness in any theory or model, which she noted discreetly and with compassion. Schwartz left Carnegie-Mellon in 1970 but not before becoming a tenured associate professor and being awarded a Ford Foundation Faculty Research Fellowship.

In 1970, she joined the Graduate School of Management at Northwestern

University as a full professor. She would spend the rest of her career at North-western's J. L. Kellogg School of Management, which had not yet achieved the world-class stature it would attain under the leadership of legendary dean Donald Jacobs. Schwartz joined Northwestern as a member of a group of faculty teaching managerial economics, quantitative methods, and operations management. Eventually, this conglomerate of disciplines would be organized into the Department of Managerial Economics and Decision Sciences (MEDS). Besides her scholarly agenda and helping recruit top scholars for Kellogg's quantitative programs, Schwartz headed the MEDS's Ph.D. programs. She chaired the department from 1977 to 1979 and then when on to become the director of all the Ph.D. programs in the Kellogg School.

Schwartz was a member of the Council of the Institute of Management Sciences, and in 1981 she was appointed to the editorial board of the *American Economic Review*. She also served as an associate editor of *Econometrica*. These and related activities raised the visibility and prestige of graduate business education at Northwestern University. In 1981, she was appointed as the Morrison Professor of Managerial Economics and Decision Sciences, becoming the first woman to hold a chaired professorship at the Kellogg School. On December 7, 1981, Schwartz committed suicide. She left no note or clue as to why.

CONTRIBUTIONS

Schwartz published more than forty professional articles, books, and chapters in books during a career that spanned less than twenty years. Most of her publications were coauthored with Morton I. Kamien, whom she first met while both were teaching at Carnegie-Mellon University and who is now the Joseph and Carole Levy Distinguished Professor of Entrepreneurship at Northwestern University. Schwartz and Kamien came to Northwestern from Carnegie-Mellon, where the two had a fledgling scholarly partnership that eventually blossomed into one of the most productive professional relationships in all of economics. Her research was clustered mainly into three categories: methods of dynamic optimization with a special emphasis on applications, theoretical issues in industrial organization, and papers and articles in which dynamic optimization was used as a tool to explore the effects of industrial structure on technological innovation.

Schwartz's fascination with dynamic optimization was evident in her Ph.D. dissertation, which became the basis of one of her early publications ("Discrete Programs"). In it, Schwartz "involved a generalization of the standard transportation problem . . ." (Kamien, 387). The problem Schwartz tackled—optimal coordination of two means of conveyance instead of one—required her to develop a novel simulation procedure to approximate the optimal solution. Schwartz generally used dynamic optimization as a tool of analysis, a means to an end and not an end in itself. As exception to this principle was her coauthored book *Dynamic Optimization*, a how-to manual designed to expose students to the tricks that were "employed in the application of these techniques rather than provide a rigorous treatment of the theory behind them" (Kamien, 391).

A second important area of Schwartz's research focused on theoretical issues in industrial organization, especially the relationship between industrial structure and innovation. Representative of the work she published in this field was the paper she coauthored on the effects market structure and elasticity have on the process of invention ("Market Structure, Elasticity"). Building on the works of Kenneth Arrow and Harold Demsetz, the article sought "to demonstrate conditions under which monopoly organization will give greater invention incentive than would competitive structure, and conditions under which it will give small incentive" (242). The theoretical analysis generated two important conclusions concerning structure, elasticity and invention: "In comparing industries of like structure, we found that the industry with the greater demand elasticity has the greater invention incentive since the resultant output expansion will be greater. . . . In comparing a competitive industry with a monopoly, we found that the monopoly will have the greater invention incentive provided that the industry demand curves are equally elastic. However, it was also shown that if the competitive industry faces a demand curve which is sufficiently more elastic than the demand for monopolist's product, than the competitive industry can provide a greater incentive to create a drastic cost-reducing invention of given magnitude" (251).

Schwartz and Kamien became so well regarded in this field that they penned a lengthy review article on market structure and innovation, complete with a 100-item bibliography ("Market Structure and Innovation: A Survey"). This paper evolved into a book in which Schwartz and Kamien expanded and updated the material in the article (Market Structure and Innovation).

Most of Schwartz's scholarship involved the application of dynamic optimization to investigate theoretical issues in industrial organization. The first major paper ("Optimal 'Induced' Technical Change") she coauthored in this area appeared in Econometrica in 1968 and represented an extension and refinement of J. R. Hicks's theory of induced inventions. Four years later, the duo of Schwartz and Kamien explored a firm's rate of expenditure for technical improvement under different market conditions, where market structure was defined by "aspects of rivals' behavior and of consumers' demand for competing goods," and not by the more conventional measures of firm numbers and size distribution ("Market Structure, Rivals' Response," 160). In toto, Schwartz and her coauthor produced some twenty articles, books, and contributions to books investigating market structure and firm behavior, and in the process the two literally defined this subfield of industrial organization from the mid-1960s through the early 1980s.

BIBLIOGRAPHY

Works by Nancy L. Schwartz

"Optimal 'Induced' Technical Change" (with M. I. Kamien). Econometrica 36(1), January 1968: 1–17.

"Discrete Programs for Moving Known Cargoes from Origins to Destination on Time at Minimum Bargeline Fleet Cost." Transportation Science, May 1968: 134–45.

"Market Structure, Elasticity of Demand, and Incentive to Invent." *Journal of Law and Economics,* April 1970: 241–52.

"Market Structure, Rivals' Response, and the Firm's Rate of Product Improvement" (with M. I. Kamien). *Journal of Industrial Economics* 20(2), April 1972: 159–72.

"Market Structure and Innovation: A Survey" (with M. I. Kamien). *Journal of Economic Literature* 13(1), March 1975: 1–37.

Dynamic Optimization (with M. I. Kamien). Amsterdam: Elsevier-North Holland, 1991. Originally published 1981.

Market Structure and Innovation (with M. I. Kamien). New York: Cambridge University Press, 1982.

Works about Nancy L. Schwartz

Kamien, M. I. "Nancy L. Schwartz (1939–81)." In *A Biographical Dictionary of Women Economists,* edited by R. W. Dimand, M. A. Dimand, and E. L. Forget, 387–93. Northampton, MA: Edward Elgar, 2000.

Reiter, S. "Schwartz, Nancy Lou (1939–1981)." In *The New Palgrave: A Dictionary of Economics,* edited by J. Eatwell, M. Milgate, and P. Newman, 268. New York: Macmillan, 1991.

Frances Julia Stewart
(1940–)

The daughter of a noted economist, Frances Julia Stewart also became an economist and in the process established a reputation for excellence in scholarship and service quite independent of her well-known father. Stewart ranks among the giants in the field of economic development, having made several seminal contributions to the study of how countries with different political, economic, and social systems can sustain the growth of per capita real income long enough to move into the ranks of developed nations.

BIOGRAPHY

Frances Julia Stewart was born on August 4, 1940, in Kendal, Westmoreland, England. Her father was the famous neoclassical economist Nicholas Kaldor, and her mother was Clarissa Goldschmidt. Stewart graduated from the Cambridge High School for Girls and then went to Oxford University, where she earned her bachelor's degree in philosophy, politics, and economics in 1961. As an undergraduate at Oxford, she won the Webb Medley Prize in Economics, once as a junior in 1960 and again as a senior in 1961. In 1962, she married Michael James Stewart; the couple had three children.

After college, Stewart held a number of posts in the national government of the United Kingdom in London during the period 1961–67. She was an economic assistant at the Treasury from 1961 to 1962. For the next five years, she served as an economic assistant, then as an economic adviser in the Department of Economic Affairs. She earned her master's degree from Oxford in 1967, then became a lecturer at the University of East Africa in Nairobi, Kenya. By 1970, Stewart had landed an academic post at Queen Elizabeth House at the University of Oxford, an institution with which she is still affiliated. She received her Ph.D. from Oxford in 1976.

At Oxford, Stewart began as a research officer but quickly became a senior research officer. She also held a concurrent position as a fellow of Oxford's Somerville College. She eventually became director of the International Development Centre at Queen Elizabeth House. Stewart supplemented her academic experience with professional assignments at various international agencies, including the International Labor Organization Employment Mission to Kenya (1971), consulting full-time with the World Bank (1978–79), and participating in UNICEF's project on the impact of economic stabilization policies on the poor in developing nations, particularly children and other vulnerable groups. Her academic work and practical professional experience earned her a long-term membership of the editorial board of *World Development*, a major journal in the field.

CONTRIBUTIONS

With one of her first major publications, Stewart established herself as an advocate for alternative approaches to the prevailing theory of economic development. In her coauthored essay on the effects of wage changes in developing countries ("Employment Effects"), Stewart took exception to the conventional wisdom that a rise in the wage rates in the modern sector of a developing nation would reduce employment opportunities because of factor substitution. This standing belief provided a rationale for keeping wages low as a country's economy matures, a proposition to which Stewart objected vehemently. Even assuming high elasticities of substitution for labor, she posited that under certain conditions a rise in the wage rate might increase total employment in a developing nation. This discovery led Stewart to champion an alternative theory of economic development, one in which the emphasis is placed on reducing the incidence of poverty and not merely keeping the level of wages constant, or actually decreasing in real terms.

In arguing against the growth of gross domestic product (GDP, formerly GNP) as the main target of development strategy, Stewart pointed to two factors that made increasing real GDP a less-than-optimal approach. First, many developing countries that have experienced rapid rates of growth of GDP "have also and simultaneously generated increasing amounts of unemployment and underemployment. The growth rate of employment in the modern sector has been much slower than the growth rate of GNP and much slower than the growth in numbers seeking modern sector jobs. Second, rapid growth in GNP has often been accompanied by a more unequal income distribution and increasing relative and, in some cases, absolute impoverishment of sections of the community" ("New Strategies," 381). In considering the best sequence of changes for promoting development, Stewart argued for reversing the usual approach of "grow first, redistribute later" to a policy of "redistribution with growth" (404).

Stewart consolidated her thinking about economic development in *Technology and Underdevelopment*, a book some consider her seminal contribution to the field. In this classic work, she asserted that the modern sectors of developing economies "have large imperfections which cause poor countries to be dependent on overpriced, and often inappropriate, technology from rich countries" (Rodgers and Colley, 1401). This dependency causes patterns of uneven growth, leading to the underutilization of human resources, which, in turn, creates more inequality in the distribution of incomes. To Stewart's way of thinking, the solutions to these interrelated problems lay in the use of machines and methods better suited to the needs of developing countries, the adoption of less-than-state-of-the-art technology in poor nations, and the encouragement of developing nations to adopt technological changes appropriate to their level of advancement. With respect to the latter, Stewart stressed the nature of the product mix of a developing country in guiding the selection of technology, and the importance of product characteristics in choosing the appropriate technology. "This research helped policy makers to better understand how appropriate technology policies, such as the promotion of labor-intensive production methods, could create more productive jobs and reduce the underutilization of workers in poor countries" (1401).

In subsequent research, Stewart extended the sophistication of her theory of economic progress described in *Technology and Underdevelopment* with the addition of two key variables: the international payments system ("Inequality"), and trade among southern economies ("Recent Theories"). With respect to the payments system, she noted that it played an important but not pivotal role in promoting income equality within developing nations. Stewart still emphasized the significance of technology as the major factor contributing to an improving income distribution, but she observed that any reform in the payments system would make the achievement of desirable outcomes in emerging countries easier and faster. "Southern" economies, for Stewart, are traditional underdeveloped nations whose very nature puts them at a disadvantage when trading with "northern," or developed, countries. Because of this natural disadvantage, she proposed a variety of policy initiatives that would encourage trade among and between southern economies as a way for these nations to capture more of the benefits of international trade than would otherwise be the case.

Stewart's approach to the process of economic development as expressed in her book *Planning to Meet Basic Needs* morphed into a cross between W. W. Rostow's five stages of economic growth and Abraham Maslow's hierarchy of needs. For Stewart, the basic-needs perspective "is one which gives priority to meeting the basic needs of *all* the people" (1). This means fulfilling certain standards of nutrition and universal provision of health and education services. Basic needs could also include certain material needs such as clothing and shelter, and even certain nonmaterial needs such as employment and political participation. She firmly believed that most developing countries could improve their basic-needs achievements markedly by simply changing their welfare-state style of government. Always the realist, Stewart observed that true development depends on a comprehensive appreciation of many interrelated factors: ". . . appropriate policies can only be devised if there is understanding of each level and of the interactions among levels and that serious policy mistakes have occurred as a result of rather simpleminded pursuits of humanitarian objectives, without analyzing the other aspects" ("Food Aid," 560).

BIBLIOGRAPHY

Works by Frances Julia Stewart

"Employment Effects of Wage Changes in Poor Countries" (with J. Weeks). In *Employment, Income Distribution, and Development,* edited by F. Stewart, 93–107. London: Frank Cass, 1975.

"New Strategies for Development: Poverty, Income Distribution, and Growth" (with P. Streeten). *Oxford Economic Papers* 28(3), November 1976: 381–405.

Technology and Underdevelopment. Boulder, CO: Westview Press, 1977.

"Inequality, Technology, and Payment Systems." In *Work, Income, and Inequality,* edited by F. Stewart, 1–31. London: Macmillan, 1983.

"Recent Theories of International Trade: Some Implications for the South." In *Monopolistic Competition and International Trade,* edited by H. Kierzkowski, 84–108. Oxford, England: Clarendon Press, 1984.

Planning to Meet Basic Needs. London: Macmillan, 1985.

"Food Aid during Conflict: Can One Reconcile Its Humanitarian, Economic, and Political Economy Effects?" *American Journal of Agricultural Economics* 80(3), August 1998: 560–65.

Works about Frances Julia Stewart

Rodgers, Y. V. D. M., and Colley, J. C. "Outstanding Female Economists in the Analysis and Practice of Development Economics." *World Development* 27(8), August 1998: 1397–1411.

"Stewart, Francis Julia." In *Who's Who in Economics,* edited by M. Blaug, 1066–67. Northampton, MA: Edward Elgar, 1999.

Diane C. Swonk
(1962–)

The chief economist and a senior vice president for the Bank One Corporation in Chicago, Diane Catherine Swonk is a darling of the media, better known to the nation's corporate elite than most Nobel laureates in economics, whose economic theories are developed in creative anonymity. Knowledgeable and articulate, Swonk is regularly quoted in the financial pages of the *Wall Street Journal,* the *New York Times,* the *Chicago Tribune,* and national news magazines such as *Business Week.* She has appeared on the major television news networks—CNN, CNBC, and PBS—speaking about her primary area of expertise, the trends of the U.S. economy with special emphasis on the economic growth and development of the Midwest. Married and the mother of two children, Swonk continually demonstrates the ability to perceive emerging trends long before others can see through the confusion and chaos that perpetually shroud everyday business. She is one of those rare economists whose views are eagerly sought by those who use economics as well as those who create it.

BIOGRAPHY

Diane Swonk was born in Kalamazoo, Michigan, on April 8, 1962. The only child in an educated, two-income family, Swonk learned the value of money at an early age. When she was four and a half years old, her father, James Swonk, took her to open her first bank account, and in so doing reflected and reinforced the family's belief in the values of saving, investing, and planning for the future. Swonk's father, an executive with General Motors, was a practical, strategic thinker, and her mother, Phyllis Swonk, an art teacher, was creative. Swonk credits these combined influences for shaping her as an economist with an inclination for creative mathematics. In 1984, she earned a B.A. with honors in economics at the University of Michigan. She continued her studies at Michigan on a merit fellowship, receiving in 1985 an M.A. in applied economics, also with honors, no small accomplishment for someone with a learning disability.

Swonk began her career in 1985 as an associate economist with the First Chicago Corporation, a large, staid Midwest bank. In 1987, she was promoted to regional economist and immediately proved her worth by forecasting an economic renaissance for the industrial Midwest, a region of the country once written off as the Rust Belt. She continued her education part-time while working full-time, earning an M.B.A., again with honors, in finance and strategic planning from the University of Chicago in 1989. In 1990, she married Arthur W. Murray III, a vice president and commercial lender for American National Bank in Chicago. It was her second marriage. Over the next few years, Swonk quickly moved up the ranks, becoming a staff officer, then an associate vice president, and eventually senior regional economist and vice president in 1991. Two years later, she added the title editor, for in addition to designing and running the bank's regional economic model, she assumed editorial supervision of the bank's economic publications. By this time, Swonk had forged a national reputation as one of the country's leading regional economists (Stangenes).

In 1995, she became deputy chief economist/vice president, and in 1996, when the First National Bank of Chicago reorganized and changed their name to First Chicago NBD, Swonk was elevated to deputy chief economist and first vice president. In 1998, the bank merged with Bank One of Columbus, Ohio, and the new organization, Bank One Corporation, established its headquarters in Chicago. As with many financial mergers, redundancies of upper-level managers led to the early retirement of some senior staffers and the separation of others. Swonk was such a valuable asset to the new bank that she was effectively insulated from these personnel shifts.

At the time of its formation, Bank One Corporation was the nation's fifth-largest bank holding company, with assets of more than $250 billion. Besides offering a full range of financial services to commercial and business customers and consumers, the bank was the world's largest issuer of Visa credit cards, the third-largest bank lender to small businesses, among the top twenty-five managers of mutual funds, and a leading national provider of automobile loans. In 1998, Swonk became the bank's deputy chief economist and senior vice president, and one year later she was promoted to the post of chief economist/senior vice president. In that capacity, Swonk heads the bank's Corporate Economic Group and serves as the bank's principal spokesperson on economic issues.

In addition to her work in banking, Swonk has developed a parallel career in civic and professional activities. In 1995, the mayor of Chicago named her to the Workforce Board, a special board to direct approximately $40 million in human resource training-and-development funds. She has been a long-time member of the National Association of Business Economists (NABE), a 3,000-plus member organization for people who use economics in their work. After having held a number of leadership positions in that organization, she was elected president of NABE for the 1999–2000 business year. At the age of thirty-seven, Swonk became the youngest person to hold the position that other luminaries, including Alan Greenspan, chair of the Board of Governors of the Federal Reserve, once occupied. Besides the presidency of NABE, she has also been honored as a "Top 40 Executive under 40" by *Crain's Chicago Business* (1993), voted "A Baby Boomer to Keep an Eye on in Chicago" by the *Chicago Sun-Times* (1993), and named a "Star Forecaster" by the *Wall Street Journal* (1999).

CONTRIBUTIONS

In the early 1980s, the Midwest was the scene of soaring unemployment and rapid downsizing, rightsizing, and capsizing in the industrial sector. Heavy industry from automobiles to steel was under siege. Economists virtually stopped reporting the region's economic statistics because the numbers were so bad. In 1985, James Annable, the chief economist at First National Bank of Chicago, completed a forecasting model that projected a set of industrial winners and losers for the whole nation. His preliminary results indicated that heavy industry—the very core of the Rust Belt's economy—was likely to make a strong comeback. With a large presence in the Midwest, First Chicago would be well positioned to benefit from this anticipated turnaround. Believing there was something to be gained at the bank from pursuing a Midwest strategy, Annable set out to convince senior management of the wisdom in his thinking. This was no small task in an organization more interested in mimicking the success of its counterparts on the coasts than in leveraging a regional advantage ("The Business Economist").

To move this agenda forward, the position of regional economist was created to shape the bank's policies regarding the Midwest economy. Annable filled it with an incredibly young, bright, yet untested economist from the University of Michigan. In her first professional job after graduation, Swonk, that freshly minted economist, was given a dual assignment: create an accurate and honest regional economic model with a forecast that validated Annable's hunch and, in the process, become the best-known regional economist in the country. The second task was in some ways more important than the first, as a regional banking strategy would be viable only if a well-regarded regional economist were making the case for it.

In 1986, Swonk completed the initial stages of the analysis that gave credibility to the hypothesis that the Midwest was poised for an economic rebound of unprecedented proportions. She also linked the regional model to the bank's model on the national economic outlook—an important connection, for it made the leap from national planning to regional planning all the more rational. The regional predictions thus became an offshoot of, but nonetheless integral with, the bank's national forecasts. By the late 1980s, the bank's regional model was fully integrated into its macroeconomic forecasting, and the resulting economic predictions were proving both accurate and robust. Swonk continually updated the model ("Regional Winners," "Regional Winners . . . Revisited," "The Economic Outlook"), and its reliability and validity were repeatedly demonstrated, making the Swonk model one of the most respected macroeconomic forecasting instruments of the 1990s.

By the early 1990s, Swonk had established a reputation as one of the foremost regional economic forecasters in the country. By the end of the decade, she was widely regarded as one of the premier forecasters of the U.S. economy. She made the transition from regional celebrity to national phenomenon by correctly predicting that the economic expansion of the mid-1990s would not only continue but accelerate. Swonk did so at a time when other forecasters seemed convinced that the Asian economic collapse of 1998 would slow U.S. growth, if not reverse it. Swonk perceived, quite rightly, that the economic slowdown in Japan, Korea, Malaysia, and Indonesia—the so-called Asian contagion—would actually fuel the already robust growth taking place in the West, particularly in the United States.

Swonk based her prognosis on her personal forecasting mantra, "It just doesn't pay to bet against the American consumer." She predicted that the worldwide decline in interest rates associated with the Asian downturn would put billions of dollars of disposable income in the hands of U.S. consumers eager to refinance mortgages. The resulting surge in consumer spending would fuel U.S. economic growth, propelling the expansion of the mid-1990s into the longest continuous period of prosperity in the country's history. Where others saw doom and gloom, Swonk saw genesis and light. The accuracy of her vision and her courage in articulating those views at a time when seasoned forecasting veterans were predicting stagnation or possibly worse made Swonk a superstar among the nation's economic prophets.

On September 11, 2001, Swonk was in a hotel near the World Trade Center participating at a professional conference. The experience transformed Swonk. From that date forward, as is evident in her book *The Passionate Economist: Finding the Power and Humanity behind the Numbers*, she became more concerned with economics as a behavioral science built on the foundation of human activity and less concerned with the numeracy of economics. For Swonk, economics is as much social policy as it is financial policy. To her, more than merely moving and counting currency, economics is a global force with the power to remake the world.

BIBLIOGRAPHY

Works by Diane C. Swonk

"Regional Winners and Losers." *Economic Issue Backgrounder*. Chicago, IL: First National Bank of Chicago, May 1990.

"The Business Economist at Work: Marketing a Specialty." *Business Economics* 30(2), April 1995: 61–65.

"Regional Winners and Losers Revisited." *Economic Issue Backgrounder*. Chicago, IL: First Chicago NBD Corporation, February 1996.

"The Economic Outlook and Undercurrents in the Consumer Credit Market" (with E. K. Fossett and G. Mount). *Economic Issue Backgrounder*. Chicago, IL: First Chicago NBD Corporation, August 1997.

The Passionate Economist: Finding the Power and Humanity behind the Numbers. New York: John Wiley & Sons, 2003.

Works about Diane C. Swonk

Martin, P., "Watching Those Cross Currents: An Interview with Diane Swonk." *Journal of Lending and Credit Risk Management* 82(2), October 1999: 8–16.

Stangenes, S. "A Voice of Growth." *Chicago Tribune,* December 18, 1994: section 7.

Nancy Hays Teeters
(1930–   )

The Federal Reserve System was established in December 1913, and for the next sixty-five years, its seven-member Board of Governors regulated the nation's banking and credit without once soliciting the input of a woman. Then, in August 1978, President Jimmy Carter announced the appointment of Nancy Hays Teeters to the board, and another glass ceiling was broken. Teeters's appointment to the Federal Reserve was something of a homecoming; she had worked as a staff economist there from 1957 to 1966. Prior to being named a Fed governor, Teeters had served as assistant staff director and chief economist for the U.S. House of Representatives Budget Committee for four years. When she assumed her position as the first woman governor of the Fed, Teeters brought with her impeccable credentials as an economist and policy maker, and the experiences she had acquired during more than twenty years of government service.

BIOGRAPHY

Nancy Teeters was born on July 29, 1930, in Marion, Indiana, the daughter of S. Edgar Hays and Mabel Drake Hays. In 1952, she earned her B.A. degree from Oberlin College, where she received the Comfort Starr Award in economics. She married Robert D. Teeters, also an Oberlin graduate, in 1952, and together they went to graduate school at the University of Michigan. At Michigan, Teeters earned her M.A. in economics in 1954, then did additional graduate studies while working as a teaching fellow from 1954 to 1955 and again from 1956 to 1957. During the 1955–56 academic year, Teeters was an instructor at the University of Maryland's overseas division in Stuttgart, Germany.

As an undergraduate, Teeters had her first exposure to life in the nation's capital as part of Oberlin's semester in Washington, D.C., program. Teeters found the experience so exciting and interesting that she and her husband secured employment in Washington in 1957—Robert with the Bureau of the Budget (now the Office of Management and Budget), and Nancy as a staff economist at the Federal Reserve. At the Fed, Teeters worked in the government finance section, which keeps track of federal fiscal (spending) policies and manages government indebtedness and the Treasury cash balance.

In 1962, the Federal Reserve Board loaned Teeters to the president's Council of Economic Advisers as a staff economist for one year. She returned to the Fed and continued there until 1966, when she moved to the Bureau of the Budget to work with Charles L. Schultze, who would go on to become chair of the Council of Economic Advisers under President Carter. She served as a fiscal economist at the bureau during the last years of the Johnson administration and the first year of the Nixon administration. In 1970, Teeters became a senior fellow at the Brookings Institution in Washington, D.C., a liberal think tank. There she teamed with Schultze, Edward Fried, and **Alice M. Rivlin** to coauthor a series of annual analyses of the federal budget called "Setting National Priorities." After three years at the Brookings Institution, Teeters became a senior specialist with the Congressional Research Service, Library of Congress, where she worked directly with members of Congress and other policy makers.

In the July 15, 1974, issue of *Time,* the magazine singled out Teeters as one of 200 "rising leaders" of the United States. *Time* characterized Teeters as "one of Washington's most knowledgeable people on the federal budget, government programs, and the impact of federal spending and taxing on the economy." Others chosen with Teeters as future leaders of the country included Gloria Steinem, one of the principal architects of the women's movement in the United States; Dan Rather, who succeeded Walter Cronkite as CBS-TV's evening news anchor; Herbert Stein, who became chair of the Council of Economic Advisers under Presidents Richard Nixon and Gerald Ford; and James Thompson Jr., who was governor of Illinois in the 1980s.

The future that the editors of *Time* predicted for Teeters became reality sooner than expected. In December 1974, Teeters was selected to be chief economist of the House of Representatives' Committee on the Budget, a position she held until September 1978. In August, President Carter nominated her to serve on the Federal Reserve Board of Governors, and on September 18, 1978, she became its first woman governor. Her appointment was largely a recognition of her experience and expertise, but it also helped that she had friends in high places.

During her twenty years in the nation's capital working at a variety of federal jobs, Teeters had developed so many relationships and acquaintances that it was said she would never run out of friends in Washington. Senator Paul Sarbanes, a Democrat who was a member of the Senate Banking Committee that confirmed Teeters, had worked with her on the Council of Economic Advisers back in 1962. On the Republican side, Senator Richard Lugar, another Banking Committee member, was Teeters's cousin. With the approval of the U.S. Senate, Teeters—the widely respected expert on the federal budget and the mother of three children—had earned a position on one of the most influential and important economic policy-making bodies in the Western world.

Teeters began her service on the board when G. William Miller was chair and continued as a governor when Miller left the Fed to become Treasury Secretary. Paul Volker succeeded Miller as chair in August 1979. For the rest of her term on the Fed's Board of Governors, Teeters served with the strong-willed Volker. On July 1, 1984, she left the Fed to become director of economics at IBM. In March 1986, she was promoted to vice president and chief economist. In that capacity, she supervised the preparation of economic forecasts for the United States and the foreign countries in which IBM operated. The economics department she headed at IBM maintained its own econometric model of the United States, with particular emphasis on the demand of all producers for durable equipment, that is, machines, tools, and plants. Her department was also responsible for preparing microeconomic models of the demand for office equipment and computer products.

During her long and distinguished career, Teeters received honorary doctorates from Oberlin College, Bates College, the University of Michigan, and Mount Holyoke College. In 1980, she was given the Distinguished Alumni Award (Economics) by the University of Michigan. She served as vice president (1973–74), president (1974–75), chair of the board (1975–76), and governor of the National Economists Club; and from 1975 to 1978 she was a member of the AEA's Committee on the Status of Women in the Economics Profession. In 1990, Teeters retired from IBM.

CONTRIBUTIONS

When asked once if she was philosophically linked to the Keynesian–interventionist–big government camp that dominated government thinking in the 1960s, Teeters replied, "I consider myself an eclectic, and strictly middle of the road. I am for what *works*, even if it's ideologically impure" ("Thoughtful Answers," 98). Given her broad and varied experiences in the federal government, shouldering responsibilities that required her to work with politicians of every stripe, Teeters had staked out a position as a middle-of-the-road liberal long before she got to the Fed's Board of Governors. This was evident in the mid-1970s, when she coauthored the Brookings Institution's annual counterbudget publication.

> There are two principal means by which the federal government could try to influence the behavior of individuals and institutions: by regulation, and by changing the incentives that individuals and institutions face. Explicit federal attempts to influence behavior through incentives are relatively new. The more traditional approach has been to change behavior by regulation. Projects or individuals receiving federal aid are required to have specified characteristics or to meet certain detailed standards. In some instances certain kinds of behavior are simply declared illegal. The regulatory approach, however, has often proved inefficient and ineffective, necessitating constant tightening of the rules or frequent administrative decisions about exceptions necessary to

meet local conditions. Hence, in many areas it would be preferable to de-emphasize the regulatory approach in favor of creating incentives for desirable behavior. (*Setting*, 458)

Teeters then applied her reasoning to three areas—pollution control, ensuring that welfare recipients who can work do so, and controlling medical costs and quality—recommending policy approaches that combined regulation and incentives to achieve desired outcomes and influence behavior. Clearly, she anticipated by twenty years the policy approach of President Bill Clinton and the New Democrats.

When she went to the Fed's board to fill the seat vacated by Arthur Burns, Teeters brought her pragmatic liberalism with her. Her service on the board began when the United States was experiencing one of the most inflationary periods in its history. The cartel of oil-producing nations, the Organization of Petroleum Exporting Countries (OPEC), had caused the price of oil to roughly quadruple in 1973–74 with an embargo aimed at the United States, western Europe, and Japan. In 1978–79, OPEC again restricted oil outputs, causing prices to more than double. The "oil shock," as economists dubbed it, increased the price of virtually every product Americans bought and sold. Long lines at gas stations made people angry, and rising gasoline prices fueled that animosity. The consumer price index had risen at an annual rate of nearly 11 percent in the first three months of 1979. Not since the elimination of price controls at the end of World War II had the country experienced double-digit inflation.

The public was demanding action, and President Carter responded by appointing Paul Volker to replace G. William Miller as chair of the Fed's Board of Governors. When Volcker took over in August 1979, inflation was hovering around 14 percent. His job was to bring inflation under control, and that meant convincing the financial community that the Fed would restrain the growth of money and credit for as long and as much as necessary to achieve this objective. As a governor of the Fed, Teeters was concerned about inflation, but she was also worried about the trade-off between inflation and unemployment. She understood the need for higher interest rates to cool the economy and slow inflation. She was also aware of the damage higher rates could do to the economy by destroying jobs, especially in the automobile and housing industries, which had been historically sensitive to interest-rate changes. As the hawks on the Board of Governors—those who believed the Fed had to raise interest rates rapidly to check inflation—pushed the federal funds rate to nearly 20 percent, Teeters, a monetary dove more concerned about the consequences of unemployment than the costs of inflation, repeatedly voted against the majority.

Teeters's thinking was obviously out of step with the prevailing monetarist view. She believed that a more gradual approach to raising interest rates, while taking longer to slow the economy, would cause less social disruption and still be effective. From her liberal perspective, she viewed the increase in interest rates as too much, too soon. She considered the recession of 1981–82 too high a price to pay to bring inflation under control. Even with the return of prosperity in 1983, the board, in Teeters's judgment, was still preoccupied with inflation and continued to limit the growth of the money supply when there was no need to. Always leery of tight monetary policy, Teeters continued to argue against what she perceived as the Fed's tight rein until the end of her term of office in June 1984.

BIBLIOGRAPHY

Works by Nancy Hays Teeters

Setting National Priorities: The 1973 Budget (with C. L. Schultze, E. R. Fried, and A. M. Rivlin). Washington, DC: Brookings Institution, 1972. Teeters also coauthored the 1974 and 1972 versions of this book.

Works about Nancy Hays Teeters

Cicarelli, J. "Nancy Hays Teeters" In *Biographical Dictionary of the Board of Governors of the Federal Reserve,* edited by B. S. Katz, 317–21. Westport, CT: Greenwood Press, 1992.

Greider, W. *Secrets of the Temple: How the Federal Reserve Runs the Country.* New York: Simon & Schuster, 1987.

"Lady Governor." *Bankers,* March 1979: 61–62.

"Natural for a Liaison Role at the Fed." *Business Week,* September 25, 1978: 46.

"Special Section: 200 Rising Leaders." *Time,* July 15, 1974.

"Thoughtful Answers from New Fed Governor." *ABA Banking Journal,* May 1979: 96–102.

Mabel F. Timlin
(1891–1976)

In the field of economics, Mabel F. Timlin may very well be the ultimate late bloomer. She was thirty-seven years old when she earned her B.A. degree, forty-eight years old when she received her Ph.D., and fifty years old when her first and most important work was published. She received her first regular academic appointment—instructor of economics—at forty-three and retired just twenty-three years later, at sixty-seven. Yet her late start and brief career did not prevent Timlin from becoming one of Canada's foremost economists and, in 1950, Canada's first tenured woman economist.

BIOGRAPHY

Mabel Frances Timlin was born on December 6, 1891, in Forest Junction, Wisconsin, one of four children of Edward Timlin and Sarah (Halloran) Timlin. "Although the family was poor, they were a 'two-newspaper-a-day' family and the children were well read. Apparently she developed an early interest in economics and could say 'free trade' and 'free silver' before she could say 'Mama' and 'Papa' " (Ainley, 29). Timlin attended school in Wisconsin Rapids and Port Edwards, Wisconsin, and from 1910 to 1912 she trained as a teacher at the Milwaukee State Normal School. Timlin taught elementary school until 1916, when, "After her parents' death . . . , she answered an ad for teachers in rural Saskatchewan and moved to Canada as a landed immigrant" (29).

She taught school in Bounty and Wilkie, Saskatchewan, before moving in 1918 to Saskatoon to study at the Saskatoon Business College (SBC). While enrolled at SBC, Timlin taught English and other subjects in night school. After three months of study at SBC, she began teaching shorthand and typing at the college. In 1921, she became a secretary in the Department of Agricultural Extension at the University of Saskatchewan, where she was employed in a variety of capacities until her retirement in 1959 (Ainley, 30).

While Timlin worked as a department secretary for nine years, she completed the requirements for a bachelor's degree by taking one course at a time. "At first she intended to take the honours degree in economics, a subject which had caught her imagination at an early age. . . . However, the courses given by the Economics Department disappointed her; after taking a fourth course she turned to the more agreeable offerings of the English Department" (Spafford, 279). Through systematic reading on her own, Timlin clearly learned as much if not more economics than she would have absorbed in formal classes.

From 1929 to 1942, she was director of the University of Saskatchewan's program of correspondence courses. During this period, she also served as a reader in economics, a position that included reading papers or other assignments, including extramural papers written especially for economics correspondence courses. In 1932, Timlin resumed her formal education, enrolling in the Ph.D. program at the University of Washington in Seattle. "She did most of her graduate work during the summer months, though she spent the winter term in 1934, as well as the 1939–40 academic year, at the University of Washington" (Ainley, 30). Timlin completed her dissertation, "Keynesian Economics: A Synthesis" in 1940 and earned her Ph.D. The next two summers were spent revising her dissertation for publication in 1942. Her book *Keynesian Economics* "was well received, though not necessarily understood, by her contemporaries" (30). After completing her Ph.D. course work in 1935, Timlin held the position of instructor of economics. With her doctorate in hand, she was appointed an assistant professor in 1941 and was subsequently made an associate professor (1946) and then full professor and the first tenured woman Canadian economist in 1950 (Dimand, 425).

Once Timlin became a full-fledged academic, she served on a number of economics and/or higher education associations. She was a member of the executive committee of the Canadian Political Science Association (which at the time included economists) from 1941 to 1943 and later served as the vice president (1953–55) and president (1959–60) of the association. She was elected to the executive committee of the AEA for the term 1958–60, one of very few Canadian economists so honored.

With her fame as a scholar and teacher came a steady stream of awards and recognition for Timlin. She received a Guggenheim Fellowship in 1945–46 and a Canada Council Special Senior Fellowship in 1959–60. She was elected to the Royal Society of Canada in 1951 and served as a consultant to the Federal Commission on Prices in 1950–51 and the Royal Commission for Saskatchewan River Development in 1952. In 1967, she was awarded Canada's Centennial Medal; in 1969, the University of Saskatchewan conferred on her an honorary doctorate; and in 1976, she was named to the Order of Canada. Timlin retired from the University of Saskatchewan in 1959 at age sixty-seven. She died on September 19, 1976, in Saskatoon.

CONTRIBUTIONS

Keynesian Economics was easily ten times more significant than any other work that Timlin published. It established her reputation as one of the foremost Canadian economists of the twentieth century. The title suggests that the book is a guide to John Maynard Keynes's classic *General Theory of Employment, Interest, and Money* (1936). But, as Lorie Tarshis wrote in the foreword to the reprint edition of *Keynesian Economics*, "the book is not at all a Guide to Keynes. It is incomplete, rather quirky and in many places, a student would find *The General Theory* far easier to read than the Timlin volume itself" (xii). As Timlin wrote, the purpose of the book was "to explore the system of economic analysis set out" in the *General Theory* with the intention of discovering "first its internal consistency and second its application to the world we know" (1).

Timlin introduced many refinements to the Keynesian system, and three of the most salient were the nature of expectations, the determinants of aggregate consumption, and the idea of multiple equilibrium. Keynes's analysis zeroed in on the formation and impact of short-term expectations on economic behavior. While appreciating his contribution, Timlin sought to expand the nature of expectations to the long term, suggesting that the formation and impact of long-term expectations would alter the Keynesian system in ways Keynes had not considered nor anticipated (*Keynesian Economics*, 26–37). Keynes built his consumption function on his famous psychological propensity, which Timlin readily accepted as a powerful explanation of current consumption spending. She, however, argued for a more complex and thus realistic consumption function, one that recognized other determinants such as the interest rate, windfall gains and losses, and distribution of income effects (102–8). Timlin thus anticipated James Dusenberry, Milton Friedman, and other economists who would propose alternative consumption functions in the late 1940s and the 1950s.

> Finally, Keynesian theory was couched in terms of a static equilibrium. Timlin investigated the idea of shifting or dynamic equilibrium (170–80). From her critique of Keynes's *General Theory*, Timlin drew five basic inferences: The first is that the structure of the interest-rate complex may be just as important in establishing and maintaining an equilibrium level of employment as the average level of interest-rates. The second is that very low rates of interest as well as very high rates may be damaging to the level of economic activity. The third is that lack of foresight and the variable nature of human psychology and expectations may keep an imperfectly monetized economic system running from low levels of employment to levels more or less high with no inherent tendency to reach the combination of values which gives a stable equilibrium. The fourth is that business cycles may occur even though the quantity of money is a datum because of transfers of money between active and inactive balances. The fifth and last is that the nature of a monetary economy is such that unemployment may be chronic. (*Keynesian Economics*, 181)

All of this led Timlin to conclude that effective interventionist policies would require a three-pronged approach: changing the quantity of money to manipulate the interest-rate complex; programs to stabilize expectations; and an institutional framework that shapes aggregate functions such as consumption so that the economy operates close to those ends the community deems good and appropriate (*Keynesian Economics*, 182).

Four years after *Keynesian Economics* appeared, Timlin published what could arguably be classified as her most innovative work, "General Equilibrium Analysis and Public Policy." The intent of the paper was "to conduct an inquiry into the relations between general equilibrium analysis and public policy by the indirect method of examining the place of such analysis in the solution of a definite economic problem" (483). The problem Timlin selected was the possibility of increasing wages without raising prices. "Traditional partial equilibrium theory made the solution of this problem a fairly simple one, but modern general equilibrium considerations, dynamic qualifications on these, and institutional changes in the organization of business and labour have opened up such areas of indeterminateness in the formation of prices that we may no longer trust the answers given by the simpler generalizations" (483).

Being familiar with the work of Michal Kalecki, Timlin realized that microeconomic conditions could impact on macroeconomic outcomes. Specifically, the degree of monopoly in an economy could alter the outcome of general equilibrium, which, in turn, might under certain conditions alter the effects of Keynesian macroeconomic policies:

> . . . we may find lags in investment by an oligopoly and in an economy characterized by oligopoly which would not apply in a more competitive industry or economy. In the first place, if the attempt to increase the liquidity of enterprises is already an adverse cyclical factor in recessions, a necessity for going outside the business for the investment of business savings can interpose an additional step between saving and investment and aggravate any existing tendency to substitute hoarding for investment or replacement by individual firms in periods of falling activity. In the second place, since the oligopolist may be more likely to use saved sums to buy shares leading to control of already established firms either within the oligopoly or perhaps in other and even unrelated lines of production as a substitute for direct investment, there may be lags for these reasons which will have dynamic effects upon the rate at which business savings find their way back to the market again as income. In the third place, if oligopoly is a dominant form of business organization in an economic community, the avenues of possible investment outside the oligopoly in question are narrowed by that fact, since there will almost certainly be punitive action if one oligopoly attempts to break into the investment territory of another. For this third reason, a trend toward oligopoly in an economy may therefore be accompanied for dynamic reasons as well as for general equilibrium reasons by a secular decline in the levels of net investment attached to given levels of consumption under given states of expectation. ("General Equilibrium Analysis," 492)

Timlin's thoughts on dynamic equilibrium clearly predate **Joan Robinson**'s thinking on the subject as reflected in Robinson's *Accumulation of Capital* (1956). The roots of the post-Keynesian movement have always been traced to Kalecki and Robinson, but one could argue that Timlin should also be considered a source. Regrettably, her 1946 article did not generate any perceptible reaction in the discipline, and Timlin did not follow up on her breakthrough, choosing instead to pursue other areas of economics to research.

For the remainder of her publishing career, Timlin divided her research interests between two topics: Canadian monetary policy, and immigration policy as it pertains to Canada. In the 1950s, she published several papers ("Recent Developments"; "Monetary Stabilization") about post–World War II Canadian stabilization policies. These efforts were descriptive and historical in nature and defended as much as explained the whys and wherefores of Canadian monetary policy.

By contrast, her papers on immigration policy ("Economic Theory"; "Canada's Immigration Policy") were clearly more important and attracted considerably more attention, especially in Canada, than her monetary stabilization articles. Timlin's greatest legacy, however, may have been her teaching and the effect it had on her students, one of whom paid her a tribute as great as any formal recognition she ever received from the economics community: "As a teacher she regarded it as her mission to seek out the brightest students and win from them a commitment to making a vocation of the teaching or application of economics. Her standards were exacting; those who showed they could measure up were treated henceforth, in spite of whatever diffidence they themselves might have felt about their powers, as junior members of the profession, already launched upon a career. The progress of those who went on was watched with close attention. Nor was the teacher forgotten: the Christmas mail brought dozens of letters from former students who addressed her, as all who knew her did (except her undergraduates, who dared not) as 'Timmie' " (Spafford, 280).

BIBLIOGRAPHY

Works by Mabel F. Timlin

Keynesian Economics. Toronto: University of Toronto Press: 1942. Reprint with a biographical note by A. E. Safarian and an introduction by L. Tarshis, Toronto: McClelland and Stewart, Carleton Library no. 107: 1977.

"General Equilibrium Analysis and Public Policy." *Canadian Journal of Economics and Political Science* 12(4), November 1946: 483–95.

"Economic Theory and Immigration Policy." *Canadian Journal of Economics and Political Science* 16(3), August 1950: 375–82.

"Recent Developments in Canadian Monetary Policy." *American Economic Review* 43(2), May 1953: 42–53.

"Monetary Stabilization Policies and Keynesian Theory." In *Post-Keynesian Economics,* edited by K. K. Kurihara, 59–88. London: George Allen and Unwin, 1955.

"Canada's Immigration Policy, 1896–1910." *Canadian Journal of Economics and Political Science* 26(40), November 1960: 517–32.

Works about Mabel F. Timlin

Ainley, M. G. "Mabel F. Timlin, 1891–1976: A Woman Economist in the World of Men." *Atlantis* 213(2), Spring/Summer 1999: 28–38.

Dimand, R. W. "Mabel Frances Timlin (1891–1976)." In *A Biographical Dictionary of Women Economists,* edited by R. W. Dimand, M. A. Dimand, and E. L. Forget, 423–26. Northampton, MA: Edward Elgar, 2000.

Spafford, D. "In Memoriam: Mabel F. Timlin." *Canadian Journal of Economics* 10, May 1977: 279–81.

Marjorie S. Turner
(1921–   )

· ·

A practicing humanist, an ardent institutionalist, and a lapsed Methodist, Marjorie Shepherd Turner has made a career of being a rebel with a cause. As a graduate student in the mid-1940s, she struggled through the whole of John Maynard Keynes's *General Theory of Employment, Interest, and Money.* The experience made her a liberal Keynesian who found much to admire in the lives and works of **Joan Robinson** and Nicholas Kaldor, two of Keynes's most important and prolific disciples. Turner's classic biographies of these two intellectual giants have established her as a major survivor of what is rapidly becoming an academically endangered species: liberal economists.

BIOGRAPHY

Marjorie Shepherd Turner was born on December 12, 1921, in Beaumont, Texas, one of three daughters in the family of Albert Edward Shepherd, an entrepreneur, and Mabel (Winne) Shepherd, a pianist and seamstress. Turner graduated with high honors in 1943 from the University of Texas at Austin, where she was elected to Phi Beta Kappa. She earned her M.A. at the University of Texas in 1945. She was married, then divorced, leaving her as a single parent raising one son while a graduate student at UT-Austin through the early 1950s. Her master's thesis—"Forerunners of John Maynard Keynes's *General Theory of Employment*"—reflected her early interest in and passion for Keynesian economics. In 1952, she became an instructor of economics at the University of Arizona in Tucson. In 1954, Turner received her Ph.D. from the University of Texas and became an associate dean at San Diego State University. From 1956 through 1976, she was a member of the economics faculty at San Diego State, serving as department head from 1967 to 1969 and as director of the Institute of Labor Economics from 1970 to 1974. Turner retired from the university in 1976 as professor emerita.

In 1961, Turner married Merle Brandt Turner, a psychology professor at San Diego State. Two years later, Turner and her husband took sabbaticals at Cambridge University in England. She attended lectures by Joan Robinson, Nicholas Kaldor, and R. F. Kahn—"Cambridge UK Keynesians"—who were engaged in heated exchanges in person and in professional journals with Americans Robert M. Solow, Kenneth J. Arrow, and Paul Samuelson—"Cambridge USA Keynesians." Being privy to these exchanges lead Turner to publish two scholarly articles related to the debate between the two Cambridges—"Wages in the Cambridge Theory of Distribution" and "A Comparison of Some Aspects of the Cambridge Theory of Wages and Marginal Productivity Theory."

After returning from her sabbatical in England, Turner went back to classroom teaching and did not have it in mind to write about Joan Robinson or Nicholas Kaldor. In 1974, her husband retired from teaching and Turner took another sabbatical. The Turners bought a cruising sailboat and took a retirement voyage to New Zealand, staying in the South Seas for two and a half years (Personal correspondence). When they returned in 1976, Marjorie formally retired and she and her husband took up residence in the Oregon Cascades. There, between sailing trips, Turner read Robinson's complete works as a prelude to writing *Joan Robinson and the Americans.* That book appeared in 1989. Four years later, her biography of Nicholas Kaldor was published (*Nicholas Kaldor and the Real World*). In the years since, Turner has continued sailing various bodies of water from the Great Lakes to the Gulf of Mexico, always returning to her home in Oregon. She has also continued her writings, which include an unpublished novel on the South Pacific and a book chapter, "Joan Robinson: Why Not a Nobel Laureate?" in **Ingrid H. Rima**'s *Joan Robinson Legacy* (1991).

CONTRIBUTIONS

Most of Turner's early publications were in the field of labor relations. She followed her doctoral dissertation—"The Industrial Pattern of Mexican-American Employment in Nueces County, Texas"—with a series of articles, monographs, and books that dealt with various aspects of labor economics. These works included *Women and Work* and *Prices, Production, and Profit: How Much Is Enough?* and several publications under the imprint of the San Diego State University Institute of Labor Economics. Even the two articles she published after her 1963 sabbatical at Cambridge University were extensions of her focus on labor and related issues as seen through the lens of the history of economic thought. It was not until Turner was in her mid-fifties and retired from full-time teaching that she began to work on the scholarship that would ultimately become her major contributions to the field of economics.

When in 1974 she decided to write an intellectual biography of Robinson, Turner had selected as her subject one of the most complex figures ever to grace the stage of Western economics.

> Joan Robinson the economist is inseparable from the complex person that she was. A strong woman, who as a teacher could make her men students

cry themselves to sleep in despair, who as a colleague could cause some of the world's leading economists to tremble with rage, she was never a feminist. An admirer and critic of Marx, she was never a Marxist. She approved of the communist social experiments, particularly those in China and North Korea, but was not a communist. She expressed deep sympathy for the working class, but she was sometimes a critic of the Labour Party. She was a tender mother and grandmother, and a devoted and popular teacher. She never yielded a point until she could see it plainly. Joan Robinson's family background, her education in economics at Cambridge, and the changing times through which she lived were important factors in molding her views and personality. (*Joan Robinson*, 9)

Reading all of Robinson's published works was not enough to give Turner a holistic sense of the person and the economist whose biography she was committed to write. For that, she interviewed many of Robinson's friends and professional colleagues, including Austin Robinson (Joan's husband), Phyliss Maurice, Ruth Cohen, Frida Knight, Frank and Dorothy Hahn, Sukhamoy Chakravarty, and Geoffrey C. Harcount, the economist designated to write an official biography of Robinson but who, as of this date, has not completed that project. To give her book an added perspective, Turner also interviewed many of the American economists with whom Robinson had crossed swords, among them Nobel laureates Samuelson and Solow. Additionally, Turner sought the insights of John Kenneth Galbraith and Juliet Schor, two of Robinson's American friends, as well as the input of the post-Keynesian economists Paul Davidson and Alfred S. Eichner. These and other individuals shared with Turner their anecdotes about Robinson as well as their personal and professional correspondence with her. Turner supplemented all of this information with what she could glean from Robinson's personal papers stored in the King's College archives (*Joan Robinson*, xiv).

Turner's *Joan Robinson and the Americans* begins with the most detailed history of Robinson's family background and early years available in print. Robinson's first important work—*The Economics of Imperfect Competition*—and the controversy that the book sparked with the American economist Edward H. Chamberlain are examined next. The conversion of Robinson to Keynesian economics is then discussed, with a special emphasis on the influence of Michal Kalecki had on her thinking. Turner reviews Robinson's relationship to Marxist thought and how she set about to generalize Keynes's *General Theory* in *The Accumulation of Capital*. The "war between the Cambridges" and the whole reswitching controversy are examined clearly, thoroughly, and thoughtfully. Robinson's relationships with liberal American economists such as Galbraith and her impact on the creation and development of the post-Keynesian movement are treated with equal compassion.

Turner summarizes Robinson's activities in the 1960s and 1970s, focusing as always on Robinson's intellectual accomplishments and professional development and not her personal life per se. Turner takes this approach throughout the book with good reason. As Joan Robinson herself noted, "I don't think that I am at all a suitable subject for a biography as the outward flow of my life has been quite conventional and uninteresting" (*Joan Robinson*, xiii). The book concludes with a reflective chapter on the meaning of Robinson's intellectual life and its place in the story of economics. As a special feature, the book has a dozen or so photographs of Robinson at various stages of her life, as well as pictures of some of the American economists she befriended and those with whom she had heated exchanges.

In the intellectual biography *Nicholas Kaldor and the Real World*, Turner's task was both easier and more complex. Easier, in that she could extract from A. P. Thirlwall's biography *Nicholas Kaldor* (1987) the basic facts of Kaldor's life and thus was not required to expend as much time as she had needed to develop the personal history of Robinson. More complex, in that Kaldor's body of works included few books, and none of them were singularly seminal in nature. Rather, his scholarly outcome consisted of papers and presentations "scattered to the winds—in economic journals, newspapers, and addresses" (*Nicholas Kaldor and the Real World*, 4).

Also complicating matters was Kaldor's inclination to apply economic theory to real-world problems in the form of prescriptive policies designed to produce predictable and desirable outcomes. Despite the obstacles, Turner produced a highly readable biography that captured the essence of a master economist, from Kaldor's transformation to a Keynesian from a laissez-faire economist to his wish that economists "give up their comfortable views on equilibrium economics" (*Nicholas Kaldor and the Real World*, 4). Like the Robinson biography, Turner's *Kaldor* contains several poignant photographs, of Kaldor and some of his family members and academic peers, as well as an extensive bibliography.

BIBLIOGRAPHY

Works by Marjorie S. Turner

Women and Work. Los Angeles: University of California, Institute of Industrial Relations, 1964.

"Wages in the Cambridge Theory of Distribution." *Industrial Labor Relations Review* 29(3), April 1966: 390–401.

"A Comparison of Some Aspects of the Cambridge Theory of Wages and Marginal Productivity Theory." *Journal of Economic Issues* 1(3), September 1967: 189–98.

Prices, Production, and Profit: How Much Is Enough? (with J. W. Leasure). Albuquerque, NM: University of New Mexico Press, 1974.

Joan Robinson and the Americans. Armonk, NY: M. E. Sharpe, 1989.

Nicholas Kaldor and the Real World. Armonk, NY: M. E. Sharpe, 1993.

Works about Marjorie S. Turner

Personal correspondence to the authors from M. S. T., dated March 6, 2001.

"Turner, Marjorie S." *Contemporary Authors*, 463–64. Vol. 145. Detroit, MI: Gale Research, 1995.

Laura D'Andrea Tyson
(1947–)

In August 1992, Robert Reich, a Harvard professor who was soon to be the secretary of labor in President Bill Clinton's first administration, invited Laura D'Andrea Tyson to an economic summit in Little Rock, Arkansas, with Governor Clinton, who was running for president. Among the prominent economists at that meeting were Nobel laureate James Tobin of Yale University, Laurence Summers of Harvard University, and Paul Krugman of the Massachusetts Institute of Technology. While an accomplished economist in her own right, Tyson was not considered the equal of these others in academic circles. Yet when Clinton asked those assembled how the government could stem the decline in U.S. manufacturing, it was Tyson's answers that resonated with the president-to-be. Her rejection of unfettered free trade in favor of a policy of "aggressive unilateralism" struck Clinton as pragmatic and reality-based. Clinton was so impressed with the power of Tyson's arguments that after he became president, he selected her to chair the president's Council of Economic Advisers, the first woman to hold that position. After serving with distinction in that capacity, Tyson was selected in February 1995 to serve as the president's national economic adviser, making her the highest-ranking woman in the White House and one of "the most powerful women in the president's inner circle and—along with Federal Reserve Chairman Alan Greenspan—one of the nation's most influential economists" (Fix).

BIOGRAPHY

Laura D'Andrea was born in Bayonne, New Jersey, on June 28, 1947. Her surname Tyson comes from her first marriage, which ended in divorce in the mid-1970s. Her father, a second-generation Italian-American, retired after a career as a financial officer for a fragrance company based in New York City; her mother is a homemaker. After graduating as valedictorian of the class of

1965 from Holy Trinity High School in Westfield, New Jersey, Tyson enrolled at Smith College. Initially interested in mathematics and psychology, she graduated in 1969 with a B.A. summa cum laude in economics. She enrolled in the graduate economics program at the Massachusetts Institute of Technology the same year. While initially taken aback by economics at MIT, where the emphasis was on the technical and statistical aspects of the field and not its practical applications, Tyson persevered, earning her Ph.D. in 1974. She immediately took a job as a staff economist at the World Bank in Washington, D.C., and shortly thereafter became an assistant professor of economics at Princeton University.

For the next three years, Tyson focused on her teaching and research, then in 1977 she accepted a post as an economics professor at the University of California, Berkeley. There she became well known for explaining complex economic concepts and theories in understandable and interesting ways. Her classroom effectiveness led Berkeley students to vote her one of their favorite teachers on campus in 1981. Two years later, she was promoted to associate professor, and in 1988 she became a full professor. From 1988 through 1992, Tyson was research director of the Berkeley Roundtable on the International Economy. This group focused on the analysis of world trade in high-tech industries and the advantages a government could give its national manufacturers through subsidies and import regulations. In 1989–90 she was the Henry Carol Thomas Ford Visiting Professor at the Harvard Business School and, from 1990 to 1992, a visiting scholar at the Institute for International Economics, where she began researching and writing *Who's Bashing Whom? Trade Conflict in High-Technology Industries.*

Before joining the Clinton administration in Washington in 1993, Tyson had an active academic career publishing numerous books and articles. She also served on the editorial boards of *East European Politics and Society, International Organizations,* the *Journal of Comparative Economics,* and *Eastern European Economics.* Once in Washington, however, the center of her interests shifted from academic economics to policy making.

Tyson's appointment as chair of the White House Council of Economic Advisers got mixed reviews. She had beat out a half-dozen high-profile heavyweight economists for the post, some of whom had lobbied tirelessly for the job. Besides the professional jealousies aimed at the former high school cheerleader, who favors designer suits and bouncy earrings, some detractors noted Tyson's lack of ideological commitment to free trade. Her supporters, however, were quick to note that such a commitment can bias analysis. Tyson had distinguished herself by drawing conclusions based on evidence of how the real economy works, not on how it should work. In her book *Who's Bashing Whom?,* Tyson stood in opposition to the conventional wisdom of equilibrium-based macroeconomic analysis. Instead, she favors a managed approach to international trade over free-market doctrine, which she believes ill serves the high-tech sectors.

Because of her recognized expertise in trade and trade policy, Tyson had significant influence in shaping the Clinton administration's position on international trade. Her policy of waging "aggressive unilateralism" against foreign traders who close their markets to U.S. imports was sometimes misinterpreted as protectionism. She saw it as a middle ground between free trade on one hand and protected trade on the other. She convinced President Clinton and members of his cabinet in charge of formulating trade policy to pursue this gray area when formulating trade positions with other economic superpowers, such as Japan.

In February 1995, President Clinton named Tyson chair of the National Economic Council (NEC), a coordinating group established in 1993 and made up of the president, the vice president, and select cabinet members. As a member and chair of the NEC, Tyson was responsible for managing economic policy making through the executive branch. Her related responsibilities included sitting in on the president's national security and domestic policy councils, making her one of the most influential women in government in the 1990s. She served on the NEC through 1996. In January 1997, Tyson returned to UC-Berkeley as the Class of 1939 Professor of Economics and Business Administration. Eighteen months later, she became dean of the Walter A. Haas School of Business at Berkeley. In addition to her academic duties, Tyson became an economic viewpoint columnist for *Business Week,* served as a commentator on Public Broadcasting's *Nightly Business Report* from February 1997 through July 1999, and became an editorial board member of *American Perspective* and the *California Management Review.* Married to Erik Tarloff, a screenwriter, and the mother of one son, Tyson has received many awards during her career, including honorary degrees from Smith College (1994) and American University (1995). In 2001, she moved to England to become dean of the London Business School.

CONTRIBUTIONS

Tyson's rejection of a blind allegiance to free trade in favor of aggressive unilateralism—the idea of expanding market access through tough negotiations on tariffs, and barriers to trade backed by a credible threat of retaliation (*Who's Bashing Whom?*, 255)—was a by-product of her research. In a study on the factors responsible for the 1980s decline in manufacturing employment in the United States and the general deterioration of the country's competitive position in international markets ("Trade and Employment"), Tyson and her coauthor looked beyond the usual suspects—prices, wages, technology, and location—in a search for the real reasons Japan and others had eclipsed the United States at its own game. She examined in detail the employment effects of trade in four industries—apparel, autos, semiconductors, and telecommunications equipment. Though different in terms of growth rates, wage levels, profitability, market structure, technological change, and other factors, the four industries taken together represented a broad picture of how trade impacts employment throughout manufacturing.

Tyson concluded that the oft-cited causes of the deterioration in the U.S. trade position in the early 1980s—a rising value of the dollar, protectionism, and slow growth in foreign markets—were important factors. She observed, however, that internal factors, including the government's adherence to a free trade policy when other countries played by a different set of rules, were relatively more significant contributors to the relative demise of the U.S. trading position. This led her to espouse three policy conclusions clearly at odds with prevailing free-market thinking.

> "First, . . . U.S. policymakers must be more sensitive to the effects of their decisions on the U.S. trade position. . . . Second, . . . the U.S. is now more sensitive to the stress and strain of structural change that is induced by changing patterns of trade competition. As the pace of structural change quickens, the need for a broad-based worker retraining and relocation program becomes more pronounced. . . . Third, . . . U.S. manufacturing will be increasingly high technology in both basic industries, such as apparel and autos, where high-tech inputs will transform production techniques, and in high-tech industries. A high-tech America requires a work force that has the skills and training that are needed to use the new technologies. The U.S. educational system from kindergarten through college must be modified to meet these new requirements if American workers are to be able to compete in the world economy with rising rather than falling wages." ("Trade and Employment," 34–35)

In *Who's Bashing Whom?*, Tyson applied her philosophy—that the economic gods help those who help themselves—to high-tech industries exclusively. She noted that "Flawed domestic choices, not unfair trading practices, are the main cause of the nation's long-run economic slowdown" (2). She persuaded Clinton and his economic advisers to embrace a variant of managed trade—trade agreements that established desired outcomes of trade rather than leaving the results to the free flow of goods—when seeking to promote the development and expansion of high-tech industries. This policy was instrumental in the veritable explosion in the volume of international trade that took place in the late 1990s, propelling the U.S. economy into an unprecedented boom that can only be described as the perfect expansion.

BIBLIOGRAPHY

Works by Laura D'Andrea Tyson

"Trade and Employment: An Overview of the Issues and Evidence" (with J. Zysman). In *Dynamics of Trade and Employment,* edited by L. D. Tyson, W. T. Dickens, and J. Zysman, 1–40. Cambridge, MA: Ballinger Publishing, 1988.
Who's Bashing Whom? Trade Conflict in High-Technology Industries. Washington, DC: Institute for International Economics, 1992.
"The End of the Washington Consensus." *New Perspectives Quarterly* 16(1), Winter 1994: 4–7.

Works about Laura D'Andrea Tyson

Chandler, C. "Administration's Economic Voice of Reason." *Washington Post,* April 25, 1994.
Fix, J. L. "Laura Tyson: Even Critics Give Her High Marks." *USA Today,* May 3, 1995.
"Laura D'Andrea Tyson." *Current Biography.* New York: H. W. Wilson, 1996.
Wildavsky, B. "Under the Gun." *National Journal,* June 29, 1996: 1417–21.

Phyllis Ann Wallace
(c. 1924–1993)

In the tight little world of economics, women are rare; women of color are rarer still. Phyllis Ann Wallace was a distinguished economist of the highest order; her gender and race only magnified the luster of her accomplishments and the importance of her scholarship. In the 1960s and 1970s, she shined the light of analysis on the economic status of African American women in a way that it had never been focused before or since. Single-handedly, she helped economists to understand the distinctive characteristics of black women in the U.S. labor force, forever changing the breadth and depth of economic research dealing with the status of minorities in it.

BIOGRAPHY

The exact date of Phyllis Ann Wallace's birth is unknown. She died of natural causes on January 10, 1993, and the *New York Times* obituary listed her age as sixty-nine, which implies that she was born in 1923 or 1924. Wallace was born and reared in Baltimore, Maryland. The oldest of seven children, her father, John Wallace, was a craftsman, and her mother, Stevella Wallace, a housewife. In 1939, Phyllis graduated from the segregated Frederick Douglass High School, one of the foremost high schools in the state. Although she ranked first in her class, Wallace was prohibited by state law from attending the then all-white University of Maryland. State law, however, provided for out-of-state educational expenses for African American students whose chosen field of study was not available at the local blacks-only college. Wallace took advantage of this opportunity to attend New York University, where she majored in economics and graduated magna cum laude and Phi Beta Kappa in 1943.

Initially contemplating a career as a high school teacher, she was encouraged by one of her economics professors to consider graduate school. Wallace applied to and was accepted at Yale University, where she earned a master's degree in 1944 and a Ph.D. in 1948, becoming probably the first African American—certainly the first black female—to receive a doctoral degree in economics from Yale. While studying at Yale, she did a research stint with a defense-related federal agency, and this convinced her to pursue the study of international economics. Wallace wrote her dissertation on commodity trade relationships, focusing on international sugar agreements. After completing her doctorate, she lived in New York City, where she continued her scholarship at the National Bureau of Economic Research.

In 1953, Wallace joined the economics faculty at Atlanta University, where she taught economics for the next four years. During this time, she developed what would be lifelong friendships with a number of prominent African American intellectuals at the university, including Samuel Z. Westerfield, dean of the Business School; Whitney M. Young, dean of the School of Social Work; and Carl Holman, a professor of English and communications. In 1957, she left academe to take a position in the federal government as a policy analyst with the Central Intelligence Agency. There she specialized in the economic growth and development of the Soviet Union, publishing several articles on that topic (e.g., "Industrial Growth in the Soviet Union").

The atmosphere of social change that permeated the 1960s inspired Wallace to shift the locus of her research. In 1965, she was invited to join the senior staff of the newly created Equal Employment Opportunity Commission (EEOC) as its director of technical studies. In that capacity, Wallace pioneered the development and use of occupational employment data as a tool for strengthening and enforcing the anti-discrimination-in-employment provisions of the 1964 Civil Rights Act. She did not limit herself to educating and informing EEOC staff but also reached out to scholars in the academic world who had an interest in labor economics, particularly issues in employment discrimination. In preparation for the landmark discrimination case against AT&T, Wallace assembled an advisory group of economists that included Marcus Alexis, Lester Thurow, Orley Ashenfelter, Robert McKersie, and others, most of whom were relatively unknown at the time but later gained distinction in the economics profession.

In 1968, she left the EEOC and joined the Metropolitan Applied Research Center (MARC) in New York City as vice president for research. While there, Wallace conducted research on the employment problems of urban minority youth and wrote *Pathways to Work: Unemployment among Black Teenage Females*, a pathbreaking book on the employment of young African American women in New York City. In 1972, she was invited to take a visiting position on the faculty of the Sloan School at the Massachusetts Institute of Technology, where three years later she was awarded a full faculty appointment, becoming the first tenured African American woman at MIT.

For the next eleven years, until her retirement in 1986, Wallace taught and wrote, expanding her intellectual pursuits to include issues of labor-management relations as well as participating in the Sloan School's program on managing human resources. Outside the classroom, she was involved in a variety of activities, including the Wellesley College Center for Research on

Women (1983–86), the President's Pay Advisory Committee (1979–80), the Minimum Wage Study Commission (1978–82), and the Economic Advisory Panel of *Black Enterprise* magazine (1982–85). In recognition of her many accomplishments, Wallace received honorary degrees from Valparaiso University (1977), Mount Holyoke College (1983), Brown University (1986), and Northeastern University (1987). During her career, she was elected president of the Industrial Relations Research Association, becoming the first African American and the first woman to lead that prestigious professional organization. In 1980, Wallace received the Wilbur Lucious Cross Medal from Yale University, and in 1982, she received the Samuel Z. Westerfield Award from the National Economic Association. Even in retirement Wallace was an active scholar, publishing *MBAs on the Fast Track* (1989), the results of surveys on career progress that she had administered while at MIT.

CONTRIBUTIONS

Wallace furthered the advancement of economics in a number of ways, but her most significant contributions came in the general area of labor economics, specifically, the economics of employment discrimination. As a result of working on the epochal antidiscrimination case against AT&T, she came to believe that the subtleties and consequences of institutional employment discrimination involved a number of complex and interrelated issues: "(1) Can equity be achieved in the workplace? (2) How are individuals allocated to occupational roles? (3) What kinds of trade-offs between efficiency and equity can be tolerated as different kinds of workers are assimilated into the workplace? (4) How can the present manifestations of past discrimination against some groups be minimized without imposing an unjustifiable burden on others? (5) What are the mechanics of the internal labor market that may facilitate or hinder the achievement of equal employment opportunity?" (*Equal Employment Opportunity*, 2).

Wallace exhibited her interest in finding answers to all of these questions in a number of publications, including *Black Women in the Labor Force*. The general purpose of the book was "to provide information on a significant segment of minority workers as well as produce some insights on the better utilization of *all* women in the labor market" (2). A related objective of this specific research was to correct two shortcomings evident in the "existing economic literature on black women in the labor force . . ." (1).

> The first deficiency might be termed the macro-micro dichotomy. In comparing the relative occupational position and relative incomes of black women with their white female counterparts, economists have tended to employ macroanalysis and sophisticated methodologies for handling massive amounts of data. Their findings are full of paradoxes, and for this reason we attempt to illuminate some of the inconsistencies by a more critical analysis of microdata. . . . A second deficiency is that although many social science researchers claim objectivity, their personal value systems intrude on the analysis. To some extent their findings are distorted not only by sins of misspecification

of economic models but, more important, by unwarranted inferences from rigorous analysis, for example, the tendency to speculate about the psycho-sociological characteristics of individuals, the inheritance of economic status, or the structure of black families. (*Black Women*, 1–2)

The consummate scholar-activist, Wallace never let her passion distort her professionalism. Her work for the EEOC convinced Wallace that the use of general intelligence tests by employers as selection devices for hiring and promotion deprived African Americans and members of other minorities of equal employment opportunities. Her response to this situation was not to call for a cessation of such testing but to search for ways that such tests could be modified to measure ability to do the job without the cultural biases inherent in many aptitude tests. Wallace believed that culture-free—or at least culture-fair or culture-equivalent—testing was possible as long as employers used commonsense guidelines when establishing objective standards for the selection, screening, and promotion of workers ("Proposed Solutions").

Wallace the economist "was a woman who refused to be defined by her race, gender, or occupation. Those who knew her well defined her by her compassion, by her willingness to make space for outsiders in an inside world. She did this by her scholarship, through her quiet activism, in the leadership roles she accepted, in the work that she did. Her academic work in the post-1965 period is distinguished by her efforts to deconstruct exclusion and to make it obsolete" (Malveaux, "Tilting," 97).

BIBLIOGRAPHY

Works by Phyllis Ann Wallace

"Industrial Growth in the Soviet Union" (with R. V. Greenslade). *American Economic Review* 49(4), September 1959: 687–95.

"Proposed Solutions to the Problem of Cultural Bias in Testing" (with B. Kissinger and B. Reynolds). In *Black Americans and White Business*, edited by E. M. Epstein and D. R. Hampton, 281–86. Encino, CA: Dickerson Publishing, 1971.

Equal Employment Opportunity and the AT&T Case (editor). Cambridge, MA: MIT Press, 1976.

Black Women in the Labor Force. Cambridge, MA: MIT Press, 1980.

Works about Phyllis Ann Wallace

Anderson, B. E. Introduction to "The Economic Status of African-American Women: Special Session in Honor of Phyllis A. Wallace." *American Economic Review* 84(2), May 1994: 91–92.

Malveaux, J. "Phyllis Ann Wallace." In *Notable Black American Women*, edited by J. C. Smith, 1197–98. Detroit, MI: Gale Research, 1992.

———. "Tilting against the Wind: Reflections on the Life and Work of Phyllis Ann Wallace." *American Economic Review* 84(2), May 1994: 93–97.

Barbara M. Ward
(1914–1981)

Barbara Mary Ward lived her life according to one overriding tenet—that human beings, particularly those such as herself who had adequate finances, should dedicate themselves to creating a better world. Guided by her firm religious faith, she was a brilliant woman who for more than forty years brought her prodigious talents to the world stage, where she advocated goals and policies that she believed would achieve a more harmonious, peaceful, and prosperous world. She became a friend and respected adviser to world leaders, sharing her vision of the future with decision makers operating at the highest levels of world governments and international organizations.

BIOGRAPHY

Barbara Mary Ward was born in York, England, on May 23, 1914, to Walter Ward, a solicitor, and Teresa Mary (Burge) Ward. Her family was very religious; her father was a Quaker, and her mother came from a prominent Catholic family. Ward was raised a devout Catholic, and this faith would always underlie her life decisions. In her early years, she was educated at the Convent of Jesus and Mary at Felixstowe, and at age fifteen she went to the Continent to study, first in Paris at the Lycée Molière and the Sorbonne, and then for one year at the Jugenheim in Germany. In 1932, she entered Somerville College at Oxford, graduating in 1935, taking first class honors in Modern Greats: philosophy, politics, and economics. From 1936 until 1939, she was an extension lecturer in foreign affairs at Cambridge University and became active in the Labour Party. She earned a Vernon Harcourt scholarship to travel to Italy, Austria, and the Balkans for three summers. In 1938, she published her first book, *The International Share-Out*.

That year, the internationally known journalist Geoffrey Cowther asked Ward to freelance for the periodical the *Economist*, and soon after he made her foreign editor. Early on in her life, she decided that journalism instead of politics or academe would be the best career to further her goals in social justice. During the war years, she worked to keep the *Economist* relevant and continued to write books and articles for other journals. She also became an active speaker for causes she believed in. Ward was known as a multitalented woman, but it was as a powerful and persuasive speaker that she is most remembered. In a wartime newspaper poll, she was voted the second-most-popular speaker in Great Britain. In 1943, she joined the staff of the British Broadcasting Corporation's popular *Brains Trust* radio program, and by age thirty, she was a well-respected and popular British star. She was a talented singer who seriously considered an operatic career, and she served on the boards of the BBC, the Sadler's Wells Ballet, and the Old Vic Theatre. In 1945, she was asked to stand for elections for the Labour Party. She declined but gave eloquent speeches for Labour policies that she favored, including the need for full employment.

In a 1944 article in *Foreign Affairs*, Ward spoke in favor of equal wages and opportunities for women. Twenty-four years later, she commented that "one of the pleasant things I shan't live to see will be the day when it's not re-markable for a woman to be doing things, and then she'll have a greater psychological ease and ability to do things for their own sake" (*The Lopsided World*, 46). On the issue of women's rights, as in her many other concerns, Ward was ahead of her time.

After the war, Ward was concerned with cold war policies and European unity. In her writings for the *Economist* and *The New York Times Magazine*, she urged implementation of the Marshall Plan. She wrote *The West at Bay*, *Policy for the West*, and *The Interplay of East and West*, which were all internationally read and reviewed. In advocating for the Marshall Plan, Ward urged Americans and Europeans not to try to restore the past, but to work instead to create a new society based on an equitable and just global economy.

In 1950, Ward married Robert G. A. Jackson, who worked for the United Nations as an international development adviser. The couple traveled widely in India and Pakistan. Like her husband, she believed that with adequate financial and technical support, developing countries could acquire the means to sustain their own economic development. She and her husband lived briefly in Australia and India, and then for six years in Ghana. They had a son, Robert, born in 1956, and were legally separated in 1966. Because of Ward's Catholicism, the couple never divorced.

In 1957, Ward began her distinguished academic career, serving as a visiting scholar (1957–68) and a Carnegie fellow (1959–67) at Harvard University and Radcliffe College during the winter terms. She taught classes in government and economics, usually in the Graduate School of Public Administration, while continuing to write and give lectures at conferences. Many of her lectures and lecture series were published as books. Among her publications that started as lectures are *Five Ideas That Changed the World*, *The Rich Nations and the Poor Nations*, *India and the West*, and *Nationalism and Ideology*. *The Rich Nations and the Poor Nations* would go on to become one of her most influential books, one that President Lyndon Johnson would later call his "other Bible"

(Ryan and Vaitheswaran, 456). Other books were *Spaceship Earth* and *The Lopsided World*.

During these years, Ward's concerns turned from the cold war to international development. She recognized that the postcolonial world was one of extreme imbalance, and in her writings and speeches, Ward advocated that the rich nations had a moral imperative to share their scientific and technological advances to help the developing nations. In 1967, she was made Albert Schweitzer Professor of International Development at Columbia University, a controversial appointment because it was in the Department of Economics. She organized the 1970 Columbia Conference on International Economic Development, which gathered representatives from the World Bank, the UN Development Program, the International Monetary Fund, and the Canadian aid program. Ward also invited economists from the developing world who challenged the prevailing wisdom about foreign aid. She edited a collection of essays from the conference, which was published as *The Widening Gap*.

While at Columbia, Ward became increasingly concerned about the environment. In 1973, she resigned her chair to devote her energies to her environmental concerns. She was president of the Conservation Society in 1972 and helped prepare a preliminary report for the 1972 Stockholm Conference on the Human Environment. She understood that concerns for the environment should be made equally relevant to the poorer countries as well as to the more affluent developed ones. *Only One Earth: The Care and Maintenance of a Small Planet*, written in collaboration with René Dubos, resulted from a preliminary report for the conference. This conference was pathbreaking, but at the time Ward and the other participants were disappointed with the results. Ward was also the director of the International Institute of Environment and Development, which would play a significant role in many UN conferences. In 1979, she completed her book *Progress for a Small Planet*.

Throughout her career, Ward played an active role in her church and in church-related organizations, such as the Sword and Spirit movement, which worked toward unity in international relations. In 1941, she published *A Christian Basis for the Post-War World*. She served as president of the Catholic Women's League from 1948 to 1950 and on the Pontifical Commission for Justice and Peace from 1967 to 1981. She became the first woman to address a session at the Vatican in 1971 when she spoke to the Synod of the Bishops on World Justice. She wrote three works commissioned by the Vatican: *A New Creation: Reflections on the Environmental Issue* (1973), *The Angry Seventies* (1976), and *Peace and Justice in the World* (1981). Although she was a devout Catholic, Ward campaigned for change within the Church, and she worked to bring about an understanding of all the world's great religions.

In the mid-1950s, Ward was struck by throat cancer. This disease would cause her great suffering over the last twenty-five years of her life. She endured five major operations, and the disease impaired one of her greatest talents, her speaking voice.

Over her lifetime, Ward was awarded many honors. In 1949, Fordham University and Smith College granted her honorary doctorates, as did many other universities during her career. In 1976, the London School of Economics made her an honorary fellow, and two years later, her college at Oxford University, Somerville, gave her the same honor. In 1973, the National Audubon Society awarded her the Audubon Medal, making her the second woman honored, after Rachel Carson. In 1974, she was awarded the Jawaharlal Nehru Prize in India for her work against illiteracy. She was proclaimed Dame of the British Empire in 1974, and in 1976, she became Baroness Jackson of Lodsworth when Queen Elizabeth II made her a life peer.

In 1979, Ward published her last book, *Progress for a Small Planet: New Directions for the Industrial Order*. By the 1980s, her illness had robbed Ward of her prodigious energy. She was awarded the Royal Society of the Arts Gold Medal, but she was too ill to accept it in person. By 1980, she resigned from the directorship of the International Institute for Environment and Development, turning the directorship over to her longtime colleague William Clark. Ward died on May 3, 1981, in the village of Lodsworth and, with special permission from Pope John Paul II, was buried at the local Anglican parish church.

CONTRIBUTIONS

To limit Ward's contributions to one intellectual discipline would be to minimize a lifetime of global achievements. The nonacademic public viewed her as an economist, but she never professed to be one. Much of her writing dealt with economic concerns such as the European postwar recovery, economic development, and environmental questions. Her numerous books and hundreds of articles were read all over the world. Popes, leaders at the United Nations, and four World Bank presidents asked her to write or speak on their behalf. She was a close adviser to world leaders, including President Lyndon Baines Johnson of the United States, Prime Minister Harold Wilson of Great Britain, and Prime Minister Lester Pearson of Canada. Through her forty-year career, she advocated for her causes: U.S. leadership of the noncommunist world; western European unity; the need for economic assistance to the developing countries of Asia and Africa; and the need to preserve the fragile ecology of our planet.

A comprehensive review of Ward's numerous writing is not possible here. A selective analysis of two of her more popular works—admittedly an incomplete sample at best—can still reveal the depth and breadth of her thinking. Her best-known book was *The Rich Nations and the Poor Nations*. In it, Ward describes the characteristics of rich nations and poor ones, then enunciates the roles capitalism and communism can or might play in closing the gap, both economic and political, between the two. Her motivation for writing the book, so on the mark in 1962, has an uncomfortable relevancy even now. "So our world today is dominated by a complex and tragic division. One part of mankind has undergone the revolutions of modernization and has emerged on the other side to a pattern of great and increasing wealth. But most of the rest of mankind has yet to achieve any of the revolutions; they are caught off balance before the great movement of economic and social momentum can be launched. Their old traditional world is dying. The new radical world is not yet born. This being so, the gap between the rich and the poor has become inevitably the most tragic and urgent problem of our day" (36).

A decade after publishing *The Rich Nations and the Poor Nations,* Ward trained her prodigious skills on an issue that transcends the level of prosperity of individual countries—namely, the environment, a global concern with scientific, social, economic, and political dimensions. The result was *Only One Earth,* coauthored with René Dubos, an eminent microbiologist and Pulitzer Prize recipient who had achieved distinction as a scientific humanist. In preparing this unofficial report commissioned by the UN secretary general, Ward and Dubos received assistance from a Committee of Corresponding Consultants, which consisted of 152 persons from fifty-two countries who represented a cross-section of disciplines including natural sciences, the humanities, engineering, commerce, law, and philosophy.

Simultaneously published in nine languages, the book—a unique experiment in international collaboration—was meant to provide the factual background and conceptual framework for a UN conference scheduled for Stockholm in June 1972. To prepare the attendees for the conference on the human environment, Ward and Dubos reviewed the evolution of the planet; the roles of science and technology in understanding and shaping how humans use and abuse the earth; human population and its impact on the planet; and strategies for survival. With respect to the future, they concluded that "The first step toward devising a strategy for planet Earth is for the nations to accept a *collective* responsibility for discovering more—much more—about the natural system and how it is affected by man's activities and vice versa. This implies cooperative monitoring, research, and study on an unprecedented scale. It implies an intensive world-wide network for the systematic exchange of knowledge and experience. It implies a quite new readiness to take research wherever it is needed, with backing of international financing. It means the fullest cooperation in converting knowledge into action—whether it be placing research satellites in orbit or reaching agreements on fishing, or introducing a new control for snail-borne disease" (*Only One Earth,* 213–14).

The Ward prescription for progress, a clarion call a generation ago, has been a motivating factor in the degree of global collaboration, however modest, currently practiced. It also reflected her values, abundantly evident from her very first publication to the last words that she wrote.

BIBLIOGRAPHY

Works by Barbara M. Ward

The West at Bay. New York: W. W. Norton, 1948.
Policy for the West. New York: W. W. Norton, 1951.
Five Ideas That Changed the World. New York: W. W. Norton, 1957.
The Interplay of East and West. New York: W. W. Norton, 1957.
The Rich Nations and the Poor Nations. New York: W. W. Norton, 1962.
India and the West. New York: W. W. Norton, 1964.
Spaceship Earth. New York: Columbia University Press, 1966.

Nationalism and Ideology. New York: W. W. Norton, 1967.

The Lopsided World. New York: W. W. Norton, 1968.

Only One Earth: The Care and Maintenance of a Small Planet (with R. Dubos). New York: W. W. Norton: 1972.

Progress for a Small Planet: New Directions for the Industrial Order. New York: W. W. Norton, 1979.

Works about Barbara M. Ward

Beloff, N. "Ward, Barbara Mary." In *Dictionary of National Biography,* edited by L. Blake and C. S. Nichols, 410–11. Oxford, England: Oxford University Press, 1990.

Ryan, C. K., and Vaitheswaran, R. "Ward, Barbara Mary." In *A Biographical Dictionary of Women Economists,* edited by R. W. Dimand, M. A. Dimand, and E. L. Forget, 445–60. Northampton, MA: Edward Elgar, 2000.

"Ward, Barbara Mary." In *Who's Who in Economics*, edited by M. Blaug, 1149. 3rd ed. Northampton, MA: Edward Elgar, 1999.

Beatrice Potter Webb
(1858–1943)

In a time when for women a professional career and a happy marriage were thought to be mutually exclusive, Beatrice Potter Webb had both. For fifty years she was married to Sidney Webb, and together the two combined their love for each other and their work into a partnership virtually without equal in the annals of the intellectual history of economics (MacKenzie, 141). More than any other two people, Beatrice and Sidney Webb were responsible for the creation of the modern British welfare state; he was the team's writer and publicist, and she, its heart and soul.

BIOGRAPHY

Beatrice Potter Webb was born on January 2, 1858, at Standish House, near Glouchester, England. The eighth of nine daughters, she was part of an affluent and socially prominent family whose one son died as a small child. Richard Potter, Beatrice's father, was a successful Victorian business professional and railroad magnate. Her mother, Laurencina (Heyworth) Potter, an intelligent and energetic woman, was the daughter of a Liverpool merchant and came from the same social stratum as her father (Cole, 6). The Potters were married in 1844. By the time Beatrice was born, they had firmly established themselves in the ranks of the Victorian upper class.

A frail and often ill child, Beatrice was schooled at home. The lack of a formal education, however, did not inhibit her intellectual development. "Her education was determined by her own reading interests, by her association with domestic servants, and by conversation with many distinguished family guests" (Thomson, 77). During her formative years and because of her family's position in society, Beatrice had the good fortune to interact on a regular basis with the likes of Francis Gaston and T. H. Huxley. By far the most prominent and influential thinker to frequent the Potter household was the Liberal philosopher Herbert Spencer.

Spencer, considered one of the greatest British minds of the day, had a singular affection for Beatrice. He became a dominant influence in her young life even though he was nearly forty years her senior. Never married, Spencer had a fondness for little girls, like many other eminent Victorian bachelors. "In those days . . . , mothers were merely touched and amused if an elderly unmarried friend fell in love with their pre-pubescent daughters, confident that the prevailing sexual code was strong enough to protect them. It was an entirely allowable *tendresse,* openly expressed . . ." (Mutteridge and Adam, 40). The Potter children, especially Beatrice, looked forward to Spencer's visits. Although her philosophy as an adult would contrast sharply with Spencer's individually narcissistic Social Darwinism, Potter admired his intellectual prowess and "cherished a tender affection for him to the day of his death in 1903" (42).

In 1882, Potter's mother died, and as the eldest unmarried daughter Beatrice became the mistress of the household, a position she held until her father's death in 1892. During this ten-year period her friendship with Spencer began to show its true significance. Her studies of Spencer's works had convinced Potter that social ills could be discovered by fact-finding and cured by recommendations for scientific-based reform. "She decided that the scientific investigation of social institutions was to be her vocation in life" (Thomson, 78). As she put it, "To win recognition as an intellectual worker was, even before my mother's death, my secret ambition. I longed to write a book that would be read; but I had no notion about what I wanted to write" (*My Apprenticeship,* 106).

During the mid-1880s, while volunteering for the Charity Organization Society, she developed some ideas that embodied the Victorian ideal of using charity as a means to prevent poverty, not just relieve it. Her experiences with the working poor in the sweatshops of Lancashire led her to conclude that "destitution is a disease of society itself" (*Our Partnership,* x). She began to document her findings in a number of small publications, the most important of which was *The Cooperative Movement in Great Britain* (1891). In 1890, she met Sidney Webb, then a member of the Fabian Society, a non-Marxist organization founded in 1883 and committed to the attainment of British socialism through gradual political change. Two years later, Beatrice Potter and Sidney Webb were married and began a partnership that literally shaped the course of British history.

Over the next half-century, she and Sidney dedicated more than twenty years to public service and published more than thirty books. With a sense of grace and dignity, the two exercised unimaginable influence over the development of the British welfare state. Beatrice, especially, never had an ax to grind. "She bore no malice; she accepted and forgave—and even forgot—insults and attacks which would have rankled forever in lesser minds. She was almost entirely immune from those mental diseases of the enlightened which so often turn any community of the socially virtuous into an inferno of injured vanity and a succession of furious battles on points of prestige or principle" (Cole, 217). After a brief illness, Webb died in 1943 and Sidney followed her in 1947. Their ashes are buried in Westminster Abbey, London.

CONTRIBUTIONS

The contributions of Beatrice and Sidney Webb fall into three broad categories: scholarship, public service, and the creation of important social institutions. While no précis of their life's work is possible, certain achievements stand out among their many accomplishments. Among their writings, *Industrial Democracy*, published in 1897, is the book that has best stood the test of time. It "was well received upon publication, and it continues to be a useful source book for students in labor economics" (Thomson, 91). As a sequel to their *History of Trade Unionism* (1894), *Industrial Democracy* was devoted to an analysis of the structure, function, and theory of trade unionism. The Webbs sought to demonstrate that unionism was compatible with democracy and not in conflict with it, as many Victorians believed.

The Webbs, however, were not knee-jerk unionists but believed that British trade unionism needed to modify some of its doctrines to be truly consistent with modern democratic principles (*Industrial Democracy*, 809–10). In particular, they held that "resistance to inventions, or of any obstruction of improvements in industrial processes" (809) would put trade unionism in conflict with interests of the community as a whole. Likewise, the Webbs believed that political attempts to restrict the numbers of workers in a particular trade should be "unreservedly condemned" (810).

Industrial Democracy contained more than the Webbs' prescriptions for the behavior of trade unionists; it also proposed a number of programs for the state to follow to ensure a democratic workplace. The most notable among these policy proposals was the idea of the "national minimum" (766). By this they meant that government would prescribe "the minimum conditions under which the community can afford to allow industry to be carried on; and including not merely definite precautions of sanitation and safety, and maximum hours of toil, but also a minimum of weekly earnings" (767). With this proposal, the Webbs gave voice to the modern notion that the state has an obligation to prevent poverty, not just relieve it.

The Webbs did more than advocate change; they worked hard to implement it. Their public service in the interest of promoting industrial democracy was legendary. Sidney Webb was a leading member of the London County Council, and in 1922 he was elected to Parliament at the age of sixty-three. One year later, when the Labour Party came to power, he was appointed to the cabinet as president of the Board of Trade. When Labour came to power again in 1929, he was appointed secretary of state for the colonies. While Beatrice Webb was less of a public figure, she too played a role in bringing to reality the Webbs vision of the British welfare state. During the 1890s, she served on the Royal Commission on Capital and Labour, and in 1906, she was appointed to the Royal Commission on the Poor Law, writing the famous Minority Report of that commission, which laid the foundation for much of the welfare state in Britain.

The Webbs were also energetic organizers and created several important social institutions to support and popularize their brand of socialism. In 1895, they founded the London School of Economics, and in 1913, they launched the liberal weekly magazine the *New Statesman.* Their many endeavors were not, however, all equally successfully or well received. In the 1930s, after only a three-week stay in the Soviet Union, the Webbs published *Soviet Communism: A New Civilisation* (1935). This sympathetic account of Soviet communism, based mostly on material and statistics supplied to them by the Soviet government, appeared in print just about the time Joseph Stalin's purges were subjecting the Soviet Union to one of the cruelest reigns of terror in history. Years later, Beatrice Webb attributed their uncritical admiration for the Soviet Union to senility: "Old people often fall in love in extraordinary and ridiculous ways—with their chauffeurs for example: we felt it more dignified to have fallen in love with Soviet Communism" (Mutteridge and Adam, 245). There were other lapses of judgment during their lives, though none as colossal. In retrospect, these were truly minor miscues in the sweep of a lifetime partnership that was broad, rich, and full of accomplishments.

BIBLIOGRAPHY

Works by Beatrice Potter Webb

Industrial Democracy. New York: August M. Kelley Reprints of Economic Classics, 1965. Originally published 1897.
My Apprenticeship. New York: Longmans, Green, 1926.
Our Partnership, edited by B. Drake and M. I. Cole. New York: Longmans, Green, 1948.

Works about Beatrice Potter Webb

Broschart, K. R. "Beatrice Webb." In *Women in Sociology: A Bio-Bibliographical Sourcebook,* edited by M. J. Deegan, 425–31. Westport, CT: Greenwood Press, 1991.
Cole, M. *Beatrice Webb.* New York: Harcourt, Brace, and Company, 1946.
MacKenzie, J. *A Victorian Courtship: The Story of Beatrice Potter and Sidney Webb.* New York: Oxford University Press, 1979.
Mutteridge, K., and Adam, R. *Beatrice Webb: A Life, 1858–1943.* London: Secker & Warburg, 1967.
Thomson, D. L. "Beatrice Potter Webb." In *Adam Smith's Daughters.* New York: Exposition Press, 1973.
"Webb, Beatrice Potter." In *Who's Who in Economics,* edited by M. Blaug, 1151. Northampton, MA: Edward Elgar, 1999.

Marina von Neumann Whitman
(1935–)

During her career, Marina Whitman has been a business economist, government adviser, author, distinguished teacher, television personality, and prominent business strategist. In the male-dominated field of international economics, Whitman became an influential decision- and policy maker, paving the way for other women to follow. She is known for her intellectual brilliance and her expertise in international economics. Early in her career, she served as senior staff economist in international affairs on the President's Council of Economic Advisers, and later, as the only female member of the Federal Price Commission. When she was thirty-six, President Richard Nixon nominated her as the first woman to serve on the three-member President's Council of Economic Advisers. Later she became vice president and chief economist at General Motors Corporation, shaping the company's views on import restrictions. She eventually returned to academe to teach, write, and do research on international trade and investment and the changing role of U.S. multinational corporations.

BIOGRAPHY

Marina von Neumann, the only child of John von Neumann and Mariette (Kovesi) von Neumann, was born in New York City on March 6, 1935. Her father was an eminent mathematician, games theorist, computer pioneer, and research professor at the Institute of Advanced Study in Princeton, New Jersey. Her parents divorced when Marina was two years old but remained close friends. Her mother, an administrator, married James B. Kuper, a physicist at the Brookhaven National Laboratory, and Marina spent her childhood in New York City with her mother and stepfather. However, her mother felt very strongly that Marina should get to known her renowned father, so Marina spent her teenage years absorbing the intellectual atmosphere John von Neumann and his colleagues provided. Marina would say later that she was fifteen before she realized that her life—filled with incredibly interesting people, such as the world-famous scientists Edward Teller, Norbert Wiener, and Robert Oppenheimer, and their fascinating conversations—was not the typical American teenage experience.

A brilliant student and a government major, Whitman graduated summa cum laude from Radcliffe College as a Phi Beta Kappa in 1956. On June 23, 1956, the weekend after graduation, she married Robert Freeman Whitman, who held a Ph.D. in English from Harvard University. The couple settled at Princeton University, where Robert taught English. Marina Whitman worked as an administrative assistant at the Educational Testing Service until she realized that she needed more education and went back to school. She chose Columbia because in those days Princeton did not admit women. She received her M.A. in economics in 1959 and a Ph.D. in 1962. While finishing up her doctoral studies, Whitman served as a consultant and staff economist for the Pittsburgh Regional Planning Association, helping to prepare a comprehensive economic plan for the greater Pittsburgh area. In 1963, she became a lecturer in economics at the University of Pittsburgh and worked her way up to full professor in 1971. During this time, she published three books on international economics: *Government Risk-Sharing in Foreign Investment*, *International and Interregional Payments Adjustment: A Synthetic View*, and *Economic Goals and Policy Instruments: Policies for Internal and External Balance*.

In 1970, she took a leave from the University of Pittsburgh when she was invited to spend a year in Washington, D.C., as a senior staff economist in international affairs, one of six economists advising the President's Council of Economic Advisers. She specialized in coaching council members on a variety of international economic problems, including the need for a realignment of currency-exchange rates. Impressed by her ability, President Nixon appointed her to the Federal Price Commission on October 1971. She was the youngest member of the commission and its only woman. On it, she was known for using a middle-of-the-road approach to price controls in a time of spiraling inflation and for her incredible ability to quickly get to the heart of a problem.

Citing her outstanding intellect, Nixon announced Whitman's nomination to his three-member Council of Economic Advisers on January 29, 1972. As the first woman nominated to serve on the council, Whitman graciously answered questions—How did the family's gerbils make the trip to Washington?—that would never have been asked of a man. Reporters commented on her clothes, her attractiveness, and her glamorous auburn hair. "Not relevant," said Whitman, "and it's plain old moss brown" (Byers).

Herbert Stein, the new chairman of the council, assigned Whitman to international affairs. He also asked her to serve as liaison with the Nixon administration's Phase II system of wage and price controls. Representing the council, she spoke and wrote extensively on the restructuring of the international monetary system and worked on the bumpy transition out of wage and price controls. She also helped prepare the council's *1973 Economic Report to the President*. Although she had taken pains not to be pigeonholed as the "women's-issues person," Whitman wrote a groundbreaking special section of the report addressing for the first time the economic role of women in U.S. society. The report stated that, despite ten years of civil-rights legislation and the fact that 43.8 percent of all working-age women were employed, women's unemployment rate was consistently higher than men's. Their salaries averaged only 66.1 percent of men's wages, and their jobs had relatively low occupational status.

In August 1973, when the Watergate scandal became an issue, Whitman resigned from the council as a matter of conscience. She returned to the University of Pittsburgh, where she was named Distinguished Public Service Professor of Economics and also served as administrative officer of the economics department. She published widely about the United States' role in a global economy. In 1979, General Motors, aware of her abilities and her expertise in global economics, offered her the position of vice president and chief economist for the corporation. Whitman saw this as an opportunity to be a problem-solving economist. At this time, GM was looking to hire more women as top executives, and Whitman became one of the highest-paid and most influential economists in the country. She managed the corporation's economics, environmental activities, industry/government relations, and public affairs staffs. She helped shape GM's opposition to import restrictions on Japanese automobiles and worked to convince other executives to abandon a restrictive domestic outlook in favor of a broader, global outlook. Her skills in dealing with a large corporate bureaucracy were shown when she managed to keep her job while convincing GM to adopt a global perspective, even though this was an unpopular view within the automobile industry. Within that industry, Whitman became known as the corporate guru of global economics.

In 1992, she went back to academe as a professor of business administration and public policy at the University of Michigan Business School. In 1999, drawing on her experiences at General Motors, she published *New World, New Rules: The Changing Role of the American Corporation*. In it, she discusses how corporate practices have been changed by the expanding global marketplace and examines the ways that the evolving global markets have changed corporations and U.S. society. She also describes her experiences as a board member of publicly held companies. In the 1970s, she was often the only woman on a corporate board. Before then, most corporate directors were chief executives of other corporations and often friends or close associates of the board's chairman. In the 1970s, this began to change. The general public demanded that corporate boards become more diverse by adding women, members of minority groups, and outside or nonemployee directors. By the 1990s, corporate boards were more diverse, and international experience, technological know-how, and other specific business skills began to replace social standing as a prerequisite for board membership.

Whitman's career has been distinguished and varied, but it has never been her first priority. A strong proponent of the nuclear family, she has always based her career choices on what was best for her family. She and her husband, who is now a professor of English emeritus, had two children, Malcolm and Laura. Whitman declined lucrative television offers to spend time with her family. When working for the Council of Economic Advisers, Whitman and her family opted to live in Washington so she could be home for dinner. When she accepted the GM offer, the family moved back to Princeton and she commuted to New York. Since 1985, Whitman and her husband have been residents of Ann Arbor, Michigan, and are very involved in community and cultural organizations. Their son, a Ph.D., teaches at the Harvard Medical School, and their daughter is a medical doctor specializing in primary care and a clinical instructor at Yale University.

In 2001, Whitman served on the board of directors of Alcoa, Chase Manhattan Corporation, Proctor and Gamble, and Unocal, and over her career she has served as a trustee, director, or member of many educational, professional, and governmental organizations. She has received honorary degrees from more than twenty colleges and universities and is a former board member of Harvard and Princeton Universities. She served on the boards of the National Bureau of Economic Research and the Institute for International Economics and was a member of the American Academy of Arts and Sciences, the Council on Foreign Relations, and Phi Beta Kappa. She has moderated a TV series, *Economically Speaking,* seen on some 200 public broadcasting stations. At the University of Michigan, her research activities included international trade and investment, trade policy and labor-market adjustments, and the changing role of the U.S. multinational corporation.

In 1972, when Marina Whitman went to Washington at age thirty-six, she was viewed as a curiosity—an attractive woman who was known for her keen intellectual abilities and economic expertise. Because of her determination, patience, and hard work in times of economic upheaval in the world financial community, Whitman went from a curiosity to a well-respected and influential economist whose views have continued to matter. Throughout her career, Whitman has blazed a trail for other hardworking and intelligent women to follow.

CONTRIBUTIONS

Whitman's first major publication *(Government Risk-Sharing)* grew out of her Ph.D. dissertation and was a narrowly focused study that sought to answer the questions "... what contribution has American private capital channeled through the risk-sharing agencies made to economic development abroad, and what contribution can it be expected to make?" (6). The scope of her expertise in international economic theory and policy is truly revealed in *Reflections of Interdependence*, a book composed of articles Whitman published from 1967 to 1977 in a variety of journals including the *Brookings Papers on Economic Activity*, the *American Economic Review*, and the *Journal of Money, Credit, and Banking*. Also included in the volume is Whitman's classic monograph on international and interregional payment adjustments *International and Interregional Payments Adjustment: A Synthetic View*. The articles presented in it deal with multiple aspects of interdependence, defined as "the extent to which developments in one country affect the economies of others, stimulating responses that in turn have feedback effects on the economy of the original country" *(Reflections*, ix). The topics covered include payment adjustments, global monetarism, and the reduction in the economic leadership of the United States during the 1970s. Each article is written with balance, brilliance, and thoroughness, the signature features of Whitman's scholarship. All reflect her deep interest in learning how the interplay of economic theory and foreign policy can be used to coordinate and manage the international economy.

Her early scholarship reflected a career-long interest in international economics, especially the role of public policy in shaping the global economic environment. After serving as a corporate officer at General Motors, Whitman developed an appreciation for the capacity of the private sector to define the contours of the international economy, and this new perspective is reflected in her recent writings. In *New World, New Rules*, Whitman chronicles the changing nature of the U.S. corporation, once the bedrock of stability and security, a benevolent institution whose power and influence was a trusted force in commerce and society alike. Sweeping changes in the U.S. economy caused by global competition, deregulation, and technology have, Whitman argues, radically reshaped the ways big companies interact with competitors, both domestic and international. This new slant in her scholarship is an extension of Whitman's perception that socially responsible firms are subject to many forces, and that reacting to each of these is complicated if not contradictory. "The concept of corporate social responsibility has as many facets as there are stake-holders, that is, individuals or groups who feel they are affected in some significant way by the actions of a corporation and therefore should have some say in what it does or does not do. Among the most important of these stakeholder groups, for any corporation, are customers, stockholders, employees and retirees, labor unions, . . . suppliers, communities, and government legislators and regulators at every level, who at least purport to represent the interests of society at large" ("The Socially Responsible Corporation," 130).

The challenge in this new world, as Whitman sees it, is for U.S. government and business to work together to reap the benefits of global liberalization while preserving the leadership and socially responsible behavior of U.S. companies.

BIBLIOGRAPHY

Works by Marina von Neumann Whitman

Government Risk-Sharing in Foreign Investment. Princeton, NJ: Princeton University Press, 1965.

International and Interregional Payments Adjustment: A Synthetic View. Princeton Studies in International Finance, no. 19. Princeton, NJ: 1967.

Economic Goals and Policy Instruments: Policies for Internal and External Balance. Princeton Special Papers in International Economics, no. 9. Princeton, NJ: 1970.

Reflections of Interdependence. Pittsburgh, PA: University of Pittsburgh Press, 1979.

"The Socially Responsible Corporation: Responsible to Whom for What?" In *Is the Good Corporation Dead?*, edited by J. W. Houch and O. F. Williams, 129–48. Lanham, MD: Rowman & Littlefield, 1996.

New World, New Rules: The Changing Role of the American Corporation. Boston, MA: Harvard Business School Press, 1999.

Works about Marina von Neumann Whitman

Byers, M. "Nixon's New Economist Has Trouble with Her Checkbook." *Life,* February 25, 1972.

Contemporary Authors, 435–37. New Revision Series, vol. 89. Farmington Hills, MI: Gale Group, 2000.

Current Biography, edited by C. Moritz, 432–34. New York: Wilson Company, 1973.

McGoldrick, B. "The Corporate Guru of Global Economics." *Working Woman,* November 1988.

"The Rise of the Role Model." *Time,* November 20, 1978.

Tristram, C. "The Upside of Downsizing." *CIO Enterprise,* February 15, 1999.

Ann Dryden Witte
(1942–)

Within the field of economics, most scholars build a reputation by centering their research on a single topic or subfield in the discipline. Ann Witte achieved prominence by training her highly developed analytical skills on a variety of interesting and eclectic problems. In the process, she established herself as a noted and prolific author of books, monographs, and professional articles that reflect the scope and breadth of economics.

BIOGRAPHY

Ann Dryden Witte was born on August 28, 1942, in Oceanside, New York. Her father, Harry Clifford Dryden, was a business executive, and her mother, Frances (Ferguson) Dryden, was an office manager. In 1963, she earned her B.A. with highest honors in political science and history from the University of Florida in Gainesville. For the next four years, Witte worked for the federal government in Washington, D.C. From 1963 to 1966, she was an economic analyst specializing in Russia with specific duties related to Soviet agriculture and labor. She then shifted jobs, becoming a systems analyst in the programming, planning, and budgeting systems of the U.S. government, a post she held from 1966 to 1967. While working for the federal government, Witte continued her education at the graduate school of Columbia University, receiving her M.A. in economics in 1965.

Witte landed her first teaching position in 1967 as an instructor of economics at Tougaloo College in Tougaloo, Mississippi, where she taught courses in economic development and minority economic development. After one year at Tougaloo, she left teaching to pursue her doctorate in economics at North Carolina State University. On June 2, 1969, she married Leo Witte, a manager; the couple has one son. Witte received her Ph.D. in 1971 and from 1970 to 1972 was an instructor at North Carolina State, teaching courses in economic development and doing research on employment in developing economies. Her Ph.D. dissertation is titled "Employment in the Manufacturing Sector of Developing Economies: A Study of Mexico, Peru and Venezuela."

Witte began teaching at the University of North Carolina, Chapel Hill, as a visiting assistant professor of economics in 1972. She left Chapel Hill in 1985 after having served as an assistant professor (1974–79), an associate professor (1979–83), and a professor (1983–85). Since 1985, she has had a permanent position as a professor of economics at Wellesley College, while taking time to serve as a fellow in law and economics at the Harvard Law School (1987–88) and a professor of economics at Florida International University (1992–2000). She has also maintained the title of research associate with the National Bureau of Economic Research since 1984.

During her career, Witte has been the recipient of numerous awards including Phi Beta Kappa, Fellow of the American Statistical Association, Fellow of the Royal Statistical Society, and Fellow of the American Society of Criminology. She has been or is a member of the editorial boards of the *European Journal of Law and Economics* (since 1993), *Policy Studies Review* (1988–95), the *Journal of Quantitative Criminology* (since 1988), the *Law and Society Review* (1985–88), and the *Review of Regional Studies* (1976–79). She has held Fulbright lectureships at Victoria University in Wellington, New Zealand (1988), the Central School of Planning and Statistics in Warsaw, Poland (1987), the Federal University of Ceara in Fortaleza, Brazil (1984), and the Federal University of Pernambuco in Recife, Brazil (1981). Her community and professional service is legendary. It includes chairing the Child Care Policy Research Consortium (1999–2000), serving as a member of the National Science Foundation's Economic Advisory Panel (1992–94), and sitting on the board of directors of the National Tax Association (1990–93).

CONTRIBUTIONS

Witte has made a highly diverse set of contributions to economic knowledge. She began her career analyzing agriculture and labor in the Soviet Union for the U.S. government. These research efforts were a natural extension of her study of political science and history as an undergraduate. After earning her master's in economics, Witte altered her scholarly focus toward the study of employment in Latin America, a research interest reflected in her Ph.D. dissertation. Eventually, she developed an interest in applying microeconomics and econometrics to a wide range of issues and problems. This approach to research took her into the economics of criminal justice, the interrelationship of law and economics, and the study of real-estate markets and the location of businesses and households.

Witte's first major publication was characteristic of her research on labor and its various conditions, especially in developing countries. In "Employment in the Manufacturing Sector of Developing Economies: A Study of Mexico and Peru," Witte investigated "the extent to which the relatively slow growth of employment in the manufacturing sector of developing economies, . . . can be explained by production functions with relatively high elasticities of substitution and a shifting of relative prices which makes it profitable for companies to substitute capital for labour" (35). The growing body of scholarship showing that developing countries experience constant or even declining rates of employment growth despite expanding manufacturing sectors motivated Witte to undertake this study. She concluded that in Mexico and Peru, variations in relative prices and the elasticity of substitution explained from one-third to virtually all of the variation of employment in manufacturing, depending on the specific industry and time period in question, confirming in quantitative detail the anecdotal hunches of others.

A cross-section of Witte's writings on the economics of criminal justice (*Work Release*; "Estimating"; *An Economic Analysis*; "Crime") covers a variety of interrelated topics, all handled with her signature analytical approach. In a monograph about the work-release system in the South Piedmont area of North Carolina (*Work Release*), Witte reviewed and evaluated the four major goals of the program: reducing recidivism, reducing the tax burden of incarceration, rehabilitation, and rewarding good behavior. This research formed the basis of an article published several years later ("Estimating"). The coauthored book *An Economic Analysis of Crime and Justice* is a synthesis of Witte's work and thinking in the field, covering numerous topics including, but not limited to, a statistical analysis of recidivism, testing the validity of an economic model of crime, and the use of production and cost theory in criminal justice research. In a recent publication, Witte altered her approach to model testing by introducing the use of vector autoregressive methodology to the mainstream of applied criminological research as an alternative to the estimation of structural models of crime ("Crime").

The balance of Witte's research defies characterization. She has authored or coauthored several professional articles on real estate economics, including a study that applied portfolio theory to the acquisition and holding of vacant urban land ("Vacant Urban Land Holdings") and an examination of the long-run effects of increasing energy and construction costs on land values and the equilibrium density of firms ("Increased Costs"). As an alternative to traditional hedonic techniques for measuring quality, Witte developed a quality index for the service sector and applied it to the day-care industry using national and Massachusetts-specific data ("Measurement"). Using data from the Minneapolis Domestic Violence Experiment, she devised a dynamic model to analyze the probability of observing domestic violence, research sparked in part by the more than 18 million incidents per year that fit the criminal-justice classification of an assault ("The Dynamics"). As a counterbalance to these narrowly defined studies, Witte published a comprehensive work on the underground economy, defined as economic activities that involve payments in money or kind but which are not recorded in official statistics (*Beating the System*). The book covered virtually every aspect of the underground economy, from tax evasion and cigarette smuggling to illegal drugs and loansharking. Witte's hallmark thoroughness and probing analyses are evident throughout the work.

BIBLIOGRAPHY

Works by Ann Dryden Witte

"Employment in the Manufacturing Sector of Developing Economies: A Study of Mexico and Peru." *Journal of Development Studies* 10(1), October 1973: 33–49.

Work Release in North Carolina: An Evaluation of Its Post-Release Effects. Chapel Hill, NC: University of North Carolina, 1975.

"Vacant Urban Land Holdings: Portfolio Considerations and Owner Characteristics" (with J. E. Bachman). *Southern Economic Journal* 45(2), October 1978: 543–58.

"Estimating the Economic Model of Crime with Individual Data." *Quarterly Journal of Economics* 94(1), February 1980: 57–84.

Beating the System: The Underground Economy (with C. P. Simon). Boston, MA: Auburn House, 1982.

"Increased Costs of Office Building Operation and Construction: Effects on the Costs of Office Space and the Equilibrium Distribution of Offices" (with H. Tauchen). *Land Economics* 59(3), August 1983: 324–36.

An Economic Analysis of Crime and Justice (with P. Schmidt). Orlando, FL: Academic Press, 1984.

"Measurement of Output and Quality Adjustment in the Day-Care Industry" (with S. Mukerjee). In *Output Measurement in the Service Sector*, edited by Z. Griliches, 343–69. Chicago, IL: University of Chicago Press, 1992.

"The Dynamics of Domestic Violence" (with H. Tauchen). *American Economic Review* 85(2), May 1995: 414–18.

"Crime, Prison, and Female Labor Supply" (with R. Witt). *Journal of Quantitative Criminology* 16(1), March 2000: 69–85.

Works about Ann Dryden Witte

"Witte, Ann Dryden" In *Who's Who in Economics*, edited by M. Blaug, 1186–88. Northampton, MA: Edward Edgar, 1999.

Theresa Wolfson
(1897–1972)

Theresa Wolfson's life as a labor economist and educator was devoted to studying the economy, wage-earning women, and trade unionism, all in an effort to strengthen the labor movement and ultimately benefit the lives of American workers, particularly women. Early in her career, she became convinced that workers in the 1920s could only achieve economic and social justice through trade unions, and in order to achieve these goals, workers must be educated. She was a lifelong educator who started teaching in union-sponsored schools in the 1920s and went on to combine this teaching with a more traditional academic career at Brooklyn College. Her work as an educator and researcher offered her students and succeeding generations a better life as well as a better understanding of the economy and women's roles in it.

BIOGRAPHY

Theresa Wolfson was born in Brooklyn, New York, on July 19, 1897, the daughter of Adolph Wolfson and Rebecca (Hochstein) Wolfson. Her parents were Jewish Russian immigrants who had moved to New York a few years before her birth. Her father worked as a news dealer, and, after the family bought a large house, both parents shared household chores and took in boarders to support Theresa and her two brothers. Her parents were considered radical in their political beliefs, and by the time she entered Adelphi College as an undergraduate, Wolfson was already politically active, helping organize a chapter of the Intercollegiate Socialist Society, later the League for Industrial Democracy. In the summer of 1916, she took a job investigating the wage standards in the ladies' garment industry. After receiving her B.A. in 1917, Wolfson worked as a health worker for the Meinhardt Settlement House in New York and occasionally spoke at socialist rallies. Her belief in socialism as a political movement was broken by the October 1917 Russian Revolution, after which her belief in industrial democracy was more important to her than party politics.

From January 1918 until June 1920, Wolfson worked as a field agent and investigator for the National Child Labor Committee, a job that took her to a number of states in the South and the Midwest and led to her first published articles. While working for the Labor Committee, Wolfson met Iago Galdston, a medical student beginning a career in public health. The two were married on July 19, 1920. Wolfson, who retained her maiden name, went on to graduate studies in economics at Columbia University. From 1920 to 1922, she campaigned for minimum-wage legislation and an eight-hour workday. She also became part of a loosely organized network of trade unionists, socialists, and academics who believed that effective trade unionism required educated workers. In 1921, Wolfson began teaching labor history and economics to workers in a variety of union-sponsored schools, a practice she would continue throughout her lifetime. She was also busy investigating the working conditions of sewing-machine operators for the ladies' garment industry's Joint Board of Factory Control. As basic data for her investigative study, she used the information that she gathered for her master's thesis, which Wolfson completed in 1923. In 1925, she became education director for the Union Health Center of the International Ladies' Garment Workers' Union (ILGWU), where her husband also worked. The couple had two children, Richard, born in 1926, and Margaret Beatrice, born in 1930.

While working at the ILGWU, Wolfson became intrigued by the exclusion of women in leadership roles in trade unions and decided to devote her doctoral thesis to exploring the reasons for their absence. This groundbreaking study earned Wolfson a Ph.D. from the Brookings Institution in 1926 and was published as her first book, *The Woman Worker and Trade Unions* (1926). In 1928, Wolfson began teaching at the Bryn Mawr Summer School for Women Workers, which was organized in 1921 to provide a forum for women workers and educators to come together and share their knowledge of industry. That year, she also began her forty-year career as professor of economics and labor relations at the Brooklyn branch of Hunter College, which later became Brooklyn College. During the 1930s and 1940s she also taught in summer schools for office workers and other white-collar workers. The American Labor Education Service sponsored these schools. In 1935, she divorced Galdston, and three years later she married a Brooklyn College colleague, Austin Bigelow Wood, who was a professor of psychology.

During World War II, Wolfson used her economic expertise as a member of the public panel of the War Labor Board and saw firsthand the increasing number of women who worked at well-paying unionized jobs that men had vacated to serve in the military. She urged a continuing role for these women after the war, saying they should not "be cast aside like an old glove" (Kessler-Harris, 743). Following the war, Wolfson joined the national panel of arbitrators of the American Arbitration Association, an organization concerned with resolving labor-management disputes. In 1957, Wolfson was a corecipient of the John Dewey Award of the League for Industrial Democracy for her work in mediating union-management disagreements. Wolfson retired from Brooklyn College in 1967, then began teaching a course in continuing education for older women at Sarah Lawrence College. She continued teaching until her death on May 14, 1972, at age seventy-four.

CONTRIBUTIONS

Wolfson's scholarship dealt exclusively with labor economics, especially the challenges and opportunities of working women. An ardent supporter of the union movement, she nonetheless took organized labor to task for its failure to represent women workers. In an early article ("Where Are the Organized Women Workers?"), Wolfson questioned the absence of women in trade unions and the emerging industrial unions of the time. Citing the work of the Federal Women's Bureau, the National Bureau of Economic Research, and the Russell Sage Foundation, she noted that in 1920, 21 percent of the total U.S. female population, or 8.5 million women, were in the workforce but only about 400,000 were organized. Forty-two percent of unionized women were in the needle trades, particularly the clothing industry. Disturbed by what she discovered, Wolfson was determined to find out why so few women compared to men were organized.

Her answers were embodied in her Ph.D. dissertation, published as *The Woman Worker and the Trade Unions*. Part of the problem was plain old male chauvinism. Wishing to reserve trade and industrial jobs for themselves, men were reluctant to organize women who, once unionized, would expect the same wages and employment opportunities as their male counterparts. Another obstacle was the prevailing belief among leaders that women were not organizable because of the temporary nature of their involvement in the labor force due to marriage, child bearing, and dead-end jobs designated as women's work. Wolfson dismissed all of these reasons as convenient rationales that prevented women from using unionization to change their dismal economic status. She firmly believed that unions would have to organize women if the labor movement was to succeed.

The 1930s proved to be a pivotal era for the U.S. labor movement. The harshness of the Great Depression gave unions the fortitude to organize with a survivalist mentality, while the progressive milieu of President Franklin Delano Roosevelt's New Deal created the external environment that allowed big labor to acquire the political status to challenge the power of big business. As Wolfson noted in her research, this was particularly evident in the clothing industry: "The history of American trade unions indicates that for many years the needle trades unions have been among the strongest, the most aggressive, and the most liberal in their political and economic philosophy. It is not strange, therefore, that in the present economic set-up, the [NRA] codes that evolved in the needle trades' industries should be among the best as far as the status of labor is concerned. . . . It is no miracle that the codes in the industries organized by the clothing bloc—such as the Amalgamated Clothing Workers of America, the International Ladies' Garment Workers' Union, the

Millinery Workers' Union—are among the best, as far as wages, hours, and working conditions are concerned" (*Labor*, 27).

The success experienced in the trade or craft unions was not easily replicated in the industrial unions. Wolfson clearly discerned that "The basis of the craft union is the organization of workers according to the tools used," while "The basis of the industrial union is the organization of workers according to the product created by an industry" ("Industrial Unionism," 3). The process of organizing the trades versus organizing an industry was easier to describe than to implement. "Labor has come of age. It has many problems . . . which organized labor has not faced with maturity and responsibility. Many attacks are now being hysterically levelled against the American labor movement—efforts to regulate trade unions—to eliminate strikes—to do away with collective bargaining. Representatives of American industry who are backing these efforts are short-sighted. On the other hand, friends of organized labor must urge and stress the necessity for a thorough study of its own responsibilities—for a cleaning of its own house, . . . and for an intellectual and emotional maturity in keeping with its own physical development" ("Labor's Coming of Age," 24).

Wolfson was convinced that the resolution of these and related problems would characterize the coming of age of the labor movement, a prophecy that proved poignantly correct, as the period from roughly 1940 through 1970 must be considered the golden age of organized labor in the United States.

BIBLIOGRAPHY

Works by Theresa Wolfson

"Where Are the Organized Women Workers?" *American Federationist,* June 1925: 445–57.

The Woman Worker and the Trade Unions. New York: International Publishers, 1926.

Labor and the N.R.A. (with L. MacDonald and G. L. Palmer). New York: Affiliated Schools for Workers, 1934.

"Industrial Unionism in the American Labor Movement" (with A. Weiss). *New Frontiers* (Periodical Studies in Economics and Politics) 5(2), February 1937.

"Labor's Coming of Age." *Ethical Frontiers.* New York: Society for Ethical Culture, 1946.

Works about Theresa Wolfson

Kessler-Harris, A. "Wolfson, Theresa." In *Notable American Women, the Modern Period: A Biographical Dictionary*, edited by B. Sicherman and C. Green, 742–44. Cambridge, MA: Belknap Press of Harvard University Press, 1980.

Phillips, L. W. "Wolfson, Theresa." In *American National Biography*, 740–41. Vol. 23. New York: Oxford University Press, 1999.

"Wolfson, Theresa." *Biographical Dictionary of American Labor*, edited by G. M. Fink, 592–93. Westport, CT: Greenwood Press, 1984.

APPENDIX: BIOGRAPHEES BY BIRTH YEAR

In those instances where two women have the same birth year, they are listed chronologically by the complete date of birth.

(1769–1858)   JANE HALDIMAND MARCET
(1802–1876)   HARRIET MARTINEAU
(1807–1858)   HARRIET HARDY TAYLOR MILL
(1847–1929)   MILLICENT GARRETT FAWCETT
(1850–1944)   MARY PALEY MARSHALL
(1857–1915)   KATHARINE COMAN
(1858–1943)   BEATRICE POTTER WEBB
(1870–1919)   ROSA LUXEMBURG
(1876–1957)   EDITH ABBOTT
(1886–1957)   HAZEL KYRK
(1891–1976)   MABEL F. TIMLIN
(1896–1991)   MARGARET GILPIN REID
(1897–1972)   THERESA WOLFSON
(1903–1983)   JOAN ROBINSON
(1908–1998)   JEAN TREPP McKELVEY
(1908–2002)   MARY JEAN BOWMAN
(1912–1962)   SELMA F. GOLDSMITH
(1913–1979)   SELMA J. MUSHKIN
(1914–1981)   BARBARA M. WARD
(1915–   )   ANNA J. SCHWARTZ

(1920–)	CAROLYN SHAW BELL
(1921–)	JUANITA M. KREPS
(1921–)	MARJORIE S. TURNER
(1923–)	MARIANNE A. FERBER
(c. 1924–1993)	PHYLLIS ANN WALLACE
(1925–)	INGRID H. RIMA
(1927–)	BARBARA ROSE BERGMANN
(1930–)	IRMA GLICMAN ADELMAN
(1930–)	NANCY HAYS TEETERS
(1931–)	ALICE M. RIVLIN
(1935–1975)	SHIRLEY ALMON
(1935–)	MARINA VON NEUMANN WHITMAN
(1936–)	ANN HOROWITZ
(1937–)	ISABEL V. SAWHILL
(1938–)	ELIZABETH ELLERY BAILEY
(1938–1992)	ANN FETTER FRIEDLAENDER
(1939–1981)	NANCY L. SCHWARTZ
(1939–)	M. KATHRYN EICKHOFF
(1940–)	FRANCES JULIA STEWART
(1942–)	ANN DRYDEN WITTE
(1942–)	DEIRDRE N. McCLOSKEY
(1945–)	KATHLEEN BELL COOPER
(1945–)	HEIDI I. HARTMANN
(1946–)	FRANCINE D. BLAU
(1947–)	LAURA D'ANDREA TYSON
(1952–)	ABBY JOSEPH COHEN
(1952–)	NANCY FOLBRE
(1955–)	JENNIFER F. REINGANUM
(1955–)	REBECCA M. BLANK
(1962–)	DIANE C. SWONK
(1966–)	CAROLINE M. HOXBY

INDEX

About the Authors

James Cicarelli is Professor of Economics at Roosevelt University. He is the author of four books and of articles published in numerous journals such as *The American Journal of Economics and Sociology, Technological Forecasting, The New Republic,* and *The Chicago Tribune.* He is a regular contributor to *The Scribner Encyclopedia of American Lives.*

Julianne Cicarelli teaches at the Huntington Learning Center in Arlington Heights, IL. Her essays have appeared in a number of books, including *Biographical Directory of Council of Economics Advisers* (1988) and *Nobel Laureates in Economic Sciences* (1989). She contributes regularly to *The Scribner Encyclopedia of American Lives.*